Practical Guide to the
Care of the Psychiatric Patient

SERIES EDITOR

Fred Ferri, MD, FACP
Clinical Assistant Professor
Department of Medicine
Brown University School of Medicine
St. Joseph's Hospital
Providence, Rhode Island

**OTHER VOLUMES IN THE
"PRACTICAL GUIDE TO THE CARE OF" SERIES**

Ambulatory Care

Critical Care Patient

Geriatric Patient

Gynecologic/Obstetric Patient

Medical Patient

Pediatric Patient

Surgical Patient

Practical Guide to the
Care of the Psychiatric Patient

RICHARD J. GOLDBERG, MD, FAPA

Professor, Department of Psychiatry and Human Behavior and
Department of Medicine, Brown University School of Medicine
Psychiatrist-in-Chief, Rhode Island Hospital and
Women & Infants' Hospital, Providence, Rhode Island

 Mosby

St. Louis Baltimore Berlin Boston Carlsbad Chicago London Madrid
Naples New York Philadelphia Sydney Tokyo Toronto

Mosby

Dedicated to Publishing Excellence

Editor: Emma D. Underdown
Editorial Assistant: Alicia E. Moten
Project Manager: Patricia Tannian
Production: Carlisle Publishers Services
Senior Book Designer: Gail Morey Hudson
Cover Designer: Teresa Breckwoldt
Manufacturing Supervisor: Karen Lewis

Printed in the United States of America

Composition by Carlisle Communications, Ltd.
Printing/Binding by R. R. Donnelley & Sons Company

Mosby–Year Book, Inc.
11830 Westline Industrial Drive
St. Louis, Missouri, 63146

Library of Congress Cataloging in Publication Data

Goldberg, Richard J.
    Practical guide to the care of the psychiatric patient / Richard J. Goldberg
        p.   cm.
    Includes bibliographical references and index.
    ISBN 0-8151-3648-X
    1. Psychology, Pathological.   2. Mental illness—Diagnosis.
    3. Mental illness—Treatment.   I. Title.
    [DNLM: 1. Mental Disorders—diagnosis.   2. Mental Disorders—
therapy.   WM 100 06169p 1995]
    RC454.G5885 1995
    616.89—dc20
    DNLM/DLC
    for Library of Congress   94-34866
                                                                                        CIP

94   95   96   97   98   /   9   8   7   6   5   4   3   2   1

To
Emily & Jenna

Preface

This book is intended to provide a practical foundation for diagnosing and treating psychiatric problems in medical practice.

The overall goals of this book include the following:

- Clarifying diagnostic categories and terminology
- Improving recognition of psychiatric problems
- Demystifying the mental status examination
- Detailing the proper use of psychiatric medications

The text is presented in outline form for clarity, with sequential diagnostic and management strategies. However, it is *not* intended to be a superficial approach, and the content is, whenever possible, based on documented and referenced sources.

The use of the *DSM (Diagnostic and Statistical Manual of Diagnoses)* is generally followed. However, some of the categories are simplified for purposes of clarity. This text (unlike the *DSM*) is not intended primarily for research purposes but is meant to be clinically useful. Readers are urged to obtain a copy of the *DSM-IV* for reference. References at the end of each chapter direct the reader to worthwhile supplementary information. This book is intended to be useful for the following individuals:

- *Medical students* looking for a basic guide to psychiatry for their clerkship
- *Primary care residents* looking for practical information that can be applied to the psychiatric problems of their patients
- *Primary care physicians* wanting to organize psychiatric knowledge already gathered through experience and to obtain updates on new terms and treatments
- *Medical specialists* who realize that many patient problems are complicated by psychiatric issues. For example, gastrointestinal symptoms are often a somatic manifestation of depression, and atypical chest pain is frequently a result of an underlying anxiety disorder.

The "essentials" approach of this book emerges from more than 15 years of teaching psychiatry to practicing physicians, medical students, and residents in both psychiatry and general internal medicine. The intent is to avoid the confusion of most psychiatry texts and to provide practical approaches and guidelines. This core information will serve as a solid foundation and organization to which more detailed readings can be added.

Contents

The Role of Psychiatric Factors in Medical Practice

1.1   PREVALENCE OF PSYCHIATRIC PROBLEMS

1. About 28% of Americans over age 18 (a group of over 52 million) suffer from a mental or addictive disorder in a one-year period.
   a. Addictive disorders: 9.5%
   b. Anxiety disorders: 12.6%
   c. Schizophrenic disorders: 1.1%
   d. Affective disorders: 9.5%
   e. Antisocial personality disorders: 1.5%
   f. Cognitive disorders (severe): 2.7%

1.2   UTILIZATION OF PSYCHIATRIC SERVICES

1. Every year over 20 million people (over age 18) make more than 325 million outpatient visits to mental health professional or volunteer resources for mental health or substance abuse reasons.
2. About 1.5 million Americans have at least one inpatient mental health or addiction admission during a 1-year period.
3. Most treatment for psychiatric problems takes place in the general medical care setting, not in specialty psychiatry or mental health programs.
   a. Therefore, increased training of physicians in the recognition and management of psychiatric disorders is needed.
   b. Patients with mental disorders make up 5% to 20% of general medical patients and are 1.5 to 2 times as likely to visit the medical setting as patients without those disorders. More than 50% of patients with a diagnosable mental disorder have an outpatient general health visit in a 6-month period, compared with about 12% who visited a mental health specialist.
   c. There is a significant lack of recognition of mental disorders in general practice. One study found that while 26.7% of a large primary practice had a mental disorder diagnosis, fewer than 10% of these were recognized by the primary care physicians. Other studies have shown that only one third to one half of mental disorders are recognized in primary care. Only half of the cases of anxiety and depression in medical settings are recognized, and most cases are undertreated.

4. Medical illness and drug effects often masquerade as psychiatric problems (see Chapter 3).

1.3   PSYCHIATRIC CO-MORBIDITY IN MEDICAL PRACTICE

Psychiatric co-morbidity impacts the course, outcome, and cost of medical care.

1. Psychiatric problems increase medical length of stay and utilization, decrease functional level, and have a negative impact on overall prognosis and outcome.
2. Disorders secondary to smoking, drinking, and drug use account for a significant portion of the health care dollar.
3. The elderly population has a high prevalence of psychiatric co-morbidity, which is often poorly recognized.
   a. Approximately 15% to 20% suffer from depressive symptoms.
   b. Forty percent of Parkinson's patients and 20% to 30% of stroke patients have depression.
   c. Approximately 20% of the elderly have substance abuse disorders. In fact, the rates of hospitalization in the elderly for alcohol-related problems are similar to those for myocardial infarction.
   d. Between 10% and 20% suffer from anxiety disorders, including phobias. In fact, phobia is the most common psychiatric disorder in women over age 65.
   e. About 8% have progressive dementias. Within the group of those with Alzheimer's disease, 30% to 40% have delusions or hallucinations.
4. There has been repeated documentation of a significant prevalence of psychiatric co-morbidity in medical inpatients. Psychiatric consultation of medical inpatients with psychiatric complications has been demonstrated to produce a positive cost offset and improve the effectiveness of treatment.

1.4   EXAMPLES OF THE IMPACT OF THE INTERRELATIONSHIP OF PSYCHIATRIC AND MEDICAL PRACTICE

1. A study of 334 consecutive patients with acute chest pain seen in an urban hospital emergency department found panic disorder in 17.5% and depression in 23.1%. It is likely that these psychiatric symptoms significantly affect medical utilization and outcome.
2. A study of a sample of trauma patients seen in a New Jersey hospital found that 58% had abused substances in the 3 months before the trauma; 40% had an anxiety disorder; 37%, an affective disorder; and 30%, a posttraumatic stress disorder.
3. The direct and indirect cost of panic disorder that is not adequately treated is about $18,000 per year, compared to about $1000 per year for successful treatment.
4. There appears to be a five-fold higher mortality rate among depressed myocardial infarction survivors, with depression being as strong a predictor of mortality as left ventricular function.
5. Fatigue is one of the most common presenting complaints in primary care medicine. A number of studies have indicated that 20% to 40% of these patients actually have underlying depressive disorders, which are

generally not recognized or treated. These patients are often high medical utilizers and suffer from significant impairment.

6. Insomnia is another common presenting complaint in primary care practice. Reviews of this problem indicate that between one third and two thirds of patients with chronic insomnia have a psychiatric disorder.

7. Patients with chronic medical conditions such as arthritis, diabetes, hypertension, and chronic lung disease have a significantly increased prevalence of psychiatric disorders.

8. Stroke is followed by depression in about 20% of patients, with a very low rate of recognition and treatment, resulting in unnecessarily impaired function level. In addition, family problems, rather than medical factors, may be the best indicator of risk for rehospitalization in these patients.

9. Twenty percent of patients who are medically recovered from myocardial infarction fail to return to their previous level of function; the most likely reason for this failure of recovery involves psychiatric problems, especially depression.

10. Generalized anxiety disorder is estimated to have a community prevalence of 2.5% to 5%. However, because it most often manifests as somatic symptoms, these patients cluster in primary care practices where the estimated prevalence is about 15%, usually presenting as somatic symptoms such as breathing problems, nonspecific complaints, sexual dysfunction, and irritable bowel symptoms. When these are overlooked, these patients continue to complain of unexplained symptoms requiring ongoing episodic medical interventions.

11. Depression has been shown to adversely affect the course of patients with a variety of medical disorders, including chronic renal failure and irritable bowel syndrome.

12. Panic disorder has a prevalence of approximately 9% in cardiology patients. Symptoms of panic disorder often confound medical diagnosis and lead to unnecessary expenditures. For example, the performance of unnecessary angiograms because of panic disorder symptoms (i.e., racing heartbeat, difficulty breathing, chest pain, and dizziness) wastes millions of dollars each year. One in three patients presenting acute chest pain to an emergency department were found to have either panic disorder or depression.

13. Somatization patients become chronic primary care patients with time-consuming and costly workups. In 1980, the per capita expenditures for these patients were 6 times the average for hospital costs, 14 times for physician charges, and 9 times for personal health. These patients often receive unnecessary surgery and diagnostic procedures, leading to iatrogenic disorders. Though control is difficult, there is evidence that management guidelines can help reduce the level of medical utilization of these patients.

14. The behavioral problems caused by tobacco, drug, and alcohol use are associated with more than $171 billion each year in health care costs. Together, they account for 60% of all preventable deaths. More than one third of admissions to the adult ICU at Johns Hopkins Hospital were directly related to alcohol, tobacco, or other drug use. Patients who abuse drugs also stayed in the ICU longer and had higher medical bills than other patients. Physician recognition of alcohol abuse continues to

be a problem. There is reasonable evidence to support the theory that a positive cost offset can be obtained by treating alcoholism. Unfortunately, few primary care programs are tightly coupled to programs for substance abuse.

15. Psychosocial difficulties are important determinants of why patients visit their doctor and affect both physical and mental health. For example, repeated visits for chest pain may be caused by an emotional reaction to ongoing family discord; domestic violence and sexual abuse can produce a variety of otherwise puzzling medical symptoms; and bereavement may produce facsimiles of medical symptoms. Relevant psychosocial problems are poorly recognized or elicited by primary care physicians. About half of primary care patients have some significant psychosocial distress, but only about one third of these cases are detected by the physician.

As we enter an era in which the interface of psychiatry and primary care will become increasingly important, I hope this text will contribute to more effective practice and better patient outcomes.

References

Adams WL, Yuan Z, Barboriak et al: Alcohol-related hospitalizations of elderly people, *JAMA* 270:1222-1225, 1993.

Baldwin WA, Rosenfeld BA, Breslow MJ et al: Substance abuse–related admission to adult intensive care, *Chest* 103:21-25, 1993.

Borus JF, Olendzki MC, Kessler L et al: The "offset effect" of mental health treatment on ambulatory medical care utilization and charges, *Arch Gen Psychiatry* 42:573-580, 1985.

Broadhead WE, Blazer DG, George LK et al: Depression, disability days, and days lost from work in a prospective epidemiologic survey, *JAMA* 264:2524-2528, 1990.

Cottrol C, Frances R: Substance abuse, comorbid psychiatric disorder, and repeated traumatic injuries, *Hosp Community Psychiatry* 44(8):715-716, 1993.

Frasure-Smith N, Lesperance F, Talajic M: Depression following myocardial infarction: impact on 6 month survival, *JAMA* 270:1819-1825, 1993.

German P, Shapiro S, Burke J et al: Detection and management of mental health problems of older patients by primary care providers, *JAMA* 257:489-93, 1987.

Holder HD, Blose JO: The reduction of health care costs associated with alcoholism treatment: a 14-year longitudinal study, *J Stud Alcohol* 53:293-302, 1992.

Houpt JL, Orleans CS, George LK, et al: The role of psychiatric and behavioral factors in the practice of medicine, *Am J Psychiatry* 137:37-47, 1980.

Levenson JL, Hamer RM, Rossiter LF: Relation of psychopathology in general medical inpatients to use and cost of services, *Am J Psychiatry* 147:1498-1503, 1990.

Mumford E, Schlesinger HJ: Assessing consumer benefit: cost offset as an incidental effect of psychotherapy, *Gen Hosp Psychiatry* 9:360-363, 1987.

Narrow WE, Regier DA, Rae DS et al: Use of services by persons with mental and addictive disorders, *Arch Gen Psychiatry* 50:95-107, 1993.

Regier DA, Narrow WE, Rae DS et al: The de facto mental and addictive disorders service system, *Arch Gen Psychiatry* 50:85-94, 1993.

Schulberg HC, Burns BJ: Mental disorders in primary care: epidemiologic, diagnostic and treatment research directions, *Gen Hosp Psychiatry* 10:79-87, 1988.

Strain JJ, Lyons JS, Hammer JS et al: Cost offset from a psychiatric consultation-liaison intervention with elderly hip fracture patients, *Am J Psychiatry* 148:1044-1049, 1991.

Walker EA, Katon WJ, Jemelka RP: Psychiatric disorders and medical care utilization among people in the general population who report fatigue, *J Gen Intern Med* 8:436-440, 1993.

Weissman MM: The hidden patient: unrecognized panic disorder, *J Clin Psychiatry* 51:5-8, 1990.

Wells KB, Golding JM, Burnam MA: Affective, substance use, and anxiety disorders in persons with arthritis, diabetes, heart disease, high blood pressure, or chronic lung conditions. *Gen Hosp Psychiatry* 11:320-327, 1989.

Wells KB, Stewart A, Hays RD et al. The functioning and well-being of depressed patients: results from the Medical Outcomes Study, *JAMA* 262:914-991, 1989.

Yingling KW, Wulsin LR, Arnold LM et al: Estimated prevalences of panic disorder and depression among consecutive patients seen in an emergency department with acute chest pain, *J Gen Intern Med* 8:231-235, 1993.

2
The Psychiatric Interview and Data Base

The following are goals of this chapter:
1. To review the basic conditions for effective interviewing.
2. To explain the core content of the psychiatric data base, including:
   a. Sociodemographics
   b. Chief complaint and history of present illness
   c. Past psychiatric history
   d. Developmental history
   e. Psychosocial review of systems
   f. Family history
   g. Medical history
3. To provide an overview of the Mental Status Examination.
4. To explain the descriptive-behavioral component of the Mental Status Examination. (Other sections will be reviewed in separate chapters.)

2.1 THE PSYCHIATRIC INTERVIEW

Conditions of the Interview

1. Privacy
   a. Establish conditions in which the patient can speak confidentially. When consulting on medical inpatients, try to leave a two- or four-bed room and find a more private area.
2. Safety
   a. If there is any question about the patient's potential dangerousness, the interview should be conducted in a safe place, with other staff or security available. Avoid settings without easy access to a door, especially when interviewing a paranoid or potentially agitated patient.
3. Communicate a time frame
   a. Let patients know in advance about the length of the interview. This knowledge allows patients to adjust their level of detail. Also, it removes patients' fantasies that the interview is being ended prematurely because they are boring or difficult, or being extended because they are special.
4. Establish the reason for the interview
   a. As with any medical interview, establish the "chief complaint" by asking the patient, "What do you hope to accomplish by meeting with me today?"

b. If the interview has been set up as a result of a consultation request, some patients may be unclear about the purpose of the meeting.

5. Identify yourself
   a. It is helpful to begin the interview by identifying yourself by name, position, and profession.

6. Address the patient with respect
   a. Patients should be addressed by their last name.

7. Avoiding obvious barriers
   a. Try not to take detailed notes in front of the patient.
   b. Create a reasonable physical distance, (not too far or too close), between you and the patient.
   c. Be sure the patient, especially if elderly, can hear you adequately.
   d. Do not sit in the "blind spot" of a patient who has had a stroke.

8. Inform the patient what will happen after the interview
   a. For example, "After we finish today, I will give you my impression of the problem and discuss what it makes sense to do next. This may involve some diagnostic studies, an additional interview, or a referral to some other person if I feel that is necessary."
   b. Some patients assume that the interviewer will automatically become their therapist. If this is not the case, it is important to let the patient know that your role is limited to evaluation and that a referral, if appropriate, will be made afterward.

9. Basic issues of confidentiality
   a. Do not communicate with anyone about the patient without permission.
   b. Be aware that obtaining or providing records usually requires signed written consent, except in emergency situations.
   c. If the interview is going to result in a report to someone else (e.g., judge, worker's compensation board, or supervisor), make sure the patient understands and is willing to be interviewed under such circumstances.
      (1) Remember that medical records are public documents. Most states do not have laws protecting the privacy of psychiatric records. While important information needs to be recorded, use some discretion in recording sensitive material.

2.2   THE PSYCHIATRIC DATA BASE

Introductory Issues

1. The psychiatric data base (see Fig. 2-1) is a means to an end, not an end in itself.
2. The purpose of a data base is to ensure that necessary data for a differential diagnosis is recorded systematically.
3. A data base can serve a quality assurance and teaching function.
4. The data base should not be a barrier. Extensive note taking should be avoided.
5. The time required to complete a data base depends on the setting and the goal. In an emergency evaluation the relevant data base may be covered in about 30 minutes. In some outpatients or in more extended evaluations, it may take several one-hour sessions.

Rhode Island Hospital
Department of Psychiatry

Name:			Record #:				DOB:	mo - day - yr
Address:	Street	City		State	Zip	Telephone:		
Education: Grade: HS Grad Coll Grad Post Grad			Marital Status: M W S D Sep				Sex: M F	
Religion: J P RC None Other:			Insurance:					
Responsible Person:				Relation:				
Address:	Street	City		State	Zip	Telephone:		
Referred By:			Reason:					

CHIEF COMPLAINT:

HISTORY OF PRESENT ILLNESS:

PAST PSYCHIATRIC HISTORY: Hosp: N Y #:   Oupt: N Y #:   Signif Sx without Rx: N Y

DEVELOPMENTAL

Pregnancy & Perinatal:	Premature		Special Care		No Cx			
Infancy: Head Injury		Seizures	Meningitis	Hospital		Abuse	Other	No Cx
School: Phobia	Held Back, Grade:		Special Ed.		Hyperactive		L.D.	No Cx
Anti-Social: No Yes:								
Relations to age 18: Social & Close		Little Social/Close		Little Social/No Close				Isolated

Rev. 2/94

Figure 2-1   *Continued.*
The Psychiatric Data Base.

6. Not every item of the data base must be obtained on every patient. For example, in assessing confusion in an elderly person, a developmental history is unnecessary. Conversely, some sections of this data base are not extensive enough for some specialized problems.

7. The data base is not the final evaluation. Greater detail in specific areas is obtained in ongoing treatment. For example, identifying some significant family problems may be sufficient in an initial interview, but fully defining the problem may take a more thorough family assessment.

SOCIAL								
Income:	Salary	Disability	Workman's Comp	GPA	AFDC	Soc Security	Spouse's Job	None Other

Employment:	Occupation:		Full-time	Part-time	Retired
Houseperson	Student	Unemployed	**Spouse's Occupation:**		

Daily activity if not work:

Living arrangements: Alone   With:

Social Support: Adequate Inadequate Other Problem:	**Self Care:** Not Impaired Impaired:

Stressful Events:

FAMILY - First Degree Relative has:
- ❑ Affective Disorder
- ❑ Anxiety Disorder
- ❑ Alcoholism
- ❑ Schizophrenia
- ❑ Seizures
- ❑ Other

Is there a family issue?:   N   Y

MEDICAL PROBLEMS:

Head Injury: No Yes Date:	**Seizures:** No Maybe Yes	**Headache:** No Yes Change in pattern:

Surgery: No   Yes:

Allergies:

Alcohol: None Not daily, social Binges Daily Abuse Dependence	**Tobacco:** No Yes	**Caffeine:** No Yes

Street Drugs: None Narcotics Sedatives Stimulants Other	**Impairment:** Social Emotional Physical Financial

Meds:

Withdrawal risk?   No   Yes

SEXUAL				
# Pregnancies:	# Term Births:	# Premature Births:	# Abortions:	# Miscarriages:
STD: No Yes:	**HIV Status:** Neg. Pos. Unknown	**Sexual Dysfunction:** No Yes:		
Menses: None Since: Reg. Irreg.	**Menarche:** Age:	**LMP:** Date:		
Contraception:	**PMS:**	**Menopause:** No Sx & Date:		

Rev. 2/94

Fig. 2-1—Cont'd   *Continued.*

8. Sometimes it is not possible to encompass the data base in an initial interview. In that case, indicate that the interview has not been sufficient to define the problem and that another meeting will be necessary.

Section I: Sociodemographics
1. Introduction
   a. When presenting a case, present this information first, since sociodemographics define risk factors and influence clinical thinking. For example, diagnostic possibilities in an elderly widow in a nursing home are different from those in a young, postpartum mother living alone and receiving welfare.

Gen Appearance:		Exam Conditions:		Participation: Full Other:	
Consciousness: Awake		Drowsy	Fluctuating	Stuporous	Coma
Kinetics: Normal Increased Decreased Variable		**Affect:** Appropriate: N Y Labile Flat Restricted to:			
Speech Loudness: Normal	Soft	Loud	Mute	**Speech Rate:** Normal	Slow Fast Pressured
Speech Structure: Normal	Loose	Vague	Incoherent	Dysphasic	Tangential Impoverished

COGNITIVE:

WNL	Prob. Abn.	Def. Abn.		
			ATTENTION	
			LANGUAGE: Naming	
			Fluency	
			Repetition	
			Reading/Writing	
			ORIENTATION	
			MEMORY: Immediate Recall	
			Short Term	
			Visual Memory	
			Long Term	
			CONSTRUCTION	
			HIGHER FUNCTIONS: Intellect	
			Abstraction	
			Judgment	

ANXIETY:

Panic	OCD	Generalized	Phobias	Adjustment	PTSD	Somatic

AFFECTIVE: (Use arrows for increase or decrease; 0 for no change)

Mood	Energy	Conc.	Sleep	Appetite	Guilt	Anhedonia	Somatization	Pain	Function

PSYCHOSIS:

Delusions: None	Somatic	Paranoid	**Hallucinations:** None	Auditory	Visual	Command	Other
Disorganized: Behavior		Verbal Behavior	**Thought:** Content		Process		

	NO IDEAS	INDEF. IDEAS	DEF. IDEAS	NO PLANS	INDEF. PLANS	DEF. PLANS
Suicide						
Homicide						
Violence						

What Inhibits?	Reason To Live:

PERSONALITY:

Dependent	Obsessive	Histrionic	Paranoid	Narcissistic	Schizoid
Anti-Social	Borderline		Masochistic		Passive-Aggressive

OTHER CONSPICUOUS FEATURES:

INTERVIEWER:	DATE:

Rev. 2/94

Fig. 2-1—Cont'd   *Continued.*

2. Specific items
   a. Some items have obvious administrative value, such as *Name, record number, address, phone number, date of birth, sex.*
   b. *Marital status:* Separation or divorce is one of the most stressful life events. Divorced and separated individuals have poorer mental and physical health than their single, married, or even widowed counterparts.
   c. *Education:* If the patient has not completed high school, inquire about the reason. Does the patient have a history of learning disability or behavior problem? Can the patient read? Note any disparity between the level of education and work level.
   d. *Religion:* A patient's religion has potential significance. Strong religious affiliations and beliefs may influence the patient's way of understanding and dealing with medical problems.

DIAGNOSIS:			
1. **Initial assessment:** Completed Incomplete:			
2. **Definite organic factor accounts for or significantly contributes to CC:** Y N			
3. **Impressions:**			
4. **Tentative DSM III Dx:**			

RECOMMENDATIONS:			
1. **Nursing Liaison**	**Social Work**	**Clergy**	**Security**
2. **Constant Observation** start: stop:	**Close Observation** start: stop:		**Restraints** start: stop:
3. **Consultation by:**			
4. **Tests:** EEG Cranial CT T4 T3u TSH Thyroid Antibodies Renal fx lytes Ca LFTs			
ABG Glu U/A CBC ESR Serology LP B12 Folate Tox Screen			
5. **D/C or decrease following meds:**			
6. **Start following meds:**			
7. **Family Evaluation** Med System Meeting Individual Psychotherapy			
8. **Obtain Records From:**			
9. **Other:**			

DISPOSITION:		
1. **No psych f/u unless requested:**		
2. **Outpt Rx:**		
3. **Inpt Rx:**		
4. **F/u by:**		
5. **Commitment paper to:**		
6. **Nursing home**	**Hospice care**	**VNA**
7. **Other:**		

CLINICIAN:	DATE:

Rev. 1/94

Fig. 2-1—Cont'd

e. *Insurance status:* Unfortunately, insurance status is a major determinant of access to care. Private insurance plans have increasing rules for authorization of treatment, co-payments, deductibles, and total limits of coverage.

f. *Responsible person:* The billing office is interested in the party responsible for the patient's bill. The "responsible person" of interest here is the "significant other" such as spouse, parent, or roommate.
   (1) The absence of such a person indicates serious isolation.
   (2) Consider when this person should be part of the evaluation (assuming the patient consents).

g. *Referred by:* The referring professional should send pertinent background information and should receive a letter summarizing the evaluation findings. No information can be obtained or sent without the permission of the patient. If a patient does not want information shared, it is important to understand why.

  h. *Reason:* The "reason" for the referral means the reason given by the referring person (or the patient's reason if self-referred). It is well known that there are significant discrepancies between the "stated" reason for the referral and the "real" reason. The referring physician may state that the reason is to "evaluate depression," but the real meaning may be "I can't stand the way this patient refuses to listen to me."

Section II: Chief Complaint

1. As with any medical interview, establish the chief complaint, which forms the basis for the subsequent history.
   a. In patients with multiple complaints, try to establish a hierarchical list. Ask the patient to define what seems to be the most important of the problems mentioned.
   b. The chief complaint may be elicited by the question, "What is it you hope to accomplish by meeting with me today?"
2. The patient may have no chief complaint if the referral was made for a consultation. In such cases the patient should be told the reason for the referral.
   a. For example, if the consultation was to evaluate depression, you might say, "Dr. X has asked me to meet with you because of some difficulties managing stress." In patients uncomfortable with psychiatry, such an opening may be more facilitative than saying, "I'm here to evaluate your depression."

Section III: History of Present Illness

1. The history of present illness (HPI) in psychiatry does not differ from other areas of medical practice. Identify the time and setting of the onset of the symptoms and trace their development to the present.
2. Do not assume you know what a patient means by words such as *depression, confusion, upset, anxiety, and nervous breakdown.* Always ask the patient to define what the term means.
3. Always find out the reason the patient is there now. What were the precipitating factors? Include a question such as, "Are there any *other* stresses, changes, or losses that have been an issue for you?"
4. If the patient does not speak English, find a competent interpreter. Using family members can be a problem because of confidentiality and distortions.
5. Time segments of the interview
   a. Try to reserve the first half of the interview for the patient to talk freely without too much structured questioning, which prematurely closes off potential problems. Inquiries should start with open-ended questions and become more specific.
   b. The second half of the initial interview should cover remaining portions of the data base, including the mental status.
6. The process of the interview should include:
   a. Summarizing your understanding of the problem, allowing the patient a chance to correct it.

b. Asking if there is anything else that you should know.
c. Determining the patient's expectations, fears, and interpretation of symptoms, with questions such as:
   (1) "What worries or fears do you have about your health/condition/situation?"
   (2) "What do you think is the cause of your symptoms?"

Section IV: Past Psychiatric History

1. *Psychiatric hospitalizations:* Inquire about any psychiatric (or substance abuse) admissions.
   a. Record the number of admissions, dates, and locations.
   b. Obtain a release of information to request records.
2. *Outpatient treatment:* Inquire about outpatient psychiatric or substance abuse treatment.
   a. Record the names of providers and dates of treatment.
   b. Obtain a signed release to request summaries.
   c. Ask what was helpful or problematic about previous treatment to continue what worked and avoid repeating mistakes.
3. *Significant symptoms without treatment:* Ask, "Are there times you had some nervous difficulties but did not see anyone for help?" Many patients have histories of significant psychiatric symptoms without formal psychiatric treatment.

Section V: Developmental History

1. A developmental history is not necessary for every patient (e.g., an elderly patient evaluated for a change in mental status would not require a developmental history).
2. Many adults have behavior problems with developmental determinants. Reasons for obtaining developmental data include the following:
   a. Perinatal or childhood insults to the central nervous system may be associated with delayed maturation and increased risk of seizures or behavioral and cognitive problems.
   b. Some adult behavior problems are strongly influenced by childhood events (e.g., multiple hospitalizations for a chronic medical condition, foster care, abuse, or absent parenting.)
3. While developmental histories are essential (and lengthy) for child psychiatry, they are more focused for adult patients and include the following:
   a. *Pregnancy and perinatal complications:* A screening question might be, "As far as you know, were there any complications when you were born or while your mother was carrying you? For example, were you born prematurely or did you have to be in a special care nursery?"
   b. *Infancy:* "As an infant, were you told of any serious problems? . . . such as *head injury, seizures, meningitis, hospitalization, abuse,* or *other problems*?"
   c. *School:*"In your early years of school, were there any problems such as fear of going to school (*school phobia*), *being held back, being in special classes, hyperactivity,* or *learning disabilities*?"
      (1) Early phobic behavior may be the first manifestation of an anxiety disorder.

(2) Hyperactivity and learning disabilities may continue into adult years.

(3) Being held back a grade may indicate a behavior or learning problem, but also may be the result of a family's moving or other situation during childhood.

d. *Anti-social:* Because adult antisocial personality disorder begins in childhood, ask: "Were you the kind of child who got into trouble a lot?" (See Chapter 16 for fuller discussion of antisocial personality.)

e. *Relations by age 18:* By the end of high school, one's pattern of social interactions is generally in place. Therefore, determining the degree of socialization may help understand adult problems with social relations (which psychiatrists sometimes call "object relations").

(1) Adolescent isolation may be the result of many causes, such as schizoid personality, social phobia, depression or parental forced isolation.

(2) The adolescent social "baseline" would be expected to continue into adult life. Changes from this baseline must be explained.

Section VI: Psychosocial Review

1. Psychosocial issues are important determinants of visits to doctors, affecting both physical and mental health.

2. A productive doctor-patient relationship may depend on identification of relevant psychosocial issues.

3. Psychosocial impairment and stresses are important diagnostic variables in psychiatry.

4. Psychosocial content should include the following:

a. *Income:* "How do you support yourself?" Money is a critical factor for everyone.

(1) Income sources such as *disability* or *worker's compensation* may raise concern about motivation to get better and the possibility that medical symptoms provide secondary gain.

(2) Patients on entitlement programs such as general public assistance *(GPA)* or aid for families with dependent children *(AFDC)* often require updating of eligibility, which may confound their assessment. A psychiatric symptom may be presented as a basis for a new disability.

b. *Work* provides structure and is an important source of both gratification and stress.

(1) Work-related problems may be the cause or result of psychiatric problems.

(2) The ability to participate in work also gives insight into adaptive capacities and recovery from illness.

c. *Daily activity if not work:* If patients are not working, how do they spend their time?

(1) Lack of structure and involvement contributes to lack of self-worth, isolation, and motivation.

(2) Creating daily structure can be an important intervention.

(a) For this reason, structured day programs are set up for the chronically mentally ill and the elderly and during the recovery phase of many other disorders.

d. *Living arrangements:* "Whom do you live with?" is an important question since that person may be a strong influence on the patient's illness and treatment, especially if that person's opinion is different from the clinician's.

e. *Social support:* Social support is an important mediating factor of distress. Patients with inadequate or chaotic social support are at higher risk for all types of physical and mental coping problems.

   (1) How much social support is adequate? Counting family or friends is of limited use since each person has differing needs.

   (2) The real question is whether the amount available matches the needs.

   (3) Helpful questions would be: "Is there someone you can call if you have a problem?" or "Is loneliness a problem?"

   (4) Social supports may involve complex relationships. The identified support may be the very person who is inflicting physical or emotional abuse.

      (a) Make no assumptions about what relationships are like, especially given the high prevalence of domestic violence.

f. *Self-care:* Less than optimal self-care is a serious stress as well as a marker of impairment.

   (1) A general screening question is, "How does your condition interfere with taking care of yourself or your daily activities?"

   (2) To inquire about functional skills (and social support) ask, "Who does your grocery shopping? cooking? housecleaning? laundry?"

   (3) On a more basic level of self-care, ask, "Are you able to wash yourself? Get out of bed? Dress yourself? Feed yourself?"

g. *Stressful events:* Stressful events are important determinants of seeking medical help and can exacerbate underlying psychiatric vulnerabilities.

   (1) A screening question would be, "Have there been any other things going on that have been stressful for you?"

Section VII: Family History

1. Many psychiatric disorders have some genetic contribution; therefore, ask, "Are there any nervous conditions that run in your family?"
   a. Determine whether any first degree relatives had any psychiatric disorders and their treatment responses.
2. Family histories also provide clues to important or problematic relationships.
3. Include questions about "medical" history because of both the psychological and biological impact.
4. It is usually helpful to draw a genogram for the family history, indicating dates and causes of death, as well as lines to indicate especially strong or problematic relationships.
5. Family specialists might take several hours for this section of the interview. The small amount of time allocated in the initial interview is for the purpose of identifying those potentially important areas that can be returned to at a later time.

Section VIII: Medical History

1. *Medical problems:* A medical problem list is essential.
   a. Give special consideration to any medical disorders (or treatments) that can affect the central nervous system (see Boxes 3.2 and 3.3) and consider the temporal relationship between such problems and psychiatric symptoms. Several areas are of direct relevance to psychiatric symptoms, including:
      (1) History of *head injury* (a risk factor for complex partial seizures, subdural hematomas, and postconcussion syndrome).
      (2) *Headache* (new onset of severe headache raises concern for intracranial pathologic condition; in addition, migraine may present as psychiatric symptoms).
      (3) *Seizures,* including passing out or fainting spells (many psychiatric symptoms can result from complex partial seizures or postictal, or interictal phenomena).
      (4) *Chronic pain* is often associated with psychiatric problems, especially depression. Psychiatric problems cannot be assessed without addressing pain.
2. *Surgery:* Surgery is important medically and psychologically.
   a. In some instances, surgery leads directly to psychiatric symptoms. For example, GI surgery may remove part of the intestine where vitamin B_{12} is absorbed; cardiovascular surgery creates risks for intraoperative brain hypoxia.
3. *Medications and substance use:* Box 3.1 provides details of the psychiatric consequences of medications and drugs. The data base should include information on the following:
   a. *Drug allergies and reactions:* Many reactions that patients report as "allergies" turn out to be nonallergic side effects.
   b. *Alcohol use:* Because of the prevalence of alcohol abuse, this area must be given special attention. It may be helpful to categorize patients in a number of ways.
      (1) Screening questions (CAGE questionnaire and the Michigan Alcohol Screening Test) are reviewed in Chapter 14.
      (2) Alcohol use patterns include the following:
         (a) None
         (b) Not daily, social (one or two drinks)
         (c) Daily (specify quantity)
         (d) Binges (a definite sign of abuse)
   c. *Street drugs:* The patient may use narcotics, stimulants, sedatives, or others (e.g., hallucinogens) or none at all.
      (1) If the patient is using alcohol or other drugs, impairment may involve social interactions, emotional symptoms, physical symptoms, and/or financial consequences.
   d. *Tobacco* used should be quantified and noted, because nicotine has adverse physical sequelae and can be involved in creating or masking symptoms involving depression, anxiety, appetite, or energy (see Chapter 18).
   e. *Caffeine* use is extremely common. Patients vary in sensitivity, but as few as two cups of brewed coffee can cause significant anxiety, palpitations, or insomnia.

  (1) Caffeine withdrawal is usually associated with fatigue and dull headache.
f. *Is there risk of drug withdrawal?* This question must be answered at the time of the interview because of potential serious medical consequences.
g. Finally, there should be a record of all over-the-counter (OTC) drugs and prescribed (Rx) medications.
  (1) The psychiatric symptoms associated with medications are so numerous that this part of the history *must* be complete.
    (a) Ask the patient to bring in all medications.
    (b) Include substances bought at drug or health food stores.
    (c) Include recently discontinued medications.
    (d) Plasma levels can indicate inadequate or toxic levels that may be relevant to psychiatric symptoms.
    (e) Toxicology screens can be used to assess illicit substance use.

4. *Physical/neurologic examination and vital signs:*
  Some focused physical/neurological examination, including vital signs, may be an extremely important part of the initial psychiatric assessment.
  a. Further details on the screening value and interpretation of the physical examination can be found in Chapter 3, 4, and 13.

5. *Sexual history:*
  a. *Pregnancy history* and outcome can be recorded by noting the number of pregnancies, term births, premature births, abortions, and miscarriages.
    (1) Do not make assumptions that patients have not been pregnant just because they are unmarried, single, young, old, or religious.
  b. *History of sexually transmitted diseases (STDs)* can be critical, with the increasing incidence of syphilis and HIV infection.
  c. *Sexual dysfunction* is usually a meaningful problem.
    (1) Sexual dysfunction is often correctable. About one third of men referred for impotence have an organic cause. Medications are often associated with erectile and ejaculatory disturbances in men and anorgasmia in women.
    (2) Because patients are often reluctant to volunteer this information, direct questioning is important. The most basic screening questions would be:
      (a) Are you sexually active?
      (b) Are you having any sexual problems or concerns?
      (c) Have you ever been a victim of sexual abuse? (It has been estimated that as many as 30% of adults experienced sexual abuse during childhood.)
      (d) Have you been involved in any homosexual or bisexual activities?
  d. *Menstrual history* includes:
    (1) Age of onset of menses (menarche), which, if delayed or early may reveal some neuroendocrine problems.
    (2) Pattern of menses (regular, irregular, or absent) may also reveal possible neuroendocrine or medical problems.
    (3) Date of last menstrual period (LMP) can be a critical question leading to consideration of pregnancy in young women presenting with mysterious psychiatric or medical symptoms.

(4) Date of onset of menopause and symptoms can be important to understanding current psychophysical issues. Inquire about the patient's beliefs about menopause and its psychosocial impact. Consultation with a gynecologic endocrinology professional may be needed to sort out the facts and fiction.

(5) Inquiring about premenstrual syndrome (PMS) can be important because of medical (e.g., increase in seizures premenstrually) or emotional effects.

   (a) Assessment is facilitated by keeping a 2- or 3-month diary of symptoms to document any pattern.

2.3 THE MENTAL STATUS EXAMINATION

Overview: The basic components of the mental status examination (MSE) can be summarized as follows:

1. Descriptive-behavioral section (this chapter)
2. Cognitive evaluation (see Chapter 3)
3. Affective evaluation (see Chapters 5 and 7)
4. Anxiety evaluation (see Chapter 8)
5. Psychotic evaluation (see Chapter 11)
6. Personality evaluation (see Chapter 16)

Descriptive-behavioral component of the MSE involves the following:

1. *Special (examination) conditions:* These factors obviously influence the reliability and validity of the interview.

   a. Language differences make assessment difficult, even with a translator. Using family members to translate is generally not a good idea because of issues of bias and confidentiality.

   b. Who is present: Other people (e.g., students, other staff, family, friends) might facilitate or impair the interview. Again, issues of confidentiality must be considered.

   c. Setting: Was the interview done in a four-bed room, in the corridor of a busy emergency room, or some other place that would impair complete and open disclosure?

2. *Appearance of the patient:* Look for evidence that implies neuropsychiatric impairment. For example, are there signs of a craniotomy? Is there a movement disorder? Is the patient disheveled? Any unusual or inappropriate appearance should be recorded and needs to be explained.

3. *Participation:* Was the patient fully cooperative, hostile, resentful, suspicious? Any deviation from full cooperation must be taken into account in interpreting findings.

4. *Level of consciousness:* Unless the patient is fully conscious and alert, the examination cannot be reliably interpreted. It makes little sense to perform an MSE on a patient who is still groggy after extubation following an overdose.

   a. The following are categories for level of consciousness:

      (1) Within normal limits (WNL).

      (2) Decreased: patients are arousable and may provide brief, poorly sustained interactions. Decreased consciousness may be a result of just being awakened, drugs, or other central nervous system impairment.

(3) Patients in stupor are more difficult to arouse and usually not capable of meaningful interaction other than simple verbal and nonverbal responses to strong stimulation. This state of consciousness blends into early stages of coma with even less responsiveness.

(4) Fluctuating level of consciousness is a hallmark of delirium (see Chapter 3).

    (a) Statements during delirium (e.g., "I will not do anything to hurt myself now") may not be reliable.

5. *Kinetics:* Increased and decreased kinetics (body movements) are non-specific but important features to note for both diagnosis and monitoring of changes.

  a. Psychomotor agitation or retardation can be seen in mood disorders, anxiety, schizophrenia, and delirium.

  b. Variable kinetics are often seen as part of the behavioral fluctuation in delirium.

6. *Affect:* Affect refers to the expression of feelings. Normally, people show a broad range of affect (e.g., smiling, pensive, sad, angry). Pathologic affect may be:

  a. Restricted: A depressed patient may show only sad affect; a manic patient may show only euphoria, a schizophrenic patient may show no discernible affect (sometimes called "flat").

  b. Patients with frontal lobe impairment, intoxication, or mild delirium may lose the ability to regulate affect and may show labile affect with rapid fluctuations.

  c. Patients with delirium, intoxication, or frontal lobe impairment may also show inappropriate affect (e.g., laughs at something that should be sad).

    (1) In so-called "emotional incontinence" a patient cries suddenly for no apparent reason. This is usually a symptom of frontal lobe pathology or pseudo-bulbar impairment.

7. *Speech:* Descriptions of speech properties help indicate or support a variety of diagnoses:

  a. Loudness may be WNL or:

    (1) Soft as in depression.

    (2) Loud as in patients with mania, hearing impairment, or escalating psychotic patients.

    (3) Mute as in psychotically depressed patients or schizophrenics.

  b. Rate may be WNL or:

    (1) Slow as in depression or expressive aphasia.

    (2) Fast as in mania and stimulant intoxication.

    (3) Dysarthric as in patients following stroke involving the speech system.

    (4) Pressured as in mania or in some patients with brain damage.

  c. Structure, which refers to the semantic (meaning), and syntactic (grammatical) aspects of language, may be WNL or:

    (1) Vague (the listener has trouble figuring out what the patient is saying because there is so little content) as with dementia, depression, paranoia.

    (2) Dysphasic (the patient makes word or sentence errors) as with stroke involving the language cortex.

    (3) Impoverished as with severe depression, dementia, brain damage.

    (4) Incoherent as with disorganized schizophrenics, intoxicated patients, disorganized manic patients, or other brain-damaged patients.

    (5) Rapid subject changes as usually seen in manic states.

    (6) Tangential as shown by manic or schizophrenic patients.

References

Goldberg RJ, Novack DH: The psychosocial review of systems, *SocSci Med* 35:261-269, 1992.

Katz S, Ford AB, Moskowitz RW et al: Studies of illness in the aged. The index of ADL: a standardized measure of biological and psychosocial function, *JAMA* 185:914-919, 1963.

Lawton MP, Brody EM, eds: Assessment of older people: self-maintaining and instrumental activities of daily living. In *Assessment of older people.*

Thompson TL, Stoudemire A, Mitchell WE: Underrecognition of patients' psychosocial distress in a university hospital medical clinic, *Am J Psychiatry* 140:158-161, 1983.

Medical Evaluation of Psychiatric Symptoms

3

The following are goals of this chapter:
1. To review the medical causes of psychiatric symptoms.
2. To review the medications and drugs that cause psychiatric symptoms.

3.1 MEDICAL CAUSES OF SYMPTOMS

1. How do medical disorders produce psychiatric symptoms?
   a. Medical disorders can cause nonspecific stress. For example, the stress of beginning chemotherapy may trigger a major depression, especially if there is vulnerability to affective illness with previous or family history.
   b. Physical symptoms may mimic a psychiatric disorder. For example, asthma may present itself as panic attacks; multiple sclerosis may initially be regarded as a conversion disorder.
   c. Medical disorders can directly affect the central nervous system (CNS). The specific psychiatric symptoms are determined by the region and extent of CNS involvement. For example, lung cancer may metastasize to the temporal lobe and be interpreted as a mood disorder, or theophylline use may account for chronic anxiety.
2. Virtually any psychiatric symptoms may be caused by an underlying medical problem (see Table 3.1).
   a. *Visual hallucinations* are more suggestive of delirium than of schizophrenia or psychotic depression.
   b. *History of head injury* should raise suspicion for intracranial pathology.
      (1) The elderly are especially vulnerable to subdural hematoma, which may cause acute symptoms or a gradual change in behavior over months.
      (2) Schizophrenics, homeless patients, and substance abusers are at risk for trauma, assault, and head injury.
   c. *Use of medications and substances* (see Box 3.1).
      (1) Obtain a comprehensive list of every substance currently taken or recently discontinued.
      (2) When in doubt, obtain a toxicology screen.
      (3) If you are unsure whether a medication can cause a psychiatric symptom, look up and verify the information.
   d. *Medical problems that cause psychiatric symptoms* (see Box 3.2).

Table 3.1   Examples of medical causes of psychiatric symptoms

Psychiatric Symptom	Example of Medical Cause
Delusions	Amphetamine
Hallucinations	Delirium tremens
Incoherence	Delirium
Catatonia	Neuroleptic malignant syndrome
Flat or inappropriate affect	Frontal CVA
Strange speech	Language Cortex CVA
Odd beliefs	Interictal temporal lobe epilepsy
Anxiety	Hyperthyroidism
Depression	Pancreatic cancer
Irritability	Substance abuse

(1) PRINCIPLES
   (a) Construct a complete medical problem list.
   (b) If any problem could affect the CNS, consider further evaluation.
   (c) The psychiatric symptoms secondary to medical problems depend on the type of CNS involvement (see Table 3.1).
      (1) Generalized brain impairment results in delirium. Delirium may manifest as agitation, withdrawal, confusion, anxiety, psychosis, or depressive symptoms.
3. Principles of psychiatric evaluation
   a. Symptoms of disordered mood, thought, or behavior must be considered nonspecific symptoms, which require differential diagnosis.
   b. It is a mistake to assume that some psychosocial situations account for psychiatric symptoms.
   c. It is an equally serious mistake to launch into a comprehensive medical evaluation not supported by history or review of systems.
      (1) In general, medically ill patients are more likely to have secondary psychiatric problems.
4. History
   a. *Temporal onset:* In general, sudden onset of symptoms is consistent with a medical disorder.
      (1) Focal brain involvement results in specific symptoms determined by location.
      (2) Neurochemical changes (e.g., catecholamine depletion with use of reserpine) result in specific syndromes.
   b. A systematic evaluation decreases errors of omission. A useful mnemonic for the medical evaluation of psychiatric symptoms follows:

MEND A MIND	*Arterial*
Metabolic	*Mechanical*
Electrical	*Infectious*
Neoplastic	*Nutritional*
Drug	*Degenerative*

Box 3.1   Medications and Substances Causing Psychiatric Symptoms

Analgesics

Salicylates (plasma levels > 25 mg/dl): delirium, anxiety, tinnitus
Propoxyphene: euphoria, dysphoria
Narcotic mixed agonist-antagonists: euphoria, dysphoria, derealization

Antiarrhythmics: delirium, excitement, agitation

Quinidine
Procaineamide (may also cause delusions, depression or panic)
Disopyramide
Lidocaine
Tocainide
Mexiletine

Antibiotics

Penicillin (procaine form):psychosis
Nalidixic acid: delirium
Sulfonamides: delirium, anorexia
Cephalothin: delirium, paranoia
Aminoglycosides: toxic psychosis
Trimethoprim (Bactrim): psychosis, mutism, depression, anorexia, insomnia, headache

Anticholinergics

may cause a peripheral syndrome consisting of tachycardia; increased temperature; hot, dry, flushed skin; urinary retention; constipation; blurred vision; dry mouth. These drugs also cause a central syndrome consisting of confusion, memory impairment, restlessness, agitation, delirium, hallucinations, and severe anxiety.

Diphenhydramine (Benadryl)
Benzotropine (Cogentin)
Trihexyphenidyl (Artane)
Oxybutynin (Dithropan)
Pro-Banthine (Propantheline)
Tricyclic antidepressants
Meperidine (Demerol)

Anticonvulsants: drowsiness, mood change, confusion, psychosis, agitation

Phenytoin: irritability, depression, visual hallucinations, agitation
Phenobarbital: depression, confusion, disinhibition
Ethosuximide: confusion, paranoia, nightmares

Continued.

Box 3.1—cont'd

Antifungals

Ketoconazole: headache, dizziness
Amphoterocin-B: delirium, anorexia
5-Flucytosine: confusion, hallucinations

Anti-hypertensives

Reserpine: depression
Methyldopa: depression, lethargy, sedation
Clonidine: depression, hallucinations
Hydralazine: depression, euphoria, psychosis
Beta-blockers: depression, insomnia, nightmares, psychosis
Calcium channel blockers (nifedipine, verapamil): irritability, agitation, depression, hallucinations, panic

Antiinflammatories

NSAIDs: depression, anxiety, confusion
Phenylbutazone: anxiety, agitation
Indomethacin: delirium, depression, hallucinations

Antituberculars

Isoniazid: agitation, hallucinations, depression, euphoria, visual hallucinations, transient memory impairment
Cycloserine: insomnia, delirium, paranoia, depression
Rifampin: drowsiness, fatigue, anorexia
Ethambutol: headache, confusion, hallucinations

Chemotherapy Agents

Vincristine: hallucinations, weakness
Vinblastine: depression, anorexia, psychosis
Alpha interferon: depression, weakness
Bleomycin: anorexia
Methotrexate: fatigue
Procarbazine: mania, anorexia, confusion
Azidothymidine (AZT): headache, restlessness, insomnia, nightmares, agitation

Diuretics: weakness, apathy, confusion, delirium

Dopaminergics:

Antagonists cause motor symptoms including dyskinesias, dystonias, akinesia, or akathisia (see Chapter 20). Dopamine agonists may cause confusion, paranoia, hallucinations, depression, or anxiety.

DOPAMINE AGONISTS
Bromocriptine
Amantadine
Levodopa (L-dopa)
Levodopa-carbidopa (Sinemet)

Box 3.1—cont'd

DOPAMINE ANTAGONISTS
   Neuroleptics
   Metoclopramide

Sedatives and Narcotics:

These drugs cause sedation and impaired cognition. Withdrawal can produce delirium, agitation, or confusion, accompanied by tachycardia, fever, mydriasis, sweating, and tremor (see Table 14.1). Sedatives may also occasionally cause disinhibition.

   Alcohol
   Barbiturates
   Benzodiazepines
   Narcotics

Steroids

   Corticosteroids: Mood change, mania, agitation
   Anabolic steroids: aggression, paranoia, mood disorders
   Oral contraceptives: depression, anxiety, somnolence

Stimulants: may cause anxiety, agitation, paranoid psychosis, insomnia, confusion. Withdrawal may cause severe depression.

   Amphetamine
   Methylphenidate
   Cocaine
   Caffeine
   Theophylline

Sympathomimetics:

may cause anxiety, restlessness, agitation, psychosis, delirium.
   Pseudoephedrine
   Phenylpropanolamine
   Albuterol

Miscellaneous Drugs

   Pentamadine: restlessness, headache, dizziness
   Acyclovir: hallucinations, mood change, paranoia, anxiety
   Cyclobenzaprine (Flexeril): mania, psychosis
   Digitalis: confusion, psychosis, depression
   Metronidazole: depression, agitation, confusion
   Quinacrine: delirium
   Chloroquine: delirium
   Griseofulvin: depression, delirium
   Hypoglycemic agents: anxiety
   Cimetidine: hallucinations, confusion, delirium, depression, paranoia

Box 3.2   Medical causes of psychiatric symptoms

Metabolic and Endocrine Causes

    Addison's disease
    Calcium imbalance
    Carcinoid syndrome
    Cushing's syndrome
    Electrolyte abnormalities
    Hepatic failure
    Hyperparathyroidism
    Hyperthyroidism
    Hypoglycemia
    Hypothyroidism
    Hypoxia
    Magnesium imbalance
    Pheochromocytoma
    Porphyria
    Renal failure
    Wilson's disease

Electrical Causes

    Complex partial seizures
    Periictal states (depression, hallucinations)
    Postictal states (depression, dissociation, or disinhibition)
    Temporal lobe status epilepticus

Neoplastic Causes

    Carcinoid syndrome
    Carcinoma of the pancreas
    Metastatic brain tumors
    Primary brain tumors
    Remote effects of carcinoma

Medication and Drug Causes

    See Box 3.1

Arterial Causes

    Arterial-venous (A-V) malformations
    Hypertensive lacunar state
    Inflammation (cranial arteritis, lupus)
    Lupus
    Migraine
    Multiinfarct states
    Subarachnoid bleeds
    Subclavian steal syndrome
    Thromboembolic phenomena
    Transient ischemic attacks

Continued.

Box 3.2 — cont'd

Mechanical Causes

Concussion
Normal pressure hydrocephalus
Subdural or epidural hematoma
Trauma

Infectious Causes

Abscesses
AIDS
Hepatitis
Meningoencephalitis (including tuberculosis, fungal, herpes)
Multifocal leukoencephalopathy
Subacute sclerosing panencephalitis
Syphilis

Nutritional Causes

B_{12} deficiency
Folate deficiency
Niacin deficiency
Pyridoxine (B_6) deficiency
Thiamine deficiency

Degenerative and Neurologic Causes

Aging
Alzheimer's disease
Creutzfeldt-Jakob disease
Heavy metal toxicity
Huntington's disease
Multiple sclerosis
Parkinson's disease
Pick's disease

5. Physical Examination
   a. Physical examination findings provide important clues to medical causes that underlie psychiatric symptoms. A discussion of these issues may be found in Chapter 13.
   b. Follow-up and reevaluation of physical examination is especially important when the clinical course is unusual or unresponsive. Underlying medical disorders may be obscured by behavioral symptoms.

3.2   DIAGNOSTIC TESTING

The use of diagnostic testing must be guided by the history, review of systems, and physical/neurologic examination. There is no set regimen to follow for the routine laboratory evaluation of any psychiatric disorder.

1. Role of the EEG in psychiatric evaluation
   a. A waking EEG is useful for documenting the brain's background rhythm. This may be helpful in:
      (1) Detecting mild delirium.
      (2) Distinguishing dementia or delirium from depression.
         (a) Background EEG should be normal in depression but is usually slowed in delirium or dementia.
         (b) EEG may be normal in mild metabolic disorders.
      (3) The waking background rhythm decreases with age but usually does not go below 8 Hz without disease.
      (4) Slowing by more than 1 Hz per year suggests a progressive disease process.
      (5) Alzheimer's disease usually shows background slowing below 8 Hz, along with increased theta (5-7 Hz) and delta (1-3 Hz) activity and poor organization.
   b. A sleep EEG is useful in evaluating possible seizure disorders.
      (1) EEGs record only surface electrical activity for a limited period of time. Therefore, a high rate of false negatives (about 40%) exists even in patients with documented complex and simple partial seizures.
      (2) Complex partial seizures may be more accurately diagnosed by EEG (with identification rates approaching 90%) by use of:
         (a) Repeated EEG recordings
         (b) Sleep deprivation
         (c) Nasopharyngeal leads
         (d) Ambulatory monitoring
         (e) Closed circuit TV monitoring
      (3) The EEG may be useful in distinguishing generalized type seizures from pseudo-seizures, because generalized tonic-clonic seizures always have an abnormal EEG, along with postictal slowing.
   c. Ambulatory EEG monitoring can be useful for determining whether:
      (1) Some episodic behavioral problems (e.g., atypical panic attacks, episodic psychotic/autonomic symptoms) are caused by seizure activity.
      (2) Epileptic symptoms result from too much or too little medication.
   d. Effects of drugs on EEG
      (1) Virtually any psychotropic can produce EEG slowing.
         (a) The slowing effect of neuroleptics is mild.
         (b) Anti-depressant slowing is usually also accompanied with some increased fast activity.
         (c) At therapeutic doses benzodiazepines, barbiturates, and stimulants produce increased fast activity.
         (d) Lithium (even at therapeutic levels, but more commonly at high levels) can produce high voltage runs of diffuse slow activity.

      (e) Tricyclics and neuroleptics lower the seizure threshold and may induce paroxysmal activity, with spike or sharp waves. When significant abnormalities occur, the patient should be evaluated for an underlying seizure disorder.

2. Role of neuroimaging in psychiatric patients
   a. Potential indications: Neuroimaging should not be regarded as a screening test for every psychiatric patient, but should be considered in cases of:
      (1) Confusion or dementia of unknown cause
      (2) First episode of psychotic disorder of unknown cause
      (3) Movement disorder of uncertain cause
      (4) Anorexia nervosa
      (5) Prolonged catatonia
      (6) First episode of major depression
      (7) Personality change after age 50
   b. Advantages of MRI over CT Scans
      (1) Better soft tissue contrast
      (2) Unlimited scan planes
      (3) Absence of bone artifacts
      (4) Lack of ionizing radiation
      (5) Generally does not need contrast materials, although contrast agents maximize detection of brain metastatic disease.
         (a) With MRIs, a gadolinium-based agent is generally used, which does not have the disadvantages (allergic reactions and nephrotoxicity) of radiographic contrast agents used in CT scanning.
   c. Disadvantages of MRI
      (1) Motion sensitive
      (2) Longer scan times
      (3) Claustrophobia (generally can be managed with anxiolytics)
      (4) Metallic objects, including the following, are contraindications:
         (a) Cardiac pacemakers
         (b) Implanted neurostimulators
         (c) Cochlear implants
         (d) Metal in the eye
         (e) Metal aneurysm clips
      (5) Poor bone visualization
      (6) Pregnancy is a relative contraindication, especially in the first trimester. However, the unspecified risks are probably less than the risks of ionizing radiation.
   d. Diagnostic indications for MRI: For certain disorders, an MRI is clearly preferable to a CT scan and the cost differential is warranted. These situations include the following:
      (1) Demyelinating disease.
      (2) Temporal lobe abnormalities (because the sphenoid bone often obscures findings in that region).
      (3) Subcortical multiple lacunae or infarcts (often too small to show up on CT).
      (4) Abnormal endocrine function (better resolution and lack of bone artifact in visualizing pituitary).

      (5) Primary and metastatic neoplasms, along with associated features such as edema, vascularity, hemorrhage, and necrosis.

      (6) Abscess, encephalitis, meningitis. Early detection of herpes simplex encephalitis is best achieved with MRI. Other infections (often AIDS related) can also be visualized, including: toxoplasmosis, lymphoma, cryptococcosis, and neurosyphilis).

      (7) Posterior fossa lesions.

      (8) Acute stroke, especially ischemic infarcts of brainstem or cerebellum (MRI is not reliable before 8 hours after stroke).

      (9) Older collections of blood in the brain.

      (10) Progressive multifocal leukoencephalopathy.

  e. Noncontrast CT is the preferred neuroimaging technique in emergency situations.

  f. Role of SPECT scans.

    (1) Single positron emission computerized tomography (SPECT) allows imaging of blood flow patterns. Potential uses in psychiatry include:

      (a) Evaluation of dementia: the SPECT scan shows a characteristic biparietal hypoperfusion pattern in Alzheimer's disease that can be distinguished from multiinfarct dementia.

      (b) Evaluation of the site of a seizure focus.

      (c) Evaluation of cerebral infarct in a patient with recent onset of neurologic findings and a negative CT or MRI.

      (d) Evaluation of areas of poor perfusion following stroke or head trauma.

    (2) Future uses may involve identification of neuroreceptor sites utilizing receptor-binding radiotracers.

3. Role of lumbar puncture (LP): Indicated to evaluate the following:

  a. Unexplained elevated temperature in a patient with altered mental statues, which should be considered CNS infection until proven otherwise.

    (1) Especially for patients with altered immunocompetence from chronic diabetics, cancer, AIDS, immunosuppressives, or steroids.

  b. Possible CNS fungal infection (which has a high false negative rate).

  c. CNS herpes (associated with increased CSF ferritin levels).

  d. Multiple sclerosis (with findings of elevated IgG or oligoclonal bands).

  e. Alzheimer's disease. LP is not a routine test but should be considered if the patient has atypical features such as rapid progression, fever, meningeal signs, or a positive serology for syphilis.

4. Role of toxicology screens.

  a. To assist in assessing psychiatric symptoms that do not have a clear diagnosis.

  b. When in doubt about possible drug or medication use.

  c. If the patient is taking medications for which levels are available; obtain levels to see if the patient is at toxic (or subtherapeutic) level.

  d. When determining alcohol levels (for interpretation of blood alcohol levels, see Chapter 14).

  e. When determining cocaine levels: Although cocaine has a brief plasma half-life, its metabolite, benzoyl ecognine can be detected in urine for up to several days.

Note that false positive and false negative results are possible, depending on techniques. When in doubt, consult with the laboratory technician about suspicion of particular drugs.

5. Thyroid tests
   a. Because hypothyroidism can be present as depression and hyperthyroidism as anxiety, screening is often indicated.
   b. A high sensitivity thyroid-stimulating hormone (TSH) test is sufficient as a screen for both hyperthyroidism and hypothyroidism.
      (1) If the TSH is elevated (indicating possible hypothyroidism), a total or free T4 should be obtained.
      (2) If the TSH is subnormal (indicating possible hyperthyroidism), follow-up with a total or free T4 and T3.
   c. Screening for patients taking lithium should occur every 6 to 12 months (see Chapter 7).

6. Glucose and glucose tolerance tests (GTTs)
   a. Glucose screening should be considered for patients with psychiatric symptoms along with diabetes mellitus, alcoholism, or cirrhosis.
   b. Hyperglycemia can cause delirium by creating osmotic imbalances in the brain.
   c. Postprandial hypoglycemia is rarely a cause of psychiatric symptoms.
      (1) Five-hour GTTs are rarely helpful in evaluating symptoms of anxiety, fatigue, or depression.
      (2) GTT may be relevant in patients after gastric/small intestine surgery with dumping syndrome.
   d. Patients taking excessive insulin may have hypoglycemic episodes presenting as anxiety, confusion, agitation, belligerence, or fatigue, which are responsive to glucose infusion.

7. Liver function tests (LFTs)
   a. Patients with extensive liver disease resulting from malignancy, cirrhosis, or hepatitis are at risk for development of hepatic encephalopathy if liver function deteriorates further. This disorder is usually marked by generalized slow waves (triphasic waves) in the EEG.
   b. LFTs are important to evaluate patients taking medications that can cause allergic hepatic responses (e.g., carbamazepine, chlorpromazine) if the patient develops clinical symptoms such as nausea, abdominal discomfort, or jaundice.

8. Arterial blood gases (ABGs)
   a. Hypoxia: Any cause of brain hypoxia (e.g., congestive heart failure, COPD, pneumonia, cardiac arrhythmia, pulmonary embolism, or asthmatic episode) will make a patient feel anxious. Therefore, assessment of PO_2 may be an important part of evaluating anxiety symptoms in such patients.
   b. Carbon dioxide retention (elevated P_{CO_2}) can result in somnolence, confusion, and impaired attention.
      (1) Avoid using benzodiazepines in patients with elevated P_{CO_2}, because they can suppress hypoxic respiratory drive and lead to respiratory depression or arrest.
   c. Sleep apnea (see Chapter 10): Oxygen desaturation from sleep apnea, can result in a variety of psychiatric symptoms including daytime sleepiness, fatigue, depression, and cognitive impairment.

(1) Patients at risk often have short, thick necks or snore loudly; however, sleep apnea can occur in patients without these features. Observing the patient for apneic periods is a first step in moving toward a referral for a sleep evaluation.

9. Complete blood cell count (CBC) is relevant to psychiatry in a number of situations:
   a. Weekly monitoring for patients taking Clozapine.
   b. When patients taking drugs such as carbamazepine or phenothiazines develop sore throat or fever.
   c. When evaluating a postsurgical patient with altered mental status who may have had significant operative blood loss.
   d. In assessing anemia in patients with altered mental status (resulting in fatigue, confusion, anxiety, depressive symptoms).

10. BUN/creatinine levels are relevant to psychiatry in the following situations:
    a. To assess renal function in patients taking drugs that are cleared by the kidneys (e.g., lithium and amantadine).
    b. In patients having chronic renal failure: As uremia worsens, psychiatric symptoms become more prominent.
    c. As a clue to dehydration and associated orthostasis risk, especially in patients with poor oral intake.

11 Electrolytes are relevant to psychiatry in the following situations:
   a. Syndrome of inappropriate antidiuretic hormone (SIADH) may develop secondary to use of drugs such as lithium or carbamazepine.
   b. Hyponatremia from any cause (usually use of diuretics) may cause delirium.
   c. Hypokalemia leads to muscle fatigue and weakness, which many patients identify as a symptom of "depression."
   d. For patients taking lithium, anything that significantly alters sodium balance (diuretics, vomiting, diarrhea) will alter lithium levels and may lead to lithium toxicity (see Chapter 7.)

12. Creatinine kinase (CK): An enzyme elevated from muscle damage, is relevant to psychiatry in the following situations:
    a. Neuroleptic malignant syndrome (NMS)(see Chapter 11) where CK elevations (MM fraction) are usually over 800 IU/L.
       (1) Elevations up to 800 may occur in patients after intramuscular injections or in those struggling in restraints.
    b. Fractionating the CK isoenzymes ensures that the elevation is not caused by the cardiac fraction, following a myocardial infarction.
       (1) Behavioral changes in the elderly may be a result of silent myocardial infarction.
    c. High elevations of CK may be found in patients following muscle crush injuries, such as car accidents.

13. Porphyrins
    a. Porphyria is a rare cause of episodic psychiatric symptoms. Abdominal pain is the usual presenting complaint, with 30% to 70% accompanied by episodic psychiatric symptoms, usually delirium or psychosis.
    b. During attacks, there may be qualitative abnormalities of uroporphyrins and coproporphyrins in the urine. These tests are not useful between attacks.

    c. Quantitative urine measurements of aminolevulinic acid (ALA) and porphobilinogen (PBG) may be abnormal between attacks.

    d. A more definitive test involves measurement of uroporphyrinogen I synthetase; decreased activity can confirm a diagnosis.

14. Copper

    a. Wilson's disease is an autosomal recessive genetic disorder that results in abnormal accumulation of copper resulting in hepatic cirrhosis, degeneration of the basal ganglia, neuropsychiatric symptoms, and hemolytic anemia.

    b. Screening tests include serum ceruloplasmin and 24-hour urinary copper levels; 90% of patients with Wilson's disease have a very low serum ceruloplasmin; 24-hour urinary copper levels are high.

    c. Screening for Wilson's disease should be considered in patients with psychiatric symptoms and in those with the following:

      (1) A family history of Wilson's disease.

      (2) Unexplained liver disease.

      (3) Signs of basal ganglia or frontal lobe disease not otherwise explained.

15. Pregnancy test

    a. Because there are a number of fetal effects of psychotropic drugs, pregnancy status should be established before prescribing medication.

    b. At times, a mysterious behavior change in a young woman may be caused by an unannounced pregnancy.

16. Vitamin B_{12}

    a. Psychiatric symptoms (anxiety, psychosis, delirium, or dementia) occur in 35% to 85% of patients with B_{12} deficiency.

    b. Accompanying physical symptoms are paresthesias and sensory loss (particularly vibration and proprioception leading to ataxia).

    c. B_{12} deficiency may be present in the absence of classic hypochromic macrocytic anemia.

    d. If B_{12} is deficient, a Schilling test is performed to differentiate dietary deficiency from impaired absorption due to absent intrinsic factor.

17. Folate

    a. Folate deficiency frequently accompanies B_{12} deficiency.

    b. Folate levels may also be low in patients with alcoholism, patients taking anticonvulsants or on dialysis, and pregnant women.

References

Abramowicz M, ed: Drugs that cause psychiatric symptoms, *Med Lett Drugs Ther* 35:65-70, 1993.

Alarcon RD, Franceschini JA: Hyperparathyroidism and paranoid psychosis: case report and review of the literature, *Br J Psychiatry* 145:477-512, 1984.

Bluestein HG: Neuropsychiatric manifestations of systemic lupus erythematosus, *N Engl J Med* 317:309-311, 1987.

Carmel R: Pernicious anemia—the expected findings of very low serum cobalamin levels, anemia, and macrocytosis are often lacking, *Arch Intern Med* 148:1712-1714, 1988.

Cassem EH: Depression and anxiety secondary to medical illness, *Psychiatr Clin North Am* 13:597-612, 1990.

Dolan JG, Mushlin AI: Routine laboratory testing for medical disorders in psychiatric inpatients, *Arch Intern Med* 145:2085-2088, 1985.

Edelman RR, Warach S: Magnetic resonance imaging, *N Engl J Med* 328:708-716, 1993.

Garber HG, Weilburg JB, Buonanno FS et al: Use of magnetic resonance imaging in psychiatry, *Am J Psychiatry* 145:164-171, 1988.

Greenlee JE: *Cerebrospinal fluid in central nervous system infections.* In Scheld WM, Whitley RJ, Durack DT, eds: *Infections of the central nervous system,* New York, 1900, Raven Press.

Hammerstrom DC, Zimmer B: The role of lumbar puncture in the evaluation of dementia: the University of Pittsburgh study, *J Am Geriatr Soc* 33:397-400, 1985.

Hellman RS, Tikofsky RS, Collier BD et al: Alzheimer disease: quantitative analysis of I-123-iodoamphetamine SPECT brain imaging, *Radiology* (172)183-188, 1989.

Klawans HL: Levodopa-induced psychosis, *Psychiatr Ann* 8:19-22, 1978.

Leigh H, Kramer SI: The psychiatric manifestations of endocrine disease, *Adv Intern Med* 29:413-445, 1984.

Ling MH, Perry PJ, Tsuang MT: Side effects of corticosteroid therapy: psychiatric aspects, *Arch Gen Psychiatry* 38:471-474, 1981.

O'Connell RA, Sireci SN, Fastov ME et al: The role of SPECT brain imaging in assessing psychopathology in the medically ill, *Gen Hosp Psychiatry* 13:305-312, 1991.

Reus VI: Behavioral disturbances associated with endocrine disorders, *Ann Rev Med* 37:205-214, 1986.

Zubenko GS, Sullivan P, Nelson JP et al: Brain imaging abnormalities in mental disorders of late life, *Arch Neurol* 47:1107-1111, 1990.

Delirium, Dementia, and Other Cognitive Disorders

The following are goals of this chapter:
1. To provide definitions, evaluations, differential diagnoses, and treatments for delirium and dementia.
2. To provide instructions for the cognitive mental status examination.

4.1 DELIRIUM

Definition and Identification

1. The characteristic features of delirium include the following:
   a. Impaired attention and consciousness.
   b. Other cognitive changes not accounted for by dementia, such as the following:
      (1) Memory impairment
      (2) Disorientation
      (3) Language disturbance
      (4) Perceptual disturbance
   c. Development usually occurs over a short period of time (hours to days) and tends to fluctuate over the course of the day.
      (1) Mild delirium, which becomes more pronounced in the evening, is sometimes referred to as *sundowning.*
   d. Evidence of some probable underlying medical etiologic factors.
2. Delirium is **important to recognize** because
   a. It often signals an underlying (and usually correctable) medical condition affecting brain and behavior.
   b. It can be associated with inadvertent self-injury.
   c. It interferes with communication and competent participation in treatment.
   d. The associated arousal can adversely affect other medical conditions.
3. Patients with delirium may appear withdrawn, agitated, or psychotic.
   a. In addition, underlying personality traits may become exaggerated and disinhibited, leading some patients to become more paranoid, for example.
4. Underlying causes of delirium include the following:
   a. Systemic medical conditions.
   b. Substance intoxication or withdrawal.
   c. Multifactorial causes (e.g., hyponatremia, hypoxia, high digitalis levels, anemia, fever).

Incidence and Prevalence

1. Delirium is one of the most commonly encountered mental disorders in medical practice, which affects, at some point, about half of hospitalized and elderly medically ill.
2. Delirium is often misdiagnosed as depression, anxiety, dementia, or personality disorder, or it may be overlooked completely.

Prognosis

1. By definition, delirium is a transient disorder, which may be as brief as hours or may linger in a subacute form for weeks or months.
2. If the underlying medical cause is corrected, complete recovery should occur.
   a. The time required to achieve recovery depends on the degree of the brain insult and the capacity of the brain to tolerate the insult.
      (1) Older patients take longer to recover (up to several weeks).

Treatment

1. Correct the underlying medical causes (see Chapter 3).
2. Agitated behaviors are managed with neuroleptics and/or benzodiazepines.
   a. Extreme agitation requires using rapid neuroleptization or rapid loading with benzodiazepines (see Chapter 13).
   b. Mild restlessness and confusion may improve with lower doses of neuroleptics, such as haloperidol 0.5 mg or perphenazine (Trilafon) 2 mg in the evening or bid, PO (see Chapter 11).
3. Adjunctive measures must be implemented to keep patients safe.
   a. Partial or complete restraints may be necessary for a limited time (see Chapter 13 for guidelines governing use of restraints).
   b. Patients may need the continuous presence of a staff member to ensure safety.
   c. Ensure a safe environment, without loose equipment (such as IV poles, glass, metal instruments), which could be used destructively.
      (1) Patients with severe forms of delirium have been known to jump through glass windows. Ideally, such patients should be in a room with safety glass.
   d. Because of altered judgment and perception, delirious patients should not drive, walk in areas with traffic, and so on.
   e. Patients with delirium sufficient to impair function should not be allowed to sign out of a hospital against medical advice unless their safety and monitoring can be ensured.
   f. Patients need clear, simple instructions and expectations with continuous reorientation (including large clocks and calendars) and reminders.
      (1) Patients are less confused in more familiar settings.
      (2) It is important to explain to the patient and family that symptoms are secondary to identifiable and treatable medical problems.

4.2   DEMENTIA

Definition and Identification

1. Dementia is defined as the following:
   a. Memory impairment, and

    b. Cognitive impairment, such as:
      (1) Language disturbance.
      (2) Apraxia (inability to carry out motor activities despite intact motor function).
      (3) Agnosia (inability to recognize or identify objects despite intact sensory function).
      (4) Executive function problems (e.g., planning, organizing, sequencing, abstracting).
    c. An onset that is usually insidious (as opposed to the more rapid onset of delirium) and is usually characterized by progressive gradual decline.
    d. Deficits that cause significant decline in previous level of function.
2. Dementia and delirium often occur together.
    a. Patients with mild dementia often become a behavioral problem because of a new, superimposed delirium.
3. Mood disturbances, anxiety, delusions, hallucinations, and impaired sleep commonly accompany dementia (see Chapter 17).

Differential Diagnosis

1. **Medical causes of dementia: see Box 4.1.**
    a. About 5% to 20% of dementias have a reversible component.
2. **Age-associated memory impairment** (AAMI) (previously known as *benign senescent forgetfulness*) is defined as mild memory loss in the elderly without other cognitive deficits or identifiable medical or psychiatric cause for the memory difficulties.
    a. The Mini-Mental State Examination score is $\geq$ 24, indicating lack of dementia.
3. **Alzheimer's disease** (AD) is diagnosed when other specific medical (see Box 4.1) and psychiatric causes (such as major depression) have been ruled out.
    a. Chapter 17 contains a more detailed review of diagnostic issues.
    b. There are currently no definitive antemortem markers for Alzheimer's disease.
    c. AD accounts for about 70% of dementia patients.
    d. Delusions and hallucinations complicate AD in about 40% of patients (see Table 17.1 for list of associated behavioral problems).
    e. Personality change usually precedes neurological findings.
4. **Multiinfarct dementia** (MID) is also a clinical diagnosis. The relationship of cerebrovascular disease to the diagnosis is uncertain.
    a. **The Hachinski Ischemic Score** may be helpful in sorting out a dementia diagnosis (See Table 4.1).
    b. MID and mixed MID/AD accounts for 20% of dementia in elderly patients.
5. **Postconcussion disorder** is another cognitive disorder, characterized by:
    a. History of head trauma with some loss of consciousness and posttraumatic amnesia.
    b. Difficulties in attention, new learning, and memory.
    c. Other features include the following:
      (1) Easy fatigability
      (2) Disturbed sleep pattern
      (3) Headache

Box 4.1   Medical Causes of Dementia

Metabolic (includes endocrine)

Acid-base disturbances
Calcium disturbance (low or high)
Carcinoid syndrome
Electrolyte abnormalities
Hepatic encephalopathy
Hypercapnea
Hypercortisolemia
Hyperglycemia
Hypoglycemia
Hypoxia
Magnesium abnormalities
Parathyroid abnormalities
Pheochromocytoma
Pituitary abnormalities
Porphyria
Thyroid disturbance (low or high)
Uremia
Wilson's disease

Electrical

Complex partial seizures
Postictal states (depression or disinhibition)
Temporal lobe status epilepticus

Neoplastic

Any primary or metastatic brain lesion, including meningiomas

Drug

Anticholinergics
Benzodiazepines
Digoxin
Dopamine agonists
H_2 blockers
Lidocaine
Narcotics
Phenytoin
Salicylates
Theophylline

Continued.

Box 4.1—cont'd

Arterial

A-V malformations
Hypertensive lacunar state
Inflammation (cranial arteritis, lupus)
Migraine
Subarachnoid bleeds
Thromboembolic phenomena
Transient ischemic attacks

Mechanical

Hydrocephalus (normal pressure)
Trauma (concussion)
Subdural or epidural hematomas

Infectious

Abscesses
AIDS
Meningoencephalitis (TB, fungal)
Multifocal leukoencephalopathy
Subacute sclerosing panencephalitis
Tertiary syphilis

Nutritional

B_{12} deficiency
Folate deficiency
Wernicke-Korsakoff syndrome

Degenerative

Aging
Alzheimer's disease
Creutzfeldt-Jakob disease
Heavy metal exposure
Huntington's disease
Multiple sclerosis
Parkinson's disease
Pick's disease

---

  (4) Vertigo or dizziness
  (5) Irritability or increased aggressiveness
  (6) Anxiety, depression, mood lability
  (7) Personality changes
  (8) Apathy or lack of spontaneity.
6. **Pseudo-dementia:** Depression may be misidentified as dementia. This condition, often called *pseudo-dementia,* is eminently treatable by treating the depression (see Chapter 6).

Table 4.1   The Hachinski Ischemic Score

Characteristic	Score
Abrupt onset	2
Stepwise deterioration	1
Fluctuating course	2
Nocturnal confusion	1
Relative preservation of personality	1
Depression	1
Somatic symptoms	1
Emotional incontinence	1
History of hypertension	1
History of stroke	2
Evidence of associated artherosclerosis	1
Focal neurologic symptoms	2
Focal neurologic signs	2

Seven or more points indicates multiinfarct dementia.
Five or six points indicates mixed dementia.
Four or fewer points indicates primary degenerative dementia.
Hachinski VC, Iliff LD, Zihka E et al: Cerebral blood flow in dementia, *Arch Neurol* 32:632-637, 1975.

Box 4.2   Basic Workup for Dementia

Chest x-ray examination
ECG
Complete blood cell count
Electrolytes
Folate level
HIV status in high-risk groups
Metabolic studies (depending on medical status)
Neuroimagining (when diagnostic issues are unclear)
Screening test for syphilis
Thyroid function tests
Urinalysis
Vitamin B_{12} level

Evaluation

1. Identify any potential contributing medical causes (see Box 4.1).
2. All patients with new onset dementia should have some standard diagnostic studies, modified by individual circumstances. These studies include those listed in Box 4.2.
3. A useful mnemonic for the medical differential evaluation of delirium, dementia, and other behavioral symptoms is "MEND A MIND." Unless the clinician follows some systematic approach to evaluation, there is a significant risk of errors of omission.

MEND A MIND

*M*etabolic
*E*lectrical
*N*eoplastic
*D*rug

*A*rterial

*M*echanical
*I*nfectious
*N*utritional
*D*egenerative

Treatment

1. Correction of any underlying medical causes is the treatment of choice, with the hope that the patient will improve (if brain cells have not been damaged too severely) or at least not deteriorate further.
2. Adjunctive environmental measures are helpful in dementia as described in the delirium treatment section.
3. Managing the behavioral problems associated with dementia (also see Chapter 17):
   a. **Psychotic symptoms** (delusion and hallucinations) secondary to dementia.
      (1) Neuroleptics are the drugs of choice to treat psychotic symptoms. Some issues to consider:
         (a) Older patients are very sensitive to the parkinsonian side effects, and these have to be monitored very closely since the patient may become more incapacitated, especially if there is underlying Parkinson's disease.
         (b) While thioridazine (Mellaril) is the least likely of the typical neuroleptics to cause parkinsonian side effects, it does produce anticholinergic effects: orthostasis and sedation. A total daily dose below 100 mg can usually be tolerated.
         (c) Neuroleptics produce akathisia, with increased restlessness and agitation (see Chapter 11). Akathisia can be managed by lowering the neuroleptic dose or by giving small doses of beta-blockers (about 5-10 mg tid of propranolol).
         (d) Use lowest dose of neuroleptics for the shortest time possible.
   b. **Affective symptoms** (see also Chapters 6 and 17).
      (1) Antidepressants are indicated for depression, which accompanies dementia.
         (a) Because pseudo-dementia is always a possibility, it is wise to err on the side of giving a trial of antidepressants because often there is little to lose and much to gain.
         (b) Among the available antidepressants, those with high anticholinergic activity should be avoided (see Chapter 7). The tricyclics also produce orthostasis (which can lead to falls and fractures) and cardiac conduction delay.
         (c) The selective serotonin reuptake inhibitors (SSRIs) appear to be effective and well tolerated in geriatric patients. Issues with the

SSRIs to consider include increased agitation (somewhat more of an issue with fluoxetine) and nausea (see also Chapter 7).

c. **Anxiety symptoms** (see also Chapters 9 and 17).

(1) Although benzodiazepines have been the standard drug group for treating generalized anxiety, they have some liabilities for the elderly, including psychomotor impairment, drowsiness, and cognitive impairment.

(a) Use the shorter-acting agents at doses as low as possible.

(2) Buspirone (Buspar) is not sedative and therefore does not produce psychomotor impairment, drowsiness, or cognitive impairment. It has virtually no serious side effects for the elderly (see Chapter 9). Starting dose is 5 mg tid for anxiety in elderly demented patients.

d. **Agitated behaviors** (see also Chapters 13 and 17) Drug groups used for these symptoms include the following:

(1) *Neuroleptics* may help aggressiveness if that behavior is a consequence of underlying psychotic process; otherwise, neuroleptics appear to cause nonspecific sedation and extrapyramidal side effects.

(2) *Benzodiazepines* are often used to nonspecifically sedate agitated patients; however, oversedation may impair function at doses large enough to prevent aggressive outbursts.

(3) *Buspirone* can decrease episodic agitation in dementia patients, usually in doses around 5 mg tid. The effect may be seen within a week, but more often it takes several weeks.

(4) *Trazodone* has some antiaggression effects in demented patients. It may work acutely in calming agitated dementia patients, even at fairly low doses such as 50 mg orally, with a repeat dose if necessary. Used on a regular basis at doses such as 25-50 mg tid, trazodone appears to decrease aggressive behavior over 3 to 4 weeks.

(5) *Lithium, carbamazepine,* and *valproic acid* have all been tried in elderly demented aggressive patients. Case reports indicate some success with each of them. Unfortunately, there appears to be no way to predict which patients will benefit from these medications.

(6) *Beta-blockers* also have been reported to decrease episodic aggression in brain-damaged patients (often in high doses such as over 350 mg/day of propranolol). However, such doses are poorly tolerated in the elderly and probably have little role.

e. **Cognitive impairment** (see also Chapter 17) A number of medications are under study for enhancing cognitive function in Alzheimer's patients.

(1) Unfortunately, no drug, with the potential exception of Tacrine for patients with mild to moderate symptoms, has, at this time, much to offer on any consistent basis.

4.3   AMNESTIC DISORDERS

Definition and Identification

1. Amnestic disorders are defined as:

a. Impairment in both short-term memory (with an inability to learn new information) and long-term memory, sufficient to cause some impairment in patient functioning.

        (1) Long-term memory impairment likely involves more recent, rather than remote, memory.

   b. The memory impairment does not occur exclusively during delirium and does not meet criteria for dementia (i.e., there is no change in abstraction, judgment, personality, or higher cortical function).

        (1) Amnestic disorders are distinguishable from delirium and dementia because of the presence of memory problems without the other prominent cognitive impairments.

   c. History, physical examination, and laboratory results indicate a probable medical cause.

2. Amnestic disorders include the following:

   a. Amnesia caused by cerebral or systemic medical conditions, which impinge on:

        (1) The medial temporal region (e.g., tumors, head injuries, or vascular conditions).

           (a) In these cases, anterograde amnesia is the outstanding cognitive deficit, but retrograde amnesia can also occur.

        (2) The diencephalic region (often following thalamic infarction); the critical anatomic areas involved are the mediodorsal nucleus of the thalamus and the mammillary bodies of the hypothalamus.

           (a) This is the region involved with Korsakoff's syndrome, with its severe anterograde amnesia.

   b. Substance-induced amnesia (e.g., caused by benzodiazepines).

        (1) In evaluating any problems of amnesia, be sure the patient has been discontinued from benzodiazepines and other sedative drugs (including alcohol).

   c. Other disorders of amnesia.

        (1) Temporary amnesia resulting from traumatic head injury

        (2) Transient global amnesia (sudden onset, lasts for several hours)

        (3) Post-electroconvulsive therapy (ECT) amnesia (see Chapter 15).

   d. Other disorders that mimic amnestic disorders.

        (1) Frontal lobe damage may cause memory impairment, because of difficulties with organizational and retrieval strategies. The frontal disorders also include deficits involving personality and higher executive functions.

        (2) Depressed patients often show memory impairment.

           (a) In amnesia, the ability to store new long-term memories is impaired.

           (b) In depression the initial processing of new information is impaired (depressed patients may have problems encoding information but can retain some). The amnestic patient processes information but does not retain any.

        (3) Psychogenic amnesia (a rare deficit).

           (a) Usually occurs after a trauma and lasts for days or weeks.

           (b) The patient is often initially found in a fugue state, wandering and acting confused.

           (c) The memory problem is not accompanied by any other cognitive deficits.

           (d) The memory deficits are often only for specific personal memories rather than public events. The patient shows an ability to relearn personal information.

(4) Malingering (see Chapter 12).

(5) Multiple personality disorder patients are often amnesic for some aspects of their history.

4.4   THE COGNITIVE MENTAL STATUS EXAMINATION

Use of Standardized Examinations

1. Some clinicians have advocated the use of standardized mental status examinations to screen for or follow the progress of delirium or dementia.

   a. Inferences about cognitive function based solely on informal medical interviewing are often inaccurate. A patient who appears intact during casual conversation may show significant deficits when formally tested.

   b. One of the commonly used tests is the Mini-Mental State Examination (see Table 4.2).

      (1) This test is brief, easy to administer, and is widely known.

      (2) There are some limitations of this test:

         (a) Focal impairment and milder forms of dementia are poorly detected.

         (b) Performance may be related to education level.

2. When to test cognitive mental status.

   a. Not every patient needs to have a cognitive mental status examination any more than every patient needs a complete physical examination. The interviewer should assess cognitive mental status in the following situations:

      (1) Patients with known brain damage (e.g., stroke, brain tumor, trauma, dementia). There is a need to specify the types and extent of cognitive impairment and to document changes over time.

      (2) Patients with medical disorders or on medications that could potentially alter the functioning of the central nervous system (CNS) (see Chapter 3 Boxes 3.1 and 3.2).

         (a) Many medications create attention or memory deficits and may need to be changed if such alterations are detected.

         (b) Patients with borderline compensated organ failure (heart, lungs, kidney, liver) may show a change in cognitive function as an early sign that the medical condition is worsening.

         (c) Patients with malignancies that frequently metastasize to the brain (e.g., lung or breast cancer), may show some cognitive change as the first sign of CNS involvement.

      (3) Patients being evaluated for competence must have cognitive function evaluated to ascertain if they are able to function adequately to provide consent.

      (4) Patients who are depressed require some cognitive evaluation because of the association of cognitive dysfunction with depression.

      (5) Patients complaining of some cognitive impairment need to have this complaint fully defined and assessed.

Table 4.2   The Mini-Mental State Examination*

Maximum Score	Score	
		ORIENTATION
5	( )	What is the (year)(season)(date)(day) (month)?
5	( )	Where are we (state)(county)(town)(hospital) (floor)?
		REGISTRATION
3	( )	Name three objects, and ask patient to repeat them. One point for each correct. Continue until patient learns them.
		ATTENTION AND CALCULATION
5	( )	Serial 7s. One point for each correct response.
3	( )	Stop after 5 answers.
		RECALL
2	( )	Ask for the three objects from registration section. One point for each correct.
		LANGUAGE
1	( )	Name a pencil and a watch.
		Repeat: "NO IFS, ANDS, OR BUTS."
3	( )	Follow command: "Take paper in your right hand, fold it in half, and put it on the floor."
1	( )	Read and obey: close your eyes.
1	( )	Write a sentence.
1	( )	Copy a design.
30		

Assess level of consciousness
Alert   Drowsy   Stupor   Coma

*From Folstein et al: with permission.

Introducing the Cognitive Mental Status Examination (MSE)

1. Let the patient know the reason these questions are important by providing some context.
   a. For example, you could say, "It is not unusual for a patient with your condition (or taking your medications, or with your level of distress) to experience some difficulties with thinking and concentration. Have you noticed anything like that?" If the patient acknowledges some difficulties, it is easy to proceed. Even if difficulties are denied, proceed by saying, "I'm glad you haven't noticed any problems, but they can commonly be difficult to recognize. Early detection may help avoid greater difficulties later or might mean you need some changes in your medication (etc.)."
2. Do not introduce this evaluation by saying something like, "Now I'm going to ask you some questions that may seem silly," or "These are just questions we ask everybody."

Components of the Cognitive MSE

See Table 4.3. NOTE: The tests suggested are not meant to be exclusive or the only tests that can be used; they are given as common, clinically helpful examples.

1. The cognitive components can be thought of in a hierarchy, with more complex functions requiring more basic functions to be intact.
2. **Table 4.4** provides a summary of the cognitive mental status components, the associated neuroanatomical systems, and the tests commonly used for assessment.
   a. *Level of consciousness:* If the patient is not alert, the rest of the examination will be impossible to assess.
      (1) In delirium, level of consciousness may be impaired and commonly fluctuates.
      (2) In dementia, level of consciousness should not be altered.
      (3) Level of consciousness should not be impaired in affective disorder or schizophrenia. However, in extreme cases patients may be so withdrawn that ascertaining their level of alertness may be difficult.
   b. *Attention:* Ability to maintain attention (and to filter out distracting stimuli) should be the first function formally assessed because attentional disturbances interfere with all higher level functions. Attention has two categories:
      (1) **Maintenance of attention** (vigilance or concentration).
         (a) A good test of attention maintenance is *months backwards.* Ask the patient to start with the month December and name the months backwards. This test is fairly independent of age or educational level; patients should be able to perform this task, especially if they receive a little prompting to support and encourage them to complete it.
         (b) An easier test (for the impaired patient) would be to count backwards.
         (c) Spelling words backwards is also sometimes used.

Table 4.3 Cognitive Component of the Mental Status Examination*
Level of consciousness: Alert   Drowsy   Stupor   Coma

WNL[†]	PROB ABN[‡]	ABN[§]	Function	Test
			Attention	
			Language	
			Naming	
			Fluency	
			Repetition	
			Reading/writing	
			Memory	
			Immediate recall	
			Short-term	
			Visual memory	
			Long-term	
			Construction	
			Higher functions	
			Intellect	
			Abstraction	
			Judgment	

*The test actually used to assess each function can be recorded in the blank area, and the result of the assessment can be recorded as **within normal limits, probably abnormal,** or **definitely abnormal.**
[†]Within normal limits.
[‡]Probably abnormal.
[§]Definitely abnormal.

     (d) "Serial sevens" (sequentially subtracting 7 from 100 and continuing with the remainder) is often used to test attention, but simple math requires calculating ability and a high percentage of normal adults make errors.
  (2) Ability to screen out extraneous stimuli (response inhibition or **vulnerability to interference**).
     (a) The "trail-making test" is a pencil and paper test involving connecting numbers and letters from within a random pattern. It can be quite sensitive at picking up early or subtle attention problems (such as in patients with early HIV brain involvement). This test is not usually part of bedside or office screening by the primary clinician.
  (3) Disordered attention is the hallmark of delirium; however, in extreme forms of dementia, depression, mania, and schizophrenia, attentional processes will appear fragmented.
  (4) In addition, it is important to be aware of the possibility of adult attention deficit disorders, which will show attentional distur-

Table 4.4 Hierarchy of Cognitive Functions

Cognitive Function	Neuroanatomic Correlation	Sample Assessment
Attention	Brainstem reticular system and frontal lobes	Months backwards
Language	Dominant temporal lobe	Naming, fluency, repeating
Memory		
Immediate recall	Perisylvian cortex	Repeating 3 words
Short-term	Limbic structures	3-Word delay recall; Orientation
Long-term	Cerebral cortex	30-Minute delay recall; Past events
Construction	Parietal lobes	Copy figures
Higher functions		
Intellect	Cerebral cortex	Calculation
Abstraction	Cerebral cortex	Proverbs/similarity
Judgment	Cerebral cortex	Problem solving

bances from childhood and may respond to treatment with stimulants.

c. *Language:* Language is critical for most cognitive abilities, and specific language disturbances are often indicative of brain damage.

(1) Aphasia is common in early onset Alzheimer's disease.

(2) Listen to spontaneous speech for the following:

  (a) Paraphasia (using a word this is not quite right, such as "blinker" when the patient means "blanket").

  (b) Dysprosody (defined as a loss of the emotional phrasing of language).

  (c) Receptive or expressive aphasia (not understanding language or being able to express oneself).

(3) Subtle language problems may need to be elicited by specific questioning. The following are language functions worth testing in a screening MSE:

  (a) *Naming:* Impaired in almost all subtypes of aphasia. Naming abnormalities indicates there is some damage to language cortex. The patient can be asked to name common and uncommon objects until the presence or absence of a naming deficit is confirmed. Intact patients should not miss any common objects. Naming (or any other cognitive function) may be impaired in depression.

  (b) *Verbal fluency:* Patients with normal spontaneous speech and intact naming can have impaired fluency. Fluency is often tested by asking the patients to name, in 60 seconds, as many words as they can think of that begin with the letters *F, A,* and *S.* Inability to name, within one minute, 12 or more words beginning with these letters suggests reduced verbal fluency, though patients with less than 10 years of education cannot be held to this standard.

(c) *Repetition:* A patient may have intact language except for repetition. A selective deficit in repetition (e.g., inability to repeat a phrase such as "pry the tin can's lid off") usually indicates a transcortical aphasia. Such focal impairment can result from anoxia resulting from decreased cerebral circulation after cardiac arrest, occlusion of the carotid artery, carbon monoxide poisoning, or dementia.

(d) *Reading and writing:* Virtually all patients with impaired oral language have written language difficulties as well. Patients with a posterior lesion in the angular gyrus (dominant anterior parietal area) may have minimal oral language dysfunction, although they may show agraphia and alexia.

(e) *Language disorders* are a hallmark of cortical impairment. In extreme forms of affective disorder, schizophrenia, and even anxiety disorders, patients may show language errors.

d. *Memory:* Memory problems are the most common initial complaint of patients with brain disease.

(1) Both attention and language disturbances as well as depression and anxiety, can impair memory performance.

(2) Memory testing is usually divided into the following three components:

(a) *Immediate recall:* Before a patient is asked to remember words or objects for later recall, it is important to demonstrate that the patient has registered the words. Therefore, repeating words is the first step in a verbal memory test. The most likely cause of failure of registration is inattention.

(b) *Short-term verbal memory:* Ability to recall three words after several minutes is the commonly used test of short-term memory, although it neglects nonverbal memory and is not sensitive to mild deficits. Recalling fewer than two of the three words clearly shows impairment because most patients will be able to recall all three objects.

  (*i*) The first and most notable symptom for patients with Alzheimer's disease is rapid forgetting (within 10 minutes) of new information.

(c) *Nonverbal (visual) memory:* This function is often neglected in testing. Nonverbal memory tends to be abnormal in various dementias but not in normal aging. Nonverbal memory may be tested by asking the patient to copy several geometric forms from memory after a delay of several minutes.

(d) *Orientation* can be defined as a short-term memory function.

  (*i*) One inoffensive way to ask about orientation is to hand the patient a blank sheet of paper and say, "I'd like to begin our assessment by having you write your name and the date at the top of the paper."

  (*ii*) For the medically ill patient, one could say, "It is not unusual for people not feeling well to lose track of time, and I wonder whether that has happened to you. Could you tell me the day . . . date . . . month . . . year?" If the patient makes an error, it can be pointed out that such a problem is not unusual under the circumstances, and the patient should be reoriented.

(iii) The patient's orientation response should be recorded verbatim to avoid having to interpret whether an answer that is close is correct or not.

(e) *Long-term memory:* In assessing this function, avoid questions you do not know the answers to. For example, do not ask the name of a second grade teacher, or what the patient had for breakfast yesterday if you don't know the answers. One reasonable approach to testing long-term memory is by a careful history of present illness, which probes names and dates of important events. Confabulation can occasionally mislead the interviewer into misjudging the extent of a patient's memory impairment. Long-term memory problems can also be uncovered by talking to family members or noting deficits in the patient's work or social performance.

e. *Constructional ability:* Without some test of visual-perceptual processes or spatial functions, a significant portion of the brain (nondominant parietal lobe) remains untested.

   (1) Few patients complain spontaneously of constructional impairment.
   (2) Constructional ability is tested by
       (a) Asking the patient to **copy a geometric figure** (such as a cross) or
       (b) Asking the patient to **draw a clock** and put in the numbers and a specific time.
   (3) Nondominant parietal lobe lesions generally produce some impairment in this function (with neglect of one side of the figure), though deficits are most striking with bilateral lesions.
   (4) Patients with dementia show nonspecific drawing problems with poor organization, impoverishment, and fragmentation, rather than a characteristic spatial neglect.
   (5) Poor planning or poor motor control can also produce drawing problems.

f. *Higher cognitive functions:* Many of the most characteristic and important human functions remain untested by the standard MSE questions.

   (1) Such higher functions include curiosity, problem solving, and complex judgments.
   (2) Patients with such deficits may complain that something is wrong, but routine mental status testing shows no abnormalities.
       (a) Such patients may need to be referred for more complex neuropsychological assessment batteries.
   (3) Some of the higher cognitive functions tested include the following:
       (a) *Intellect:* Testing calculating abilities may be too simple a task for many patients and too difficult for others. A better approach is to assess intellectual change by determining what

the person's work is and whether or not there has been some deterioration of function in tasks associated with that job.

(b) *Abstraction:* Patients can be asked how certain objects (e.g., apple-orange; table-chair) are alike, or they can be asked to interpret proverbs. Proverb interpretation is highly variable and the determination of abnormal performance can be highly subjective. Loss of abstracting ability is a common deficit seen in patients with dementia but can also be seen in patients with low intelligence and in schizophrenia.

(c) *Judgment:* The complex functions that make up judgment can be impaired in virtually any psychiatric disorder. To test judgment:

  (*i*) Patients can be asked artificial questions such as, "What would you do if you smelled smoke in a movie theater?"

  (*ii*) As an alternative, one could ask patients questions about their current problems and about what it makes sense to do with them. Such an approach can give a glimpse into the patient's judgment in a more natural way.

References

Barry PP, Moskowitz MA: The diagnosis of reversible dementia in the elderly: a critical review, *Arch Intern Med* 148:1914-1918, 1988.

Concensus Conference: Differential diagnosis of dementing diseases, *JAMA* 258:3411-3416, 1987.

Cummings JL: *Subcortical dementia,* New York, 1990, Oxford University Press.

Engel GL, Romano J: Delirium: a syndrome of cerebral insufficiency, *J Chronic Dis* 9:260-277, 1959.

Fogel BS, Mills MJ, Landen JE: Legal aspects of the treatment of delirium, *Hosp Community Psychiatry* 37:154-158, 1986.

Folstein MF, Folstein SE, McHugh PR: Mini-Mental State, *J Psychiatr Res* 12:189-198, 1975.

Francis J, Martin D, Kapoor WN: A prospective study of delirium in hospitalized elderly, *JAMA* 263:1097-1101, 1990.

Goldberg RJ, Faust D, Novack D: Integrating the cognitive mental status examination into the medical interview, *Southern Med J* 85:491-497, 1992.

Lipowski ZJ: Delirium (acute confusional states), *JAMA* 258:1789-1792, 1987.

Liptzin B, Levkoff SE, Gottlieb GL et al: Delirium, *J Neuropsych* 5:154-160, 1993.

Nelson A, Fogel B, Faust D: Bedside cognitive screening instruments: a critical assessment, *J Nerv Ment Dis* 174:73-83, 1986.

Rosen WG, Terry RD, Fuld PA et al: Pathological verification of ischemic score in differentiation of dementias, *Ann Neurol* 7:486-488, 1980.

Squire LR, Amaral DG, Press GA: Magnetic resonance imaging of the hippocampal formation and mammillary nuclei distinguish medical temporal lobe and diencephalic amnesia, *J Neurosci* 10:3106-3117, 1990.

Szymanski HV, Linn R: A review of the postconcussion syndrome, *Int J Psychiatry Med* 22(4):357-375, 1992.

Tucker GJ, Caine ED, Folstein MF et al: Introduction to background papers for the suggested changes to DSM-IV: cognitive disorders, *J Neuropsych* 4(4):360-368, 1992.

5

Depression: Identification and Diagnosis

The following are goals of this chapter:
1. To identify depressive symptoms.
2. To provide a systematic evaluation of depressive symptoms.
   a. Medical causes
   b. Psychosocial dimensions
3. To increase recognition of major depression and other affective disorders.

5.1   GENERAL ISSUES OF IDENTIFICATION

1. The term *depression* can mean many different things. Therefore, when patients say they are "depressed," it is important to ask, "What do you mean by 'depressed'?"
2. The term *depression* may refer to any of the following:
   a. Major affective disorder (major depression)
   b. Depression secondary to some medical cause
   c. Adjustment disorder with depressed mood
   d. Dysthymia (minor, chronic depression)
   e. Brief depressive reaction
   f. Grief
   g. Bereavement
   h. Chronic emptiness of the borderline personality
   i. A component of schizoaffective disorder
   j. Boredom.
3. Because "depression" can mean so many different things, it is important to be precise. Start the evaluation by listing "depressive symptoms," as demonstrated in Box 5.1, which presents a summary of the five areas of history pertinent to evaluating depressive symptoms:
   a. Delineation of *depressive symptoms* themselves.
   b. *Accompanying symptoms* (for differential diagnosis)
   c. *Possible precipitants* (for potential psychotherapy)
   d. *Possible medical causes*
   e. *Past episodes*

5.2   STRATEGY FOR THE EVALUATION OF DEPRESSION

1. Step one
   a. Consider "depression secondary to a medical cause"

Box 5.1   Depressive Symptoms Data Base

Depressive symptoms	Duration
Depressed mood	_____
Decreased energy	_____
Poor concentration	_____
Sleep change	_____
Appetite change	_____
Psychomotor change	_____
Guilt, poor self-esteem	_____
Anhedonia	_____
Suicidality	_____
Chronic pain	_____
Poor functional level	_____
Somatized symptoms	_____

Accompanying symptoms

Delusions	_____
Panic attacks	_____
Mania	_____
Hallucinations	_____
Generalized anxiety	_____

Possible precipitants

_____

_____

Possible medical causes

_____

_____

Past episodes

_____

_____

_____

   b. Identify and correct (if possible) potential medical causes of depressive symptoms (see Boxes 5.2 and 5.3).

2. Step two
   a. Consider "adjustment disorder with depressive symptoms"
   b. Assess psychosocial problems
   c. Decide if these can be addressed by some type of psychotherapy or counseling.

3. Step three
   a. Consider the possibility of major depression or other affective disorder.
   b. Use a "target symptom approach" to decide if antidepressant medication should be a component of treatment.

Box 5.2   Medical Causes of Depressive Symptoms

Brain tumor	Hypokalemia
Cancer	Hypothyroidism
Coronary artery disease	Hypoxia
Dementia	Liver failure
Diabetes mellitus	Multiple sclerosis
Epilepsy	Parkinson's disease
HIV positivity	Renal failure
Hypercalcemia	Sleep apnea
Hypercortisolism	Stroke

Box 5.3   Medications and Substances Causing Depressive Symptoms

Alcohol	Clonidine
Alpha-methyldopa	Corticosteroids
Amantadine	Oral contraceptives
Anabolic steroids	Propranolol
Anticholinergics	Ranitidine
Anticonvulsants	Reserpine
Barbiturates	Sedatives
Benzodiazepines	Stimulant (withdrawal)
Cimetidine	Thiazides

(1) Treat depressive symptoms with medication if they are severe enough, even if it is impossible to sort out whether they are due to major depression, adjustment disorder, or some untreatable underlying medical factors.

THE DEPRESSIVE DISORDERS

5.3   DEPRESSION SECONDARY TO SOME MEDICAL CAUSE

Definition and Identification

1. In the past this category was called *organic affective disorder.* However, because major depression is an "organic disorder," this terminology is being eliminated.
   a. Therefore, depressive symptoms caused by hypothyroidism would be listed as "depression secondary to hypothyroidism."
2. Box 5.2 lists selected medical causes of depressive symptoms.
3. Box 5.3 lists medications that are associated with depressive symptoms.
4. Potential medical causes of depression should be considered in every patient. The extent of the medical evaluation should be determined by the medical history and review of systems. For example:
   a. In a healthy 28-year-old with depressive symptoms and a negative medical review of systems, it is not warranted to pursue an extensive medical workup.
   b. In a patient with a history of lung cancer, the onset of depressive symptoms should raise consideration of a metastatic brain lesion. A careful neurologic and mental status examination should be done.
5. There is no recipe for the medical workup of depression. The workup is determined by the specific medical conditions that could affect the central nervous system.

Differential Diagnosis

1. Do not assume that depression is necessarily caused by some obvious psychosocial distress.
   a. For example, it would be a mistake to dismiss an evaluation by saying, "Wouldn't you be depressed if you had cancer?" Certainly, patients with severe medical illness face difficult psychological issues; however, such patients may develop depressive symptoms because of hypercalcemia, brain metastases, or severe anemia.
2. Depression secondary to a medical cause deserves consideration in every differential diagnosis of depressive symptoms.

Prognosis

1. Depressive symptoms secondary to some medical cause usually resolve themselves when the underlying medical problem is corrected.
   a. Patients in pain often exhibit depressive symptoms that disappear when the pain is adequately treated.
   b. Patients receiving drugs that cause depression (e.g., alcohol or antihypertensives) usually recover when that drug is discontinued.
2. Since depressive symptoms may have multifactorial causes, the correction of underlying medical problems (e.g., mild hypothyroidism) may not resolve all depressive symptoms.

Treatment

1. All potential medical causes of depression should be corrected if possible.
2. In many cases the relationship between an underlying medical factor and the depressive symptoms cannot be confirmed.
   a. For example, if the patient is taking a drug that might cause depression, such as cimetidine, the practical approach would be to change to some alternative drug.
3. The presence of contributing medical factors does not exclude the need for other dimensions of therapy.
   a. For example, a patient with depression secondary to steroid therapy may need antidepressants and certainly might benefit from supportive psychotherapy for issues related to the illness experience.

5.4   MAJOR DEPRESSION

Definition and Identification

1. Major depression used to be called *endogenous depression.*
2. Major depression is defined by the presence of specific symptoms.
   a. There is no biological marker for major depression, though its diagnosis implies an underlying psychobiological disorder.
3. For criteria for diagnosing major depression, see Box 5.4. The diagnosis requires the following:
   a. **Depressed or discouraged mood must be present continuously for at least 2 weeks.** It is useful to ask medical patients if they are discouraged, since many patients deny being "depressed" because it is considered a sign of weakness and involves some stigma.
   b. **The depressive symptoms cannot be a result of some medical cause.**

NOTE: In addition, the diagnosis requires at least four of the following:
   c. **Fatigue.** Fatigue is one of the most common complaints taken to primary care physicians. Depression is one of the most common disorders underlying this symptom.

Box 5.4   Diagnostic Criteria for Major Depression

At least 5 of the following* present continuously over 2 weeks.
Depressed mood
Anhedonia
Appetite change or weight change
Sleep disturbance
Psychomotor agitation or retardation
Fatigue
Feeling worthless or guilty
Poor concentration
Suicidal thoughts

---

*One of the symptoms must be either depressed mood or anhedonia.

d. **Decreased concentration.** Depression is usually thought of as a mood disorder; however, it is also a cognitive disorder. When the cognitive impairment is prominent, especially in the elderly, clinicians often misdiagnose the problem as dementia. Memory difficulty associated with depression is sometimes called *pseudodementia.*

e. **Change in sleep pattern.** Depressed patients may have classical early morning awakening but also may have trouble initiating or maintaining sleep. Ask the patient, "Has there been a change in your usual sleep pattern?" (See Chapter 10 for a review of sleep disorders.)

f. **Change in appetite.** Depressed patients typically have impaired appetite (which may result in weight loss); however, increased appetite (and weight gain) is also possible.

g. **Psychomotor agitation or retardation** is a behavioral expression of depression. Clinicians may observe hand wringing, restless pacing, or withdrawal and slowed movements.

h. **Excessive guilt and loss of self-esteem.** Depressed patients frequently magnify their faults and feel excessively and inappropriately guilty about past actions.

i. **Anhedonia.** Anhedonia is the inability to get pleasure from or find interest in activities. Ask, "When you were last feeling well, what sort of things did you do to enjoy yourself? Are you doing those things now, and do you enjoy them?"

j. **Suicidal ideation.** It is crucial to ask about suicidal ideation as part of every depression evaluation because patients may not volunteer this information (see Chapter 13 for further discussion of suicide).

   (1) It may be helpful to pursue this topic by an escalating series of questions (see Box 5.5).

   (2) Patients acknowledging suicidal ideation and plan should be considered a serious suicide threat.

   (3) Arrangements should be made for the patient's safety until a psychiatric evaluation takes place or some other competent clinician evaluates the situation.

Box 5.5   Interview Protocol for Evaluating Suicidal Ideation

1. "You have said you are depressed; could you tell me what that's like for you?"
2. "Are there times you feel like crying?"
3. "When you feel that way, what sort of thoughts go through your mind?"
4. "Do you ever get to the point where you feel that if this is the way things are, that it is not worth going on?"
5. "Have you gone so far as to think of taking your own life?"
6. "Have you made any plan?"
7. "Do you have the means to carry out such a plan?"
8. "Is there anything that would prevent you from carrying out the plan?"

The Use of Standardized Screening Instruments

1. Because of problems in recognition or reluctance of patients to talk about symptoms, it can be useful to screen for depression using standardized instruments, such as:
   a. Beck Depression Inventory (see Box 5.6) is one of the most widely used, self-rated scales. It contains 21 items. A score ≥ 18 indicates a serious depressive condition, which should be evaluated further.

Box 5.6   Beck Depression Scale

On this questionnaire are groups of statements. Please read each group of statements carefully. Then pick out the one statement in each group which best describes the way you have been feeling during the PAST WEEK, INCLUDING TODAY. Circle the number beside the statement you have chosen. Be sure to read all the statements in each group before making your choice. If several in the group seem to apply equally well, circle each one. **(Be sure to read all the statements in each group before making your choice.)**

1. 0 I do not feel sad.
   1 I feel sad.
   2 I am sad all the time and I can't snap-out of it.
   3 I am so sad or unhappy that I can't stand it.
2. 0 I am not particularly discouraged about the future.
   1 I feel discouraged about the future.
   2 I feel I have nothing to look forward to.
   3 I feel the future is hopeless and that things cannot improve.
3. 0 I do not feel like a failure.
   1 I feel I have failed more than the average person.
   2 As I look back on my life, all I can see is a lot of failures.
   3 I feel I am a complete failure as a person.
4. 0 I get as much satisfaction out of things as I used to.
   1 I don't enjoy things the way I used to.
   2 I don't get real satisfaction out of anything anymore.
   3 I am dissatisfied or bored with everything.
5. 0 I don't feel particularly guilty.
   1 I feel guilty a good part of the time.
   2 I feel quite guilty most of the time.
   3 I feel guilty all of the time.
6. 0 I don't feel I am being punished.
   1 I feel I may be punished.
   2 I expect to be punished.
   3 I feel I am being punished.
7. 0 I Don't feel disappointed in myself.
   1 I am disappointed in myself.
   2 I am disgusted with myself.
   3 I hate myself.

Continued.

Box 5.6—cont'd

8. 0 I don't feel I am any worse than anybody else.
   1 I am critical of myself for my weaknesses or mistakes.
   2 I blame myself all the time for my faults.
   3 I blame myself for everything bad that happens.
9. 0 I don't have any thoughts of killing myself.
   1 I have thoughts of killing myself, but I would not carry them out.
   2 I would like to kill myself.
   3 I would kill myself if I had the chance.
10. 0 I don't cry any more than usual.
    1 I cry more now than I used to.
    2 I cry all the time now.
    3 I used to be able to cry, but now I can't cry even though I want to.
11. 0 I am no more irritated now than I ever am.
    1 I get annoyed or irritated more easily than I used to.
    2 I feel irritated all the time now.
    3 I don't get irritated at all by the things that used to irritate me.
12. 0 I have not lost interest in other people.
    1 I am less interested in other people than I used to be.
    2 I have lost most of my interest in other people.
    3 I have lost all of my interest in other people.
13. 0 I make decisions about as well as I ever could.
    1 I put off making decisions more than I used to.
    2 I have greater difficulty in making decisions than before.
    3 I can't make decisions at all anymore.
14. 0 I don't feel I look any worse than I used to.
    1 I am worried that I am looking old or unattractive.
    2 I feel that there are permanent changes in my appearance that make me look unattractive.
    3 I believe that I look ugly.
15. 0 I can work about as well as before.
    1 It takes an extra effort to get started at doing something.
    2 I have to push myself very hard to do anything.
    3 I can't do any work at all.
16. 0 I can sleep as well as usual.
    1 I don't sleep as well as I used to.
    2 I wake up 1-2 hours earlier than usual and find it hard to get back to sleep.
    3 I wake up several hours earlier than I used to and cannot get back to sleep.
17. 0 I don't get more tired than usual.
    1 I get tired more easily than I used to.
    2 I get tired from doing almost anything.
    3 I am too tired to do anything.

Continued.

Box 5.6—cont'd

18. 0 My appetite is no worse than usual.
    1 My appetite is not as good as it used to be.
    2 My appetite is much worse now.
    3 I have no appetite at all anymore.
19. 0 I haven't lost much weight, if any lately.
    1 I have lost more than 5 pounds.
    2 I have lost more than 10 pounds.
    3 I have lost more than 15 pounds.
    I am purposely trying to lose weight by eating less.
    _____Yes _____ No
20. 0 I am no more worried about my health than usual.
    1 I am worried about physical problems such as aches and
       pains; or upset stomach; or constipation.
    2 I am very worried about physical problems and it's hard to
       think of much else.
    3 I am so worried about my physical problems, that I cannot
       think about anything else.
21. 0 I have not noticed any recent change in my interest in sex.
    1 I am less interested in sex than I used to be.
    2 I am much less interested in sex now.
    3 I have lost interest in sex completely.

---

b. Hamilton Depression Scale is commonly used in depression research
   as a way of following progress. It requires questions and ratings by the
   clinician, who rates 21 items.

Prevalence

1. The community prevalence of major depression is 3% to 5%. The
   lifetime risk is 3% to 12% for men and 20% to 25% for women. The risk
   is higher for those with a first-degree relative with major depression,
   bipolar disorder, or alcoholism.
2. The prevalence of major depression in the elderly
   a. Community prevalence of 3% to 5%
   b. Nursing home prevalence 15% to 20%.
3. The prevalence of major depression goes up dramatically in patients with
   medical illness as shown in Table 5.1.

Recognition

1. In primary care practice, recognition of major depression is about 50%.
   Reasons for low recognition include the following:
   a. Patient reluctance to acknowledge symptoms.
   b. Predominant symptoms may mislead the clinician.
      (1) Fatigue may be seen as a medical problem
      (2) Sleep difficulty may be seen as primary

Table 5.1   Prevalence of Depression in Selected Medical Disorders

Alzheimer's disease	15%-55%
Cancer patients	
Inpatients	42%
Gastrointestinal	20%
Gynecologic	23%
Coronary artery disease	18%-26%
Cushing's syndrome	67%
Diabetes mellitus	33%
End stage renal disease	30%
Epilepsy	55%
HIV positive	7%-15%
Huntington's disease	32%-41%
Multiinfarct dementia	27%-60%
Multiple sclerosis	6%-57%
Myocardial infarction	18%
Pain (chronic)	32%
Parkinson's disease	40%
Renal disease	8%
Stroke	30%-50%

    (3) Cognitive symptoms are seen as dementia
    (4) Somatized symptoms imply a medical problem
    (5) Chronic pain may be seen as only a physical problem
    (6) Functional disability may be accepted as inevitable
    (7) Depression may be seen as a "normal" reaction.
2. Comorbidity
    a. Anxiety disorders, such as obsessive compulsive disorder, panic disorder, and generalized anxiety, often coexist with depressive disorders.

5.5   DIFFERENTIAL DIAGNOSIS

1. **Major depression with psychotic symptoms**
    a. Psychotic symptoms may accompany severe depression, increasing risk for suicide.
    b. A question to uncover psychotic symptoms might be the following:
        (1) "It is not unusual for someone who is very depressed to hear voices saying unpleasant things (like you don't deserve to live), or to have disturbing thoughts about his or her body. Has anything like that happened to you?"
    c. Somatic delusions are not unusual in severely depressed patients.
    d. Psychotic depressed patients usually need a neuroleptic along with their antidepressant.
2. **Schizoaffective disorder**
    a. Should be considered in patients with combined depression and psychotic symptoms.

(1) With psychotic depression psychotic symptoms occur only during the depression.

(2) In the schizoaffective patient psychotic symptoms also occur separately. In severe forms of psychotic depression the distinction may not be easy to make.

3. **Bipolar affective disorder with depression**

   a. In any patient with major depression, ask about manic episodes to determine if the patient is bipolar. Screening questions might be the following:

      (1) "Have there been times when you felt the opposite of depressed, that is, euphoric, or irritable, clearly different from your normal self?"

      (2) "Have there been times when you stayed up all night, spent a lot of money, or acted socially in a way you later regretted?"

   b. Bipolar depressed patients often need a mood stabilizer (e.g., lithium; see Chapter 7), along with an antidepressant. A mood stabilizer, by itself, is usually not adequate to resolve the depression.

4. **Depression secondary to a medical cause**

   a. This should always be considered (see previous section).

5. **Adjustment disorder with depressed mood**

   a. The presence of a "precipitating" event does not exclude the diagnosis of major depression. Many major depressions have an identifiable precipitant and respond to medication no differently from those that do not.

   b. Adjustment disorders:

      (1) Do not meet the full criteria for major depression

      (2) Occur in relation to a specific stress, and

      (3) Last less than 6 months.

6. **Bereavement** is associated with the death of a close relationship. During bereavement, the person may show the symptoms of major depression.

   a. The duration of bereavement may be culturally determined; it is problematic to diagnose a depressive disorder before the prescribed bereavement phase has been completed.

7. **Other depressive disorders** include

   a. **Dysthymia** (see Section 5.7).

   b. **Borderline personality disorder** with chronic emptiness, depressed mood, and suicidal ideation (see Chapter 16).

   c. **Seasonal affective disorder** (see section 5.9).

Prognosis

1. Left untreated, episodes of major depression usually last about 6 to 9 months.

2. Some cases of major depression are episodic and recurrent.

3. Some cases become chronic and may last for years.

4. Without treatment, major depression is a serious illness that affects quality of life to the same extent as chronic medical illnesses. In addition, there is a definite increased risk of suicide.

5. Treatment has a significant positive effect, with ≥70% of major depression responding to adequate trials of medication.

Treatment

Three forms of effective treatment for major depression are psychotherapy, antidepressant medication, and electroconvulsive therapy (ECT).

1. Psychotherapy.
    a. Several forms of psychotherapy have research evidence to confirm that the response of patients with moderate levels of major depression is equivalent to that obtained with antidepressants. Among the most studied psychotherapies are:
        (1) Cognitive behavioral therapy.
            (a) A patient is helped to identify and alter repetitive, distorted, maladaptive ways of thinking, which create depressive responses.
        (2) Interpersonal psychotherapy.
            (a) One problem area is chosen. The therapy process consists of:
                (*i*) Nonjudgmental exploration
                (*ii*) Active questioning
                (*iii*) Clarification
                (*iv*) Direct advice
                (*v*) Decision exploration
                (*vi*) Development of insight
                (*vii*) Facilitation of affective responses.
    b. Should you use medication or psychotherapy?
        (1) Patients whose symptoms interfere with participation in talking therapy should start with medication first.
        (2) Patients with milder symptoms who seem willing to talk about their problems should be started with psychotherapy, reserving medication for an inadequate response.
        (3) Between these extremes, the two treatments can be used conjointly.
        (4) As a generalization: Psychotherapy addresses problems; medication addresses symptoms.
2. Antidepressant medication (see Chapter 6).
3. Electroconvulsive therapy (ECT) indications and use (see Chapter 15).

5.6 OTHER DEPRESSIVE DISORDERS

ADJUSTMENT DISORDER WITH DEPRESSED MOOD

Definition and Identification

1. Transient discouragement as a response to some identifiable life stress, occurring within 3 weeks of a stressor, and lasting less than 6 months.
2. NOTE: It is also possible for adjustment disorders to be characterized by anxiety alone or by mixed anxious and depressed mood.

Prevalence

1. No one is immune from brief depressive reactions.
    a. These transient self-limited feelings generally remain separate from the medical care system; however, in many cases they contribute to medical utilization.
2. Brief depressive reactions are very common during the course of serious medical illness.

Differential Diagnosis

1. If the symptoms intensify and remain continuous for more than 2 weeks, the patient may start to qualify for an episode of **major depression.**
2. **Borderline personalities** (see Chapter 16) may have brief severe depressive reactions, which include suicidal ideation or behavior.
3. Withdrawal reactions from stimulant drugs may occur.
4. The effects of **sedating drugs,** including alcohol.
   a. Alcohol has some initial, brief mood-elevating effects, followed by worsening depressive feelings.
5. **Delirium** may appear as depression to the casual observer.
6. **Dysthymia:** the low-grade depressive symptoms are present for at least 2 years (longer than an adjustment disorder).
7. **Grief** can be thought of as a special case of an adjustment problem associated with a specific loss. Grief reactions are not limited to loss of a person through death but may be the result of loss of health, social position, job, and so on.
   a. Grief reactions are, by definition, time-limited events, which should spontaneously resolve. If they do not resolve, the person may develop another category of depressive disorder.

Prognosis

1. Adjustment disorders are generally self-limited; however, they do have the potential to become unresolved, chronic disorders. It is not unusual, for example, to find unresolved grief reactions manifesting as chronic medical symptoms.

Treatments

1. Adjustment disorders should be treated by some form of time-limited therapies, which focus on the precipitant and the development of more adaptive coping responses.
2. Anxiolytics or antidepressants can be used as an adjunct to the psychotherapy if the symptoms are severe or the patient is not psychologically minded.
3. Some patients transform their distress into a somatic symptom. In those cases the physician should educate the patient about the connection between the underlying distress and the resulting physical symptom (see Chapter 12 for a review of acute somatization).

5.7   DYSTHYMIA

Definition and Identification

1. Dysthymia refers to chronic depressive symptoms that do not become severe enough to meet criteria for major depression, present for at least 2 years.

Prevalence

1. The community-based prevalence of dysthymia is 4.5% to 10.5%, more common in women than men.

Differential Diagnosis

1. Adjustment disorder (cannot last more than 6 months).
   a. Chronic sense of emptiness and anhedonia, which may accompany borderline personality disorder (see Chapter 16).
   b. Chronic major depression (symptom number and severity is greater than with dysthymia).
   c. Dysthymia may coexist with other psychiatric disorders.
      (1) *Double depression* is sometimes used to refer to an episode of major depression superimposed on dysthymia.

Prognosis

1. Dysthymia is, by definition, a chronic condition.

Treatments

1. Dysthymia is not very responsive to either psychotherapies or pharmacotherapies.
2. Some patients appear to benefit from antidepressants, including monoamine oxidase inhibitors (MAOIs).

5.8   MIXED ANXIETY-DEPRESSION

Definition and Identification

1. There has not been a DSM category for mixed anxiety-depression, even though it is extremely common.
2. Mixed anxiety-depression is a state of general distress characterized by both anxious and depressive symptoms, with neither of sufficient number or severity to qualify for a separate anxiety or depressive disorder (see Fig. 5.1).

Prevalence

1. Mixed anxiety-depression may be one of the most common psychiatric presentations in primary care practice, with a prevalence estimated of at least 5%.

Differential Diagnosis

1. Primary depressive disorders with some anxiety symptoms
2. Primary anxiety disorders with some depressive symptoms
3. Adjustment disorder with mixed anxiety and depression
4. Coexistence of an anxiety and a depressive disorder.

Prognosis

1. The natural course is not well known.

Treatments

1. Because little data exist on the natural history, treatment effects are also not well known.
2. If symptoms are clinically significant, it would be reasonable to give the patient a trial of:
   a. Any antidepressant from Table 6.1, because all antidepressants also have antianxiety properties.

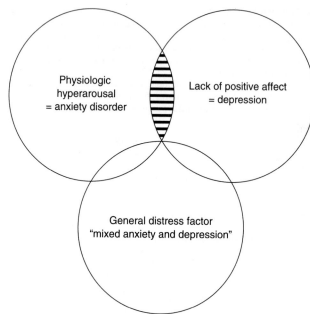

Figure 5.1.
Mixed anxiety-depression.

   b. Buspirone, because the azapirone group has both antianxiety and antidepressant activity.

5.9 SEASONAL AFFECTIVE DISORDER

Definition and Identification

1. There is a temporal relationship between the onset (or remissions) of a mood disorder and a particular period of the year.
   a. Typically illness begins in autumn or spring
   b. Carbohydrate craving and weight gain are often associated
   c. Sleep disturbance is usually hypersomnia.

Prevalence and Prognosis

1. No definitive data exist in these areas.

Differential Diagnosis

1. Bipolar disorder without clear seasonal pattern.
2. Recurrent depression without clear seasonal pattern.
3. Recurrent psychiatric symptoms triggered by seasonal events (such as seasonal pattern of lay-offs from work).

Treatments

1. Bright light stimulation at dawn or dusk has been reported to help people with "winter" depression.
2. There is no single agreed-on approach to the dose or duration of light that is most effective. Treatments often consist of about 2 hours of bright, full-spectrum light.

References

Alexander DA: Bereavement and the management of grief, *Br J Psychiatry* 153:860-864, 1988.

Avery DH, Bolte MA, Dager SR et al: Dawn simulation treatment of winter depression: a controlled study, *Am J Psychiatry* 150:113-117, 1993.

Caplan LR, Ahmed I: Depression and neurological disease: Their distinction and association, *Gen Hosp Psychiatry* 14:177-185, 1992.

Coulehan JL, Schulberg HC, Block MR: The efficiency of depression questionnaires for case finding in primary medical care, *J Gen Int Med* 4:541-547, 1989.

Depression in primary care: vol 1, *Detection and diagnosis,* Rockville, Md., 1993, U.S. Dept of Health and Human Services.

Depression in primary care: vol 2, *Treatment of major depression,* Rockville, Md., 1993, U.S. Dept of Health and Human Services.

Goldberg RJ: Depression in primary care: DSM-III diagnoses and other depressive syndromes, *J Gen Int Med* 3:491-497, 1988.

Goldberg RJ: Depression in medical patients, *Rhode Island Med J* (in press).

Katon WJ, Buchwald DS, Simon GE et al: Psychiatric illness in patients with chronic fatigue and those with rheumatoid arthritis, *J Gen Int Med* 6:277-285, 1991.

Liebowitz MR: Mixed anxiety and depression: should it be included in DSM-IV? *J Clin Psychiatry* 54(5):4-7, 1993.

Mayeux R, Stern Y, Williams JBW: Clinical and biochemical features of depression in Parkinson's disease, *Am J Psychiatry* 143:756-759, 1986.

Schleifer SJ, Macari-Hinson MM, Kahn M, et al: The nature and course of depression following myocardial infarction, *Arch Intern Med* 149:1785-1789, 1989.

Wells KB, Stewart A, Hays R, et al: The functioning and well-being of depressed patients: results from the medical outcomes study, *JAMA* 262:914-919, 1989b.

6 Antidepressants

The following are goals of this chapter:
1. Review issues in selection of an antidepressant
2. Review parameters for providing a good clinical trial of antidepressants
3. Present the medical issues in the use of antidepressants.

6.1 INTRODUCTION

1. When to use antidepressants
   a. Antidepressants are indicated primarily for treatment of depressive symptoms of
      (1) Major depression
      (2) Depressed phase of bipolar disorder.
   b. Other uses of antidepressants include
      (1) Depressive symptoms secondary to some medical disorders (assuming the medical cause is being addressed)
      (2) Dysthymia
      (3) Obsessive-compulsive disorder (clomipramine and the selective serotonin reuptake inhibitors [SSRIs])
      (4) Panic disorder (imipramine is written about most; others also work)
      (5) Generalized anxiety disorder, especially with mixed depressive symptoms
      (6) Adjunctive use for pain control (e.g., diabetic neuropathy).
2. General guidelines for using antidepressants
   a. When antidepressants are properly used, 50% to 70% of patients should respond, assuming
      (1) The diagnosis of depression is correct
      (2) The patient can tolerate the medication
         (a) Noncompliance or side effect dropouts are common
      (3) Adequate dose and duration are used.
   b. Patients who respond should remain on medication for at least 6 months; longer (or continuously) for chronic, relapsing symptoms.
   c. Doses used by many clinicians are too low. Plasma levels are useful for only a few tricyclics.
   d. Response rate can often be increased by drug combinations. However, before starting any combination, adequate trial(s) of single drugs should be confirmed.

3. Principles of using antidepressants
   a. A good trial of an antidepressant generally means
      (1) Using the medication at a therapeutic level for at least 4 weeks
      (2) Avoiding premature changes is important.
   b. If the patient cannot tolerate the medication because of side effects, clearly document the problem and switch to another medication.
      (1) Antidepressants can be stopped immediately, although withdrawal symptoms can occur. New drugs can be started the same day except when MAOIs are involved.
   c. If the patient does not respond to a good trial of a single medication
      (1) Reconfirm the diagnosis
      (2) Consider whether psychotherapy needs to address factors that may be interfering, such as
         (a) Unresolved secondary gain (e.g., disability issue)
         (b) Ongoing family disagreements
         (c) Unaddressed psychological conflict
      (3) If possible, wait a few more weeks
      (4) Document that a good trial has been completed
      (5) Consider options for continued treatment:
         (a) Switch to another antidepressant
         (b) Add a second drug such as lithium, buspirone, or another antidepressant from Table 6.1.
      (6) Patients failing two attempts should be considered for a second opinion, or, if symptoms are serious enough, for ECT. (For a review of ECT, see Chapter 15.)
   d. If the patient does respond to an antidepressant
      (1) In general, a patient with major depression should be maintained on medication for 6 to 9 months and then tapered off
      (2) Patients with recurrent depression often relapse and may need to be maintained on an antidepressant.

6.2 SPECIFIC ISSUES IN USING ANTIDEPRESSANTS

1. This table does not list MAOIs or stimulants (such as methylphenidate), which are discussed later in this chapter.
2. The first eight rows of Table 6.1 are the tricyclic (first-generation) antidepressants. The lower section contains the nontricyclic, second-generation antidepressants.
3. Choosing which antidepressant to use:
   a. There is no efficacy advantage to any of these antidepressants; therefore, the choice of medication is generally made on the basis of side effect profiles.
   b. Past patient response and response of first-degree relatives may be a predictor of a specific drug response.
   c. Cost is sometimes a consideration. Products are generally less expensive if available in generic form.
   d. Overdose danger is another consideration. The tricyclics are generally more lethal in overdose than the newer generation antidepressants, with problems including seizures and cardiac arrhythmias. In fact, several weeks' supply of a tricyclic is likely to be a potentially lethal quantity.

Table 6.1 Antidepressant summary

Medication	Anticholinergic	Sedation	Activation	Hypotension	HIS Bundle	GI Activation	Seizures	Half-Life (Hour)	Dose Range	Therapeutic Level µg/ml
Tricyclics										
Amitriptyline (Elavil)	4	3	0	3	+	0	+	20-46	100-300	75-175
Clomipramine (Anaframil)	4	2	0	3	+	0	+	20-40	50-250	
Nortriptyline (Pamelor)	2	2	0	1	+	0	+	18-88	50-150	50-150
Imipramine (Tofranil)	3	2	1	3	+	0	+	4-34	100-300	>265
Desipramine (Norpramin)	2	1-2	2	2	+	0	+	10-32	100-300	100-160
Doxepine (Sinequan)	3	4	0	2	+	0	+	8-47	100-300	
Protriptyline (Vivactil)	4	1	3	2	+	0	+	53-124	10-60	
Trimipramine (Surmontil)	3	3	0	3	+	0	+	9	100-300	
SSRIs										
Fluoxetine (Prozac)	0	1-2	1-2	0	0	1-2	+	7 DAY	20-60	
Paroxetine (Paxil)	1	0-1	1-2	0	0	1-2	0	24	10-50	
Sertraline (Zoloft)	1	1-2	1-2	0	0	1-2	+	26	50-200	
SNRIs										
Venlafaxine (Effexor)	0	1-2	1-2	0	0	1-2	+	9-11	75-300	
Others										
Amoxapine (Ascendin)	2	2	1	1	?+	0	+++	8-33	100-600	
Bupropion (Wellbutrin)	1	0	3	0	0	0	++	8-24	150-300	
Maprotilene (Ludiomil)	2	3	1	1	+	0	++	27-58	100-300	
Trazodone (Desyrel)	0	3	0	2	0	0	+	6-14	100-600	

1. **Side Effects** (as listed in Table 6.1)
   a. *Anticholinergic (Column 1):*
      (1) Some medications, such as amitriptyline, have high anticholinergic activity (indicated by a "4"), while a number of the others, indicated by a "0," have none.
      (2) Try to minimize anticholinergic activity because of
         (a) Dry mouth: May be a nuisance or may predispose to stomatitis (patients can suck on sugarless mints)
         (b) Blurred vision
         (c) Narrow angle glaucoma may be precipitated
         (d) Urinary retention: greater risk with prostatic enlargement or spinal cord problems
         (e) Constipation is common. Patients may need stool softeners. Narcotics or GI surgery can predispose to paralytic ileus
         (f) Confusion or impaired memory, especially in older patients.
      (3) Anticholinergic effects are additive with other drugs including
         (a) Benztropine (Cogentin)
         (b) Trihexyphenidyl (Artane)
         (c) Diphenhydramine (Benadryl)
         (d) Meperidine (Demerol)
         (e) Probantheline (Probanthine)
         (f) Oxybutynin (Ditropan).
      (4) If a patient develops anticholinergic symptoms, try lowering the dose or changing to another antidepressant.
         (a) In patients who have not responded to other antidepressants, the anticholinergic side effects can be counteracted by using bethanecol (Urecholine).
            (1) Bethanecol should be started in small doses (5-10 mg tid). Patients should be observed for GI hyperactivity and cardiac rhythm disturbances.
   b. *Sedation (Column 2):* due to central histamine receptor blockade or serotonin effects. Ratings are from very sedating, at "4," to not sedating, at "0."
      (1) If a patient is agitated, restless, insomniac, and anxious, using a sedating medication might be helpful.
      (2) Patients who are anergic, hypersomnic, and concerned about oversedation should not be given a sedating medication as first choice.
   c. *Activation (Column 3):* Higher numbers indicate more activating drugs.
      (1) Patients who are anergic, withdrawn, and hypersomnic should be started on a more activating medication.
      (2) Activation can consist of a positive sense of increased energy and alertness but may also consist of dysphoric agitation, tremulousness, increased anxiety, restlessness (akathisia), and sleep disturbance.
         (a) Patients sensitive to dysphoric arousal should either not continue using the drug that caused it or should have the dose lowered.
         (b) Higher doses of SSRIs and bupropion are often associated with nervousness and insomnia to a greater extent than the other drugs.

d. *Orthostatic Hypotension (Column 4)* is a result of peripheral alpha-adrenergic blockade, as well as a central brainstem mechanism.
   (1) Risks for orthostasis include
      (a) Depleted intravascular volumes
      (b) Prolonged bed rest
      (c) Old age
      (d) Autonomic disorders
      (e) Young women with labile autonomic systems
      (f) Pretreatment orthostasis.
   (2) Orthostasis can lead to falls and injuries, such as hip fracture.
   (3) Patients should be asked about light-headedness and have orthostatic blood pressure readings if at risk.
e. *Cardiac conduction delay (Column 5):* A "+" indicates delayed conduction through the intraventricular portion of the HIS bundle.
   (1) Patients older than 40 or with a history of cardiac problems should have a pretreatment ECG.
   (2) Tricyclics should be avoided with preexisting conduction problems.
   (3) The tricyclics also have quinidine-like effects.
   (4) Summary information on cardiac issues pertaining to antidepressants is shown in Table 6.2.

Table 6.2   Cardiac Issues with Antidepressants

	Nefazodone	Buspirone (Buspar)	SSRIs†	Tricyclics	Venlafaxine
Myocardial depression	0	0	0	Toxic	0
Orthostatic hypotension	0	+	0	+	0
Arrhythmias	"0"‡	"0"‡	Very rare	Quinidine-like withdrawal, tachycardia	"0"
Conduction delay	"0"	0	Very rare	+	0
Drug interactions	0	Anti-hyper-tensives	*	Clonidine Guanethidine Nitrates Quinidine	0

*SSRIs may interfere with metabolism of drugs dependent on the P-450 system
†In more than 3 million fluoxetine patients to 1991:
60 Cases bradycardia
34 Atrial dysrhythmias
26 Cases heart block
54 Ventricular dysrhythmias
24 cases CHF
42 Other dysrhythmias
‡"0" = Little experience in cardiac patients; therefore, document why, follow lytes and blood levels, monitor.

f. *GI Side effects (Column 6):*
   (1) Nausea and GI activation are the most common side effects for venlafaxine, nefazodone and the SSRIs. Up to 25% of patients experience nausea, which may decrease with time.
   (2) The tricyclics decrease gastroesophageal sphincter tone, leading to symptoms or reflux.

g. *Seizures:*
   (1) All antidepressants tend to lower seizure threshold. This is not a reason to avoid the use of antidepressants in epileptic patients as long as they are taking adequate doses of anticonvulsants.
   (2) Patients who develop a first seizure on antidepressants need a full seizure evaluation.

h. *Elimination half-life (Column 7)* of the parent compound and/or the active metabolite.
   (1) TCAs and SSRIs can usually be given once/day.
   (2) Fluoxetine and its active metabolite have a long elimination half-life. This may be an advantage for compliance and a disadvantage for elimination.
       (a) Side effects may appear after the patient has taken the drug for many weeks.

i. *Oral dose range (Column 8)* needed to obtain a therapeutic response shows wide intra-individual variation.
   (1) Underdosing is common
   (2) Starting dose is usually 50% to 100% of the lower number in the "oral dose range" column. Patients started too quickly taking higher doses have higher rates of side effects.
       (a) In general, the patient's dose should be moved up into the midrange of the oral dose range over the first few weeks.
       (b) If a patient does not respond at a midrange dose over 3 to 4 weeks, move up to the top range number.

j. *Plasma therapeutic levels (Column 9)* are available for four tricyclic medications.
   (1) For these drugs, levels can be used as an adjunct in monitoring treatment
       (a) For example: start the patient on 25 mg of nortriptyline, obtain a plasma level about 5 days later. If the level is below the therapeutic window (i.e., below 50 μg/ml), the oral dose could be raised to 50 mg hs. Another plasma level could be obtained 5 days later. If that level is within the therapeutic range, stay on that oral dose for 3 to 4 weeks to provide a good clinical trial.

k. *Other side effects*
   (1) Anorgasmia in women and either erectile or ejaculatory disturbances in men may occur in up to 30% to 40% of patients. Lower incidence is reported with bupropion and nefazodone. Cyproheptidine has been reported to reverse anorgasmia.

6.3   DRUG INTERACTIONS WITH TRICYCLIC ANTIDEPRESSANTS

1. Issues in the use of antidepressants:
   a. **Tricyclic antidepressants**

Box 6.1   Antidepressant Drug Interactions

Tricyclics

Drugs that potentiate hypotension
Prazosin and Alpha-adrenergic blocking agents

Drugs that may cause increased blood pressure
Sympathomimetics

Drugs whose antihypertensive effects may be decreased
Reserpine
Guanethidine
Clonidine

Drugs that raise antidepressant levels
Disulfiram
Methylphenidate
Cimetidine

Drugs that lower antidepressant levels
Oral contraceptives
Alcohol
Barbiturates
Dilantin

Drugs that may prolong cardiac conduction
Phenothiazines
Carbamazepine

Drugs that augment quinidine-like effects
Quinidine and Type 1A antiarrhythmics

Drugs that augment anticholinergic effects
Trihexyphenidyl (Artane)
Benztropine (Cogentin)
Diphenhydramine (Benadryl)
Oxybutynin (Ditropan)
Probantheline (Probanthine)
Meperidine (Demerol)
Tricyclics

(1) Many are available in generic form and may be less expensive
(2) May be poorly tolerated because of side effects
(3) Several (including amitriptyline and desipramine) are useful in treating chronic pain (see Chapter 14 on analgesic augmenters)
(4) Clomipramine is used to treat obsessive-compulsive disorder.
(5) Dosing

(a) For drugs with established therapeutic plasma levels (amitriptyline, nortriptyline, desipramine, imipramine), titrate oral dose to achieve desired plasma level. Generally, starting on 50 mg hs makes sense. Plasma levels can be checked about every 5 days.
- (*i*) Plasma level information is not definitive and serves only as a guideline.

(b) For drugs without known plasma levels, start on low doses and gradually increase until the patient either responds or cannot tolerate side effects.

b. **Selective serotonin re-uptake inhibitors (SSRIs)**
- (1) Often better tolerated than TCAs with nausea being the most frequent problem.
- (2) Fluoxetine dosing
  - (a) Most patients do well on 20 mgs qd, given in the morning
  - (b) Watch for onset of side effects several weeks into treatment (because of long half-life), such as tremulousness, activation, insomnia, especially in older patients
  - (c) Some older patients may do well on 10 mg/day
    - (1) Drugs metabolized by the P-450 system may have increased plasma levels if given with fluoxetine or paroxetine, but rarely with sertraline. These drugs include:
      - (*i*) Haloperidol
      - (*ii*) Digoxin
      - (*iii*) Cyclosporine
      - (*iv*) Tricyclics
      - (*v*) Diazepam
      - (*vi*) Carbamazepine
      - (*vii*) Valproic acid (Depakote)
      - (*viii*) Alprazolam.
  - (d) Some patients will respond better if dose is increased (to 60 mg/day), but there is no way to predict who needs higher doses
  - (e) Because of insomnia associated with activation, some patients may need trazodone (50-100 mg hs). These patients may be able to avoid using a hypnotic if switched to another SSRI.
- (3) Sertraline (Zoloft) dosing
  - (a) Most patients do well on 50-100 qd mg bid
    - (*i*) Dose range is generally between 50 and 200 mg/day
  - (b) There may be a lower tendency to activation than with fluoxetine
  - (c) Does not cause clinically significant effects on P-450 system at usual doses.
- (4) Paroxetine (Paxil) dosing
  - (a) Effective dose range is between 10 and 40 mg/qd (10 mg is a reasonable starting dose for older patients, 20 mg for others)
  - (b) Has no active metabolites. The parent compound is therefore cleared within several days after discontinuation.

  (5) Drug interactions
c. **Other antidepressants**
  (1) *Amoxapine (Ascendin)* has some dopamine-blocking properties (which may cause extrapyramidal side effects and even tardive dyskinesia if used for more than 4 months) and should be considered as a second line drug.
  (2) *Bupropion (Wellbutrin)* has a side effect profile similar to amphetamine and is a reasonable second choice for many patients, especially those who need some activation. Bupropion has a greater tendency to produce seizures than other drugs (incidence of about 4/1000) especially in higher doses (300 mg/day).
  (3) *Trazodone (Desyrel)* has good hypnotic properties, no anticholinergic activity, but is often too sedating for many patients in doses needed for depression (often $\geq$ 300 mg/day). Trazodone has also been reported to cause priapism in a small number of men.
  (4) *Venlafaxine (Effexor)* inhibits both norepinephrine and serotonin reuptake. It is, therefore, an SNRI (serotonin and norepinephrine reuptake inhibitor); it lacks anticholinergic, antihistaminergic, and antiadrenergic effects. Its side effect profile resembles the SSRIs, with most reported effects being nausea (dose dependent), sedation, and dry mouth. The parent compound has a 3 to 4 hour elimination half-life, and the active metabolite (o-desmethyl-venlafaxine) has a 9 to 11 hour half-life. The effective oral dose range appears to be between 75 and 375 mg/day given in a divided bid dose. A small percentage of patients (5% of those receiving a dose of 100-200 mg/day) have a dose-dependent increase in blood pressure. Therefore, monitoring of blood pressure is recommended.
  (5) *Nefazodone (Serzone),* a new agent, is chemically related to trazodone but has fewer side effects, specifically less orthostatic and less sedation. Unlike most other antidepressants, it does not suppress REM activity and does not cause sexual side effects. It acts as a potent 5-HT_2 antagonist and also exhibits selective serotonin uptake inhibition.

6.4   USE OF STIMULANTS AS ANTIDEPRESSANTS

1. Indications
  a. Stimulants should not be considered first-line drugs for the treatment of depression.
  b. Potential indications include
    (1) Geriatric and medically ill patients (such as AIDS patients) with depressive symptoms involving withdrawn behavior, lack of motivation and energy, and depressed mood.
2. Clinical use
  a. Methylphenidate (the more commonly used) and dextroamphetamine

(1) Patients are usually started on 5 mg PO in the morning When a response is seen, it is often apparent the first day. If there is no response, the dose may be raised daily by 5 mg increments up to 20 mg

(2) Because the effect may be short lived, a second dose may be needed at noon.

3. Side effects
   a. In general, these doses are well tolerated. Only about 15% of patients have side effects, including
      (1) Overstimulation without antidepressant effect
      (2) Anxiety
      (3) Confusion
      (4) Paranoia
      (5) Tachycardia (unusual)
      (6) Appetite disturbance (unusual).
4. Medical issues in clinical use
   a. These drugs have been used safely in a variety of medically ill patients, though caution should be observed because experience is not widespread.

6.5   MONOAMINE OXIDASE INHIBITORS (MAOIs)

1. Indications
   a. Treatment resistant major depression
   b. Treatment resistant panic disorder
   c. Treatment resistant mixed anxiety-depression
   d. Treatment resistant depression in bipolar patients
   e. Dysthymia not responsive to other antidepressants
   f. Atypical depression (depression characterized by anxiety, somatization, feeling better in the morning and worse as day goes on, hyperphagia, weight gain, sensitivity to rejection, trouble falling or staying asleep).

2. *MAOIs available*

	Daily dose	Starting dose
Isocarboxazid (Marplan)	20-60	10 mg at 9 am, 1 pm
Phenelzine (Nardil)	45-90	15 mg at 9 am, 1 pm
Tranylcypramine (Parnate)	20-40	10 mg at 9 am, 1 pm
Selegiline (Eldepryl) (selective for MAO-B)	10-30	10 mg at 9 am

3. Effective dose
   a. Greater than 80% monoamine oxidase inhibition must be reached for a clinical effect.
      (1) This usually requires a dose of 60 mg/day of phenelzine or 40 mg/day of tranylcypramine. Start with 15 mgs PO for phenelzine (10 mgs for Parnate) and increase by that dose increment every 7 days until reaching 45 mg and 30 mg respectively.
   b. Three to five weeks at a therapeutic dose is necessary to judge response.

4. Side effects
   a. Orthostatic hypotension is a common limiting factor (10% to 15%)
      (1) Assure adequate hydration
      (2) Use support stockings
      (3) Try to eliminate other hypotensive agents
   b. Weight gain (carbohydrate craving and/or edema)
   c. Insomnia: low doses of trazodone (50-100 mg hs) or benzodiazepine hypnotics may be helpful in counteracting this side effect
   d. Sexual dysfunction (anorgasmia)
   e. Pyridoxine deficiency may develop with phenelzine, producing paresthesias. Treatment (which some clinicians feel should be supplied prophylactically) is Vitamin B_6, 100-400 mg/day.
   f. Hypertensive crisis: This is the rare (incidence $\leq 0.5\%$ with mortality $\leq 0.001\%$), but potentially life-threatening reaction that is usually associated with mixing the MAOI with a pressor medication or food with high tyramine content (see Box 6.2).
      (1) Box 6.2 Foods and Medications to Avoid for Patients Using MAOIs: Patients started on MAOIs need to be competent and willing to follow dietary and medication restrictions. Review the list with the patient.
      (2) Some clinicians give nifedipine capsules (10 mg) for patients to take orally if they sense a hypertensive reaction (usually noted as a pounding headache). Patients should bite the capsule and swallow the contents.
      (3) Patients who think they are having a hypertensive crisis should go to an emergency room. Phentolamine 5 mg IV or nifedipine is usually given.
5. Drug interactions: Because there are so many MAOI drug interactions (see Box 6.2), it is prudent to look up every drug before a patient takes it.
   a. MAOIs increase intracellular catecholamine stores. Therefore, indirect-acting sympathomimetics, which release these stores, are contraindicated.
      (1) Indirect-acting agents include cocaine, amphetamines, methylphenidate, pseudoephedrine, ephedrine, phenylpropanolamine.
      (2) Many OTC cold remedies contain these agents.
      (3) Because intracellular dopamine is also increased, sinemet can cause hypertension with MAOIs. Direct-acting dopamine agonists are safer. Selegilene is safe to combine with dopamine agonists in doses of about 10 mg/day.
   b. Direct-acting sympathomimetics can be used safely.
      (1) Bronchodilators (inhalers are safer than oral drugs).
   c. Combining MAOIs with serotonin-augmenting drugs (e.g., tricyclic antidepressants, SSRIs, trazodone, or buspirone) can produce serotonin syndrome. Discontinue MAOIs for 2 weeks before switching to another antidepressant.
      (1) Clinical features of serotonin syndrome include
         (a) Fever
         (b) Delirium
         (c) Myoclonus and hyperreflexia
         (d) GI hyperactivation
         (e) Ataxia.

Box 6.2 Food and Medications to Avoid
for Patients Using MAOIs

Foods to avoid

Avocados (if overripe)
Banana peel
Bean curd (fermented)
Broad beans
Caviar
Cheese (cottage, cream, and pasteurized are permissible)
Chocolate (in large amounts)
Fava beans
Figs (overripe)
Fish, pickled or salted (safe if fresh)
Ginseng
Licorice
Liqueurs
Liver (safe if fresh)
Meats, aged or processed
Miso soup
Protein (powdered supplements)
Sausage
Shrimp paste
Soy sauce
Wines (especially chianti)
Yeast extracts

Drugs that increase blood pressure with MAOIs

Aminophylline
Amphetamines
Caffeine
Carbamazepine
Cocaine
Cyclic antidepressants
Cyclobenzaprine
Direct-acting sympathomimetics
Epinephrine
Ephedrine
Guanethidine
Isoproterenol
L-Dopa
Methyldopa
Metaraminol
Methylphenidate
Phenylethylamine
Phenylpropanolamine
Pseudoephedrine

Continued.

Box 6.2 —cont'd

Theophylline
Tyramine

Drugs that lower blood pressure with MAOIs

Calcium channel blockers
Diuretics
Hypoglycemic agents
Prazosin
Propranolol

Drugs with prolonged (increased) activity with MAOIs

Anticholinergics
Anticoagulants
Succinylcholine

Drugs that may create serotonin syndrome with MAOIs

Buspirone
Cyclic antidepressants
Meperidine
SSRIs
Tryptophan

Other drugs that should be avoided with MAOIs

Aldomet
Clonidine
Guanethidine
Reserpine

d. MAOIs and anesthesia
   (1) A 2-week washout before elective general anesthesia would be ideal but is not definitely necessary.
   (2) Curare should be avoided because of its indirect sympathomimetic effect.
   (3) For hypotension: volume expansion or direct-acting sympathomimetics (e.g., norepinephrine) should be used instead of indirect-acting agents (e.g., metaraminol).
   (4) Droperidol should be avoided because of reports of cardiac and respiratory depression with MAOIs.

References

Chiarello RJ, Cole JO: The use of psychostimulants in general psychiatry, *Arch Gen Psychiatry* 44:286-295, 1987.

Ciraulo DA, Shader RI: Fluoxetine drug-drug interactions. I. Antidepressants and antipsychotics, *J Clin Psychopharmacol* 10:48-50, 1990a.

Ciraulo DA, Shader RI: Fluoxetine drug-drug interactions. II. *J Clin Psychopharmacol* 10:213-217, 1990b.

Clary C, Schweizer E: Treatment of MAOI hypertensive crisis with sublingual nifedipine, *J Clin Psychiatry* 48:249-250, 1987.

Dechant KL, Clissold SP: Paroxetine: a review of its pharmacodynamic and pharmacokinetic properties, and therapeutic potential in depressive illness, *Drugs* 41:225-253, 1967.

El-Ganzouri AR, Ivankovich AD, Braverman B et al: Monoamine oxidase inhibitors: should they be discontinued preoperatively? *Anesth Analg* 64:592-596, 1985.

Goldberg RJ, Capone RJ, Hunt JD: Cardiac complications following tricyclic antidepressant overdose, *JAMA* 254:1772-1775, 1985.

Lipinski JF, Mallya G, Zimmerman P et al: Fluoxetine-induced akathisia: clinical and theoretical implications, *J Clin Psychiatry* 50:339-342, 1989.

Masand P, Pickett P, Murray GB: Psychostimulants for secondary depression in medical illness, *Psychosom* 32:203-208, 1991.

Montgomery SA: Venlafaxine: a new dimension in antidepressant pharmacotherapy, *J Clin Psychiatry* 54:119-126, 1993.

Preskorn SH, Fast GA: Therapeutic drug monitoring for antidepressants: efficacy, safety, and cost effectiveness, *J Clin Psychiatry* 52:23-33, 1991.

Preskorn SH, Othmer SC: Evaluation of bupropion hydrochloride: the first of a new class of atypical antidepressants, *Pharmacotherapy* 4:20-34, 1984.

Roose SP, Glassman AH, Giardina EGV et al: Tricyclic antidepressants in depressed patients with cardiac conduction disease, *Arch Gen Psychiatry* 44:273-275, 1987a.

Roose SP, Glassman AH, Giardina EGV et al: Cardiovascular effects of imipramine and bupropion in depressed patients with congestive heart failure, *J Clin Psychopharmacol* 7:247-251, 1987b.

Roose SP, Glassman AH, Giardina EV: Nortriptyline in depressed patients with left ventricular impairment, *JAMA* 256:3253-3257, 1986.

Roose SP, Glassman AH, eds: *Treatment strategies for refractory depression,* Washington, DC, 1990, American Psychiatric Press.

Schenck CH, Remick RA: Sublingual nifedipine in the treatment of hypertensive crisis associated with monoamine oxidase inhibitors, *Ann Emerg Med* 18:114-115, 1989.

Schweizer E, Weise C, Clary C et al: Placebo-controlled trial of venlafaxine for the treatment of major depression, *J Clin Psychopharmacol* 11(4):233-236, 1991.

7 Manic-Depressive Disorder and Mood-Stablizing Drugs

The following are goals of this chapter:
1. To define bipolar affective disorder.
2. To provide a differential diagnostic evaluation of manic symptoms.
3. To detail the use of three mood-stabilizing drugs:
   a. Lithium
   b. Carbamazepine
   c. Valproic Acid.

7.1 DEFINITION AND IDENTIFICATION

1. Manic-depressive disorder is also known as *bipolar affective disorder* because patients have mood swings including both manic and depressive episodes.
2. There is a spectrum of presentations of manic-depressive disorder:
   a. At one extreme are rapid cyclers who alternate highs and lows very frequently (as often as every few weeks or even days).
   b. At the other extreme are patients who may have an episode in their 20s, with the next episode two decades later.
   c. Patients with recurrent depressions, with subclinical hypomanic episodes are referred to as bipolar, Type II (as distinguished from Type I, who have both manic and depressive episodes).
   d. Manic and depressive features may exist at the same time during an episode.
   e. Patients whose mood swings are not severe enough to qualify for bipolar disorder may be referred to as *cyclothymic.*
3. Family history may provide a clue to diagnosis because bipolar illness has a strong familial component.
4. A depressive episode is defined in Chapter 5. A **manic episode** can be defined as:
   a. A distinct period of abnormally and persistently elevated, expansive, or irritable mood.
   b. During the period of mood disturbance, at least three of the following symptoms have persisted (four if the mood is only irritable):
      (1) Inflated self-esteem or grandiosity
      (2) Decreased need for sleep
      (3) Pressured speech
      (4) Racing thoughts

    (5) Distractibility
    (6) Physical agitation (or increased work, social, or sexual activity)
    (7) Poor judgment about activities (e.g., buying sprees).
c. The mood disturbance must be significant enough to cause work or social impairment, hospitalization, or concern over harmfulness.
d. Patients have delusions or hallucinations during the period of mood disturbance, but not otherwise.
e. Symptoms are not a result of an underlying medical cause.

Prevalence

1. The life-time risk of a manic episode is about 0.75%.
2. The 6-month prevalence of manic episodes ranges from 0.4% to 0.9%, equal in men and women.
3. The age of onset is usually in adolescence or the early 20s.

7.2 DIFFERENTIAL DIAGNOSIS

1. *Schizophrenia:* Acute manic illness may seem indistinguishable from schizophrenia. Both may be associated with agitated, paranoid, psychotic symptoms.
   a. These two disorders are distinguished by:
      (1) Family history (because the two diseases tend to segregate genetically).
      (2) Previous history (manic-depressive illness is episodic with higher functioning between episodes as well as the presence of mood disturbance).
2. *Recurrent unipolar depression:* It can be difficult to distinguish recurrent unipolar depression from bipolar Type II. However, mood stabilizers may be helpful in both disorders.
3. *Temporal lobe epilepsy* may sometimes be seen as episodic mood disturbance.
   a. Interestingly, the drugs used to treat complex partial seizures (carbamazepine and valproate) also treat manic depressive illness.
   b. Patients with episodic mood disturbance and risk factors for complex partial seizures should have an EEG, especially if the presentation is in any way atypical. Risk factors for temporal lobe epilepsy include:
      (1) Family history of epilepsy
      (2) Previous head injury
      (3) Febrile convulsions in childhood
      (4) Presence of another type of seizure disorder
      (5) Presence of cancer, which could metastasize to the brain
      (6) Central nervous system infections.
4. *Stimulant abuse* may produce periods of manic behavior followed by severe depressive withdrawals.
5. *Alcohol (or sedative) abuse* will produce "depression" during the sedative phase and "mania" during the withdrawal delirium.
   a. Attempts to self-medicate underlying mood disorders may lead to alcohol or other substance abuse, which then confuses the diagnosis.
6. *Episodic delirium* may present as agitated behavior followed by withdrawal.

7. *Adult attention deficit hyperactivity disorder (ADHD)* may present as restless and distractibility, but there is not a manic mood component.
8. *Brief reactive psychosis* may appear as a manic episode, but the episode is brief, clearly related to some stressful situation, and usually has no elevated mood.

7.3   PROGNOSIS

1. The natural course of manic-depressive illness is to have increasing number and severity of episodes as the patients gets older.
2. Drugs used to stabilize and prevent mood swings (lithium, carbamazepine, and valproate) decrease the number and severity of episodes but do not necessarily abolish them.
3. The disorder appears to be lifelong, and therefore often requires lifelong treatment.

7.4   TREATMENTS

1. The treatment of an acute manic episode is best approached as a behavioral emergency (see Chapter 13).
   a. While lithium or carbamazepine can treat mania, they do not work rapidly enough for an acute manic episode, without toxicity.
   b. Neuroleptics, alone or with benzodiazepines, are the drug(s) of choice (see Chapter 13).
2. Patients in remission are often helped by understanding the underlying medical basis of their illness, removing much of the stigma and self-deprecation. Manic-depressive societies function as information sources and support groups.

7.5   LITHIUM

1. Indications
   a. Lithium is the primary choice for the reduction of the frequency and severity of both the manic and depressive components of bipolar illness.
   b. Lithium can treat acute mania; however, it is initially supplemented with neuroleptics and/or benzodiazepines (see Chapter 13).
   c. In a small subset of bipolar patients, lithium can treat depression. However, in general, lithium should not be thought of as an antidepressant.
      (1) Bipolar patients who develop depression usually need a separate antidepressant.
   d. Lithium alone is effective in about 60% to 80% of classic bipolar patients but in a lower percentage of mixed or rapidly cycling bipolars.
      (1) For poor responders or atypical patients, carbamazepine or valproic acid (alone or in combinations) are often effective alternatives.
2. Pharmacology
   a. Lithium is excreted by the kidney with an elimination half-life of about 24 hours.

(1) Therefore, it is crucial to know a patient's renal function before and during lithium therapy.

b. Proximal resorption in the kidney is influenced by sodium levels.

(1) Therefore, lithium toxicity may develop in the context of restricted sodium intake, diarrhea, or vomiting.

3. Drug interactions

a. Drugs that increase lithium levels

(1) Thiazide diuretics

(2) Indomethacin and the NSAIDs

(3) Erythromycin

(4) Metronidazole.

b. Drugs that decrease lithium levels

(1) Theophylline.

c. Drugs that have increased toxicity when prescribed with lithium

(1) Haloperidol

(2) Succinylcholine

(3) Digoxin

(4) Alpha-methyldopa.

4. Clinical use

a. Formulations

(1) Most often prescribed as lithium carbonate, 300 mg capsules.

(2) Scored tablets can be split in half but may taste metallic and cause more GI upset.

(3) Sustained release forms may improve compliance and minimize plasma level fluctuations.

(4) Liquid form is available.

b. Dose

(1) Usually between 900 and 1200 mg/day.

(2) Initial dose is usually 300 mg tid (assuming normal renal function).

(3) Therapeutic lithium level (12 hours after the last dose) is about 1.0 mEq/L.

(a) Lithium level should be obtained on the fourth day after starting lithium therapy, in the morning (about 12 hours after night dose), and before the first morning dose.

(b) Adjust the oral dose based on the first level. If, for example, the plasma level on a starting oral dose is 0.4 mEq/L, the oral dose would be increased by 300 mg and a level repeated in another 4 days.

(c) This process can be repeated until a therapeutic level is achieved.

(d) Once a level is achieved, it can be checked in another month or so, and then every 3 to 6 months. Once established, a level remains steady unless there is a change in renal function or sodium levels, or there is a drug interaction.

5. Side effects

a. *Fine tremor* (usually dose related) is not uncommon (about 5%).

(1) It can be treated with beta-blockers (e.g., propranolol 20 mg qid).

(2) As the lithium level goes up, patients develop a **coarse tremor,** and, in toxic ranges, myoclonus and seizures.

b. *Nephrogenic diabetes insipidus,* with resulting polyurea and polydipsia. Between 10% and 40% of patients taking lithium put out more than 3 L of urine/day. If this becomes a problem, a lithium alternative is indicated. This problem is almost always reversible upon discontinuing lithium use.

   (1) If lithium must be continued despite polyurea and polydipsia, amiloride (10-20 mg/day) often corrects the problem.

c. *Hypothyroidism* may develop (in about 8%). Therefore, it is important to check thyroid function (by TSH) before starting and every 6 to 12 months while the patient is receiving lithium.

d. *Weight gain,* for unknown reason, is a problem that sometimes causes people to stop taking lithium.

e. *GI discomfort* is not uncommon. As the level becomes toxic, patients develop **nausea, vomiting, and diarrhea.**

   (1) GI side effects are lessened by giving the drug with meals or prescribing a slow-release preparation.

f. *Cardiac effects* include occasional T-wave inversions at therapeutic levels (which may be related to low potassium levels) and rare cases of sinus node dysfunction.

g. *Cerebellar and abnormal movements* often occur after overdose.

h. *Leukocytosis* without a left shift.

i. *Teratogenicity:* Lithium use has been contraindicated during pregnancy, especially the first trimester, with reports of Ebstein's anomaly. While these date have recently been reconsidered, lithium use should be avoided in pregnancy without special consultation.

j. *Calcium abnormalities* because of a change in parathyroid function are uncommon.

6. **Medical clearance and monitoring:** Before lithium therapy is started, and then at the time intervals indicated:

a. **TSH:** initially and every 6 to 12 months.

b. **BUN and creatinine:** initially and every 6 to 12 months.

c. **Electrolytes:** initially, and repeated if there is some clinical change that might alter electrolytes.

d. **ECG:** screening for T-wave and sinus node abnormalities in patients over age 40 or with a history of cardiac problems.

7.6   CARBAMAZEPINE (CBZ) (TEGRETOL)

1. Indications

a. Treatment of acute mania, but because of toxicity its use is supplemented by neuroleptics and/or benzodiazepines (see Chapter 13).

b. For reduction of the frequency and severity of both the manic and depressive components of bipolar illness.

c. Treatment of pain syndromes (herpetic pain; neuropathic pain) often in low doses (such as 50 mg tid).

d. Stabilizing episodically aggressive behavior (see Chapter 17).

2. Pharmacology

a. CBZ absorption is somewhat unpredictable, with peak plasma levels 2 to 6 hours after dose. Therefore, multiple daily doses are recommended.

b. Half-life is 13 to 17 hours; therefore, steady state is reached in 2 to 4 days.

c. 80% is protein bound, and only the unbound form crosses the blood-brain barrier.

    (1) Medically ill patients with low albumin levels may suffer toxic effects more quickly.

    (2) Plasma levels measure bound and unbound portions.

d. P 450 system metabolizes CBZ to CBZ 10,11 epoxide (not routinely measured by CBZ plasma levels), which is often present at significant levels and may be responsible for many of the toxic side effects.

3. Drug interactions

  a. Drugs that lead to increased CBZ levels

    (1) Erythromycin

    (2) Cimetidine

    (3) Propoxyphene

    (4) Isoniazid

    (5) Fluoxetine

    (6) Calcium channel blockers.

  b. Drugs that lead to decreased CBZ levels

    (1) Phenobarbital

    (2) Phenytoin.

  c. Drug levels decreased by CBZ

    (1) Oral contraceptives

    (2) Warfarin

    (3) Theophylline

    (4) Tricyclic antidepressants

    (5) Valproic acid

    (6) Haloperidol.

4. Clinical use

  a. CBZ comes in 200 mg scored tablets, as well as 100 mg chewable pediatric tablets.

  b. Oral doses in the range of 800-1200 mg/day are often necessary to achieve a therapeutic level (8-12 µg/ml).

  c. Patients need to achieve this dose gradually to avoid excessive side effects.

    (1) Start with 100 mg or 200 mg tid, raising by 100-200 mg increments every 5 days or so.

    (2) Because the plasma elimination half-life is about 13 to 17 hours, the first therapeutic level could be reached about 4 days after starting the drug.

    (3) The oral dose can continue to be raised until the therapeutic level (between 8 and 12 mg/L) is reached.

    (4) CBZ is well known for auto-induction of metabolic enzymes (P 450 system). Therefore, after a month or more of taking the drug, its own level decreases, and the oral dose needs to be raised.

5. Side effects

  a. Common initial side effects: lethargy, nausea, tremor, ataxia, double vision.

  b. Antidiuretic action by a direct effect on renal tubules may result in hyponatremia, presenting as water intoxication or seizures.

  c. Leukopenia
    (1) Low leukocyte counts, usually not below 3000, transiently occur in about 10% of patients and may persist in about 3%.
  d. Aplastic anemia (1 in 500,000 patients)
    (1) Patients should be instructed to immediately report fever, sore throat, rash, or easy bruising.
    (2) Routine blood monitoring is not indicated.
    (3) Extreme caution should be used in combining CBZ with other drugs that suppress white cell production (e.g., clozapine).
  e. Hepatic reactions (usually in first months)
    (1) About 5% show a mild increase in ALT and AST. It is usually not necessary to discontinue the drug unless the elevations are two to three times normal.
    (2) Serious, life-threatening hepatic reactions occur in only 1/10,000.
    (3) Routine monitoring is not indicated. Patients should be told to report symptoms such as anorexia, nausea or vomiting, or abdominal pain.
    (4) Underlying liver disease is a relative contraindication.
  f. Rash: may occur in 10% to 15%. Since this may develop into a serious problem, the drug should be discontinued for any rash more significant than a simple macular rash.
  g. Cardiac conduction may be slowed.
    (1) Initial ECG should be done to check for preexisting A-V delay, which may contraindicate the use of CBZ.
    (2) CBZ also has quinidine-like effects, suppressing ventricular automaticity.
  h. Teratogenic effects have been reported, including a 1% risk of spina bifida.

7.7   VALPROIC ACID (VA) (DEPAKOTE)

1. Indications
  a. Acute mania, but because of the toxicity that would result from high loading doses, it is not used alone for this indication.
  b. Reduction of the frequency and severity of both the manic and depressive components of bipolar illness.
2. Pharmacology
  a. Syrup, capsule, and tablet are absorbed in less than 2 hours. The enteric-coated formulation (Depakote) reaches peak plasma levels after 3 hours.
  b. VA is highly protein bound, and toxic effects can occur if the drug is displaced from binding sites, because only the unbound portion crosses the blood-brain barrier.
    (1) As plasma levels increase, the unbound portion increases disproportionally; the higher percentage of unbound drug is metabolized more rapidly, appearing to create accelerated metabolism.
  c. Elimination half-life is about 12 to 16 hours, with metabolism, which involves the P 450 system, and a mitochondrial pathway.
3. Drug interactions
  a. VA inhibits liver enzymes that metabolize other drugs, including:

(1) Diazepam (but not lorazepam)

(2) Phenobarbital.

b. There is increased clearance of this drug when taken with other anticonvulsants.

c. Monitor levels closely when co-prescribing with drugs that are highly protein bound. Patients may show toxicity even at therapeutic plasma levels. Changes in unbound fraction occur with:

(1) Phenobarbital

(2) Aspirin (use acetaminophen instead)

(3) Phenytoin

(4) Carbamazepine.

4. Clinical use

a. Plasma levels should be maintained between 50 and 100 µg/ml. However, the relationship between plasma level and clinical response is not tightly coupled.

b. VA comes in a noncoated form (Depakene), which is usually not used because of GI side effects. The preferred form is Depakote.

c. Depakote comes in tablets of 125, 250, and 500 mg, as well as a 125 mg sprinkle capsule.

5. Side effects

a. Nausea/vomiting and GI irritation are common, but less of a problem with the coated form (Depakote).

(1) It may help to prescribe the drug after meals, and start with a low dose.

b. Tremor (in up to 10%).

c. Lethargy.

d. Hepatic reactions (usually in first few months):

(1) A transient increase in LFTs may occur in up to 40%. The drug should be discontinued if the LFTs rise above two times the limit of normal. LFTs should be monitored every 2 to 3 weeks for the first 2 to 3 months, then every 6 months thereafter.

(2) A more severe form of hepatic reaction is rare.

e. Some patients gain weight and should reduce calories.

f. Alopecia (may be transient; zinc and selenium supplements may be helpful).

g. Transient amenorrhea.

h. Thrombocytopenia with decreased platelet aggregation.

(1) Patients going to surgery should have a full coagulation profile

i. Pancreatitis is rare.

j. Increased ammonia levels are not uncommon, but almost always asymptomatic, except for patients with underlying liver disease.

k. In 1% to 2% spina bifida has been reported if taken during pregnancy.

References

Ashton MG, Ball SG, Thomas TH et al: Water intoxication associated with carbamazepine treatment, *Br Med J* 1:1134-1135, 1977.

Benassi E, Bo GP, Cocito L et al: Carbamazepine and cardiac conduction disturbances, *Ann Neurol* 22:280-281, 1987.

Bourgeois BFD: Pharmacologic interactions between valproate and other drugs, *Am J Med* 84(1a):29-33, 1988.

Chouinard G: The use of benzodiazepines in the treatment of manic-depressive illness, *J Clin Psychiatry* 49(suppl):15-20, 1988.

Cotariu D, Zaidman JL: Valproic acid and the liver, *Clin Chem* 34:890-897, 1988.

DasGupta K, Jefferson JW: The use of lithium in the medically ill, *Gen Hosp Psychiatry* 12:83-97, 1990.

Ieiri I, Higuchi S, Hirata K et al: Analysis of the factors influencing antiepileptic drug concentrations—valproic acid, *J Clin Pharmacol Ther* 15:351-363, 1990.

Keck, PE Jr, McElroy SL, Turgul KC et al: Valproate oral loading in the treatment of acute mania, *J Clin Psychiatry* 54(8):305-308, 1993.

Kosten TR, Forrest JN: Treatment of severe lithium-induced polyuria with amiloride, *Am J Psychiatry* 143:1563-1568, 1986.

Maarbjerg K, Vestergaard P, Schou M: Changes in serum thyroxine (T_4) and serum thyroid stimulating hormone (TSH) during prolonged lithium treatment, *Acta Psychiatr Scand* 75:217-221, 1987.

McElroy SL, Keck PE, Pope HG et al: Valproate in psychiatric disorders: literature review and clinical guidelines, *J Clin Psychiatry* 50:23-29, 1989.

Mitchell JE: MacKenzie TB: Cardiac effects of lithium therapy in man: a review, *J Clin Psychiatry* 43:47-51, 1982.

Pellock JM, Willmore LJ: A rational guide to routine blood monitoring in patients receiving antiepileptic drugs, *Neurology* 41:961-964, 1991.

Pope HG, McElroy SL, Keck PE et al: Valproate in the treatment of acute mania: A placebo-controlled study, *Arch Gen Psychiatry* 48:62-68, 1991.

Post RM: *Effectiveness of carbamazepine in the treatment of bipolar affective disorder.* In SL McElroy, HG Pope (eds): *Use of anticonvulsants in psychiatry: recent advances,* Clifton, NJ, Oxford Health Care.

Simpson SG, Folstein SE, Meyers DA et al: Bipolar II: the most common bipolar phenotype? *Am J Psychiatry* 150:901-903, 1993.

Teitelbaum M: A significant increase in lithium levels after concomitant ACE inhibitor administration, *Psychosomatics* 34(5):450-453, 1993.

Vestergaard P, Amdisen AS, Schou M: Clinically significant side effects of lithium treatment: a survey of 237 patients in long-term treatment, *Acta Psychiatr Scand* 62:193-200, 1980.

Zajecka J: Pharmacology, pharmacokinetics, and safety issues of mood-stabilizing agents, *Psychiatric Ann* 23(2):79-85, 1993.

Diagnosis of Anxiety Disorders

8

The following are goals of this chapter:
1. To define and present evaluation and management issues for each of the following anxiety disorders
   a. Panic disorder
   b. Obsessive compulsive disorder
   c. Generalized anxiety disorder
   d. Phobia
   e. Adjustment disorder with anxiety
   f. Posttraumatic stress disorder

8.1 INTRODUCTION AND BACKGROUND

1. Anxiety can be defined most simply as *fear without a cause.*
2. Anxiety is not necessarily a problem. It can be a positive motivating factor.
3. Anxiety becomes a problem when:
   a. It interferes with adaptive behavior
   b. It causes physical symptoms
   c. It exceeds a tolerable level.
4. Anxious patients are likely to approach nonpsychiatric physicians with somatic complaints or substance use disorders (see Box 8.1, Physical Symptoms of Anxiety).

8.2 DIAGNOSTIC APPROACH TO ANXIETY SYMPTOMS

1. *Step One: Medical Assessment:* Do not assume that anxiety is explained by the patient's psychosocial situation. Review the medical problem list, history, and substance use.
   a. See Box 8.2, Medical Causes of Anxiety.
   b. See Box 8.3, Drugs that Cause Anxiety.
2. *Step Two: Psychosocial assessment:* Always ask the patient: "Why do you think you are so anxious?" The patient may identify some problem that needs to be addressed by counseling or therapy. For example, if a stressful marriage underlies anxiety, marriage therapy is probably indicated.
3. *Step Three: Medication:* Medication should be used to lessen symptom severity.

Box 8.1   Physical Symptoms of Anxiety

Respiratory	**Cardiovascular**	**Autonomic**
Chest pressure	Tachycardia	Dry mouth
Choking	Palpitations	Sweating
Sighing	Chest pain	Headaches
Dyspnea	Faintness	Hot flashes

Musculoskeletal	**Genitourinary**	**Gastrointestinal**
Aches/pains	Frequency	Swallowing
Twitching	Urgency	Abdominal pain
Stiffness	Sexual dysfunction	Nausea
Fatigue	Menstrual problems	Irritable bowel

Neurological

Dizziness
Numbness/tingling
Visual disturbance
Weakness
Tremor

Box 8.2   Medical Causes of Anxiety

Respiratory	**Cardiovascular**
Asthma	Angina pectoris
Chronic obstructive pulmonary disease	Arrhythmias
Hypoxia	Congestive heart failure
Pulmonary edema	Hypertension
Pulmonary embolism	Hypotension
	Mitral valve prolapse

Endocrine	**Neurologic**
Carcinoid syndrome	Akathisia
Hypercorticolemia	Delirium
Hyperthyroidism	Otoneurologic disorders
Hypoglycemia	Postconcussion syndrome
Pheochromocytoma	Complex partial seizures
	Essential tremor
	Parkinson's disease

Metabolic

Hypercalcemia
Hyperkalemia
Hyponatremia
Porphyria

Box 8.3   Drugs that Cause Anxiety

Stimulants

Amphetamine
Aminophylline
Caffeine
Cocaine
Methylphenidate
Theophylline

Sympathomimetics

Ephedrine
Epinephrine
Phenylpropanolamine
Pseudoephedrine

Drug withdrawal

Barbiturates
Benzodiazepines
Narcotics
   Alcohol
Sedatives

Anticholinergics

Benztropine mesylate (Cogentin)
Diphenhydramine (Benadryl)
Meperidine (Demerol)
Oxybutynin (Ditropan)
Propantheline (Probanthine)
Tricyclics
Trihexyphenidyl (Artane)

Dopaminergics

Amantadine
Bromocriptine
Levodopa (L-dopa)
Levodopa-carbidopa (Sinement)
Metoclopramide
Neuroleptics

Miscellaneous

Baclofen
Cycloserine
Hallucinogens
Indomethacin

a. **Therapy treats problems; medication treats symptoms.** Medication may be an important adjunct to psychotherapies if the patient has significant somatic symptoms.

8.3   PANIC DISORDER

Definition and Identification

1. Panic disorder is basically defined as the presence (or history) of panic attacks that do not have an underlying medical etiology.
   a. A **panic attack** is defined as an episode of extreme anxiety, which often comes on suddenly, and is characterized by a number of typical somatic and psychological features. See Box 8.4 for the criteria for diagnosing panic disorder.
2. Panic disorder patients often believe they are having a medical crisis and seek emergency care.
3. Not every "panic attack" is part of "panic disorder." Panic attacks may be a result of other medical or psychiatric conditions.
4. Agoraphobia frequently is part of panic disorder. Patients become fearful that they will have a panic attack and want to remain in a safe place.

Box 8.4   Panic Disorder Criteria

1. Recurrent panic attacks
   a. With worry about recurrence or consequences
2. Panic attack is defined as a discrete period of intense fear or discomfort, starting abruptly and reaching a peak within 10 minutes, with physical symptoms such as the following:
   a. Palpitations, tachycardia
   b. Sweating
   c. Shaking or trembling
   d. Shortness of breath
   e. Choking
   f. Chest pain/discomfort
   g. Nausea, abdominal distress
   h. Dizziness, faintness
   i. Feeling unreal or detached from oneself
   j. Fear of "going crazy"
   k. Fear of dying
   l. Paresthesias
   m. Chills or hot flashes

Prevalence

1. Panic disorder has a prevalence in the general population of 1% to 2%. Incidence is highest in young women, with an average onset in the early 20s; 40% have onset after age 30.
   a. In older and medically ill patients, suspect an underlying medical cause for a panic attack.
2. Because of the medical symptoms of panic attacks, these patients tend to cluster in medical practices.
   a. The prevalence in cardiology, gastroenterology, or neurology, for example, is probably about four times the community prevalence.
3. Panic disorder often occurs along with other psychiatric disorders.
   a. For example, about 33% of patients with generalized anxiety disorder or depression also have panic disorder at some point in their illness.
4. Panic disorder appears to have a genetic component, with a substantially greater risk for the disorder in first-degree relatives.

Differential diagnosis

1. *Medical disorders* presenting as panic attacks should always be considered, especially in older patients (see Boxes 8.2, 8.3, and 8.5). Millions of dollars each year are spent for unnecessary medical care for undiagnosed panic disorder.
2. *Major depression:* Panic attacks often emerge in the context of a major depression. Treating the depression often resolves the panic attacks.
3. *Other psychiatric disorders* with panic attacks:
   a. Posttraumatic stress disorder

Box 8.5   Common Medical Causes of Panic Attacks

Allergies
Hyperthyroidism
Hypoglycemia
Irritable bowel syndrome
Mitral valve prolapse
Otoneurological disorders
Structural lesions of the brain
Temporal lobe epilepsy

---

   b. Borderline personality
   c. Delirium
   d. Decompensating schizophrenia

Course and Prognosis

1. Panic disorder appears to be an episodic disorder, which may emerge, disappear, and re-emerge years later.
   a. Patients often do not need lengthy maintenance treatment. After a period of stability (of at least several months) patients may be able to taper (slowly) their treatment and remain symptom free for extended periods.
2. Do not underestimate the impact of panic disorder.
   a. Symptoms are frightening and disabling.
   b. Secondary substance abuse is not uncommon.
   c. In severe cases there has been an association with suicide.

Treatments

Overall, panic disorder is very responsive to psychopharmacologic and cognitive behavioral therapies. Medication can abolish panic attacks of any etiology; therefore, the success of medication does not imply the absence of some underlying medical cause.

1. *Psychopharmacology:* Panic disorder responds to several drug groups including benzodiazepines (especially alprazolam and clonazepam) and antidepressants (including tricyclics, SSRIs, and MAOIs).
   a. **Benzodiazepines:** Among the benzodiazepines, alprazolam (Xanax) and clonazepam (Klonopin) appear to have the most potent antipanic effects. (Further details about using benzodiazepines may be found in Chapter 9.)
     (1) Alprazolam (Xanax)
       (a) Alprazolam is very effective at abolishing panic attacks, often at fairly low doses such as 0.25 or 0.5 mg tid, although higher doses may be needed.
       (b) Some patients ask for or require increasing doses or frequency

of doses of alprazolam. For this type of patient, it may be helpful to cross over to clonazepam (because of its longer half-life) on a 2:1 ratio; that is 1 mg of alprazolam to 0.5 mg of clonazepam.

(c) Tapering off alprazolam can be quite difficult. If discontinued too rapidly, there can be withdrawal seizures (if the daily dose is about 6 mg/day or more), rebound anxiety, and rebound panic attacks. Tapering should be done slowly, by 0.5 mg/week until reaching 1 mg/day, then by 0.25 mg/week.

(2) Clonazepam (Klonopin)

(a) Also appears to be an effective antipanic medication, in doses about half those of alprazolam.

(b) Can be taken twice a day rather than four times as is needed with alprazolam (see Chapter 9).

(c) Many patients find clonazepam too sedating.

b. **Antidepressants:**

(1) Imipramine, often in very low doses (such as 25 mg/day) can effectively treat panic disorder.

(2) This effect is not unique to imipramine and appears to be a property of other antidepressants including desipramine and fluoxetine (often in low doses such as 5–10 mg/day). Start at a low dose and gradually increase until a response occurs or side effects intervene.

(3) Chapter 6 describes the side effects of antidepressants.

(4) In addition, some patients with panic disorder (about 10% to 15%) develop a dysphoric, agitated response to antidepressants. Such patients are reluctant to try antidepressants again, although they would probably do well on *very small* doses (e.g., 10 mg of imipramine or 2.5 mg of fluoxetine).

2. *Cognitive-Behavioral Therapy (CBT):* Several studies have demonstrated that CBT can be as effective as medication in the treatment of panic disorder.

a. CBT involves two basic components:

(1) A relaxation component in which the patient learns some form of relaxation exercise (see Chapter 9) coupled with:

(2) A cognitive component in which the patient learns to identify cues that may trigger panic attacks and to apply some alternate way of dealing with the situation.

b. This treatment usually requires referral to a therapist specially trained in this technique.

3. Treatment of co-morbidities: When panic attacks are treated but the patient still remains functionally impaired, there may be coexisting:

a. Agoraphobia (which may require behavioral therapy).

b. Generalized anxiety disorder (which may require a second medication, such as buspirone).

c. Depression (requiring a higher dose or additional antidepressants).

d. Anticipatory anxiety: after having panic attacks, patients become fearful of a recurrence. This component often requires some behavioral therapy to desensitize the patient.

| 8.4 | OBSESSIVE COMPULSIVE DISORDER (OCD)

Definition and Identification

1. Obsessions are persistent thoughts, ideas, or images that intrude into conscious awareness and are perceived as senseless and intrusive.
2. Compulsions are urges or impulses for repetitive intentional behaviors, performed in a stereotyped manner, to attempt to reduce anxiety. Some typical compulsions involve touching, counting, arranging.
3. OCD patients may show up at a physician's office in a number of disguised presentations:
   a. Dermatologic presentations of compulsive hand washing.
   b. Hair pulling (trichotillomania) presenting as alopecia.
   c. Some forms of hypochondriasis or chronic pain might be a form of obsessive disorder.
4. Patients may not reveal their OCD behaviors unless specifically asked. Screening questions for OCD would be:
   a. "Are there certain thoughts that go through your mind over and over that you can't seem to get rid of?"
   b. "Are there any behaviors or habits that you feel compelled to repeat?"
5. Many people have obsessive compulsive behaviors that are not of sufficient severity to qualify as a disorder. When less severe, it would be more accurate to say such people have obsessive-compulsive personality features or traits (see Chapter 16).

Prevalence

1. OCD has a community prevalence of about 2%.
2. There is a higher incidence of OCD in first-degree relatives of patients with OCD.

Differential diagnosis

1. *Schizophrenia:* Patients with severe OCD may appear to be psychotic and may be misdiagnosed as schizophrenic and prescribed neuroleptics because of the extreme and seemingly bizarre practices associated with their illness.
2. *Major depression:* About 30% of patients with major depression have obsessive compulsive symptoms. When patients with obsessive-compulsive traits develop major depression, their obsessive-compulsive traits may become magnified and exaggerated, at times misleading the clinician into diagnosing OCD as the primary disorder.
3. *Dementia:* When patients with underlying obsessive compulsive traits become demented, their underlying traits may become magnified.
4. *Gilles de la Tourette disease:* 30% to 50% of these patients have obsessive compulsive symptoms. Tourette's patients have characteristic recurrent involuntary movements and/or vocal tics.
5. *Organic personality disorder:* This is often as an aspect of temporal lobe epilepsy and may manifest compulsive, repetitive behaviors.
6. *Phobic disorders:* Phobias typically show symptoms only in relation to a specific object. At times, these two disorders may be difficult to distinguish.
7. *Somatoform disorders:* Such disorders can be difficult to distinguish from OCD, especially body dysmorphic disorder (see Chapter 12).

Prognosis

1. OCD tends to be a chronic disorder, although many patients have remissions, often for extended periods.
2. Recovery takes place in about 50% of patients.

Treatments

1. *Psychopharmacology:* Drugs that augment serotonin function are effective in decreasing OCD symptoms.
   a. Clomipramine is a tricyclic antidepressant with potent serotonin reuptake blocking activity.
      (1) Side effects are listed in Table 6.1.
         (a) Sedation and anticholinergic effects are difficult for some patients to tolerate.
         (b) There is a high incidence of anorgasmia.
      (2) Relatively high doses (e.g., 250 mg/day) are often necessary.
   b. Fluoxetine (and other SSRIs) are also likely to be effective. For details on using fluoxetine, refer to Chapter 6.
      (1) For OCD, high doses (e.g., 80 mg/day) are often necessary.
   c. Augmenters:
      (1) If OCD symptoms partially respond to one medication, there may be further improvement by augmenting with buspirone (starting with doses of 5 mg tid and increasing to 20 mg tid).
      (2) For patients with coexisting mood disorder, augmenting with lithium may be helpful.
      (3) For patients with a significant anxiety component, augmenting with a benzodiazepine may be helpful.
2. *Psychological and behavioral therapies:*
   a. OCD patients can be helped by a variety of behavioral interventions, including the following:
      (1) Exposure and response prevention
      (2) Thought-stopping techniques
      (3) Desensitization procedures
   b. Psychotherapy focused on trying to achieve some underlying psychological understanding and resolution by reasoning is usually not very helpful.
   c. Family therapy may be needed along with medication to help change the patient's habit patterns associated with this disorder.
3. For severe, unremitting cases, psychosurgery, involving stereotactic limbic leukotomy, has been used.

8.5   GENERALIZED ANXIETY DISORDER (GAD)

Definition and identification

1. GAD is defined as:
   a. Excessive anxiety and worry most of the time.
   b. Other symptoms include:
      (1) Restlessness
      (2) Fatigue
      (3) Difficulty concentrating

(4) Muscle tension
(5) Sleep problems.
2. GAD patients often go to primary care physicians complaining of somatic symptoms (see Box 8.1).
3. The significance of GAD should not be underestimated. Such patients are in distress and tend to have both social and vocational impairment.

Prevalence

1. GAD appears to have a community prevalence of about 4%.
2. Since these patients often have somatic symptoms, the prevalence in medical practices is increased. The prevalence in primary care practices may be as high as 10% to 15%.

Differential diagnosis

1. *Medical disorders:* Symptoms of generalized anxiety may be caused by some underlying medical condition or drug (see Boxes 8.2 and 8.3).
2. *Substance use disorders:* GAD patients often attempt to self-medicate with alcohol or other sedatives. Unfortunately, these "treatments" lead to substance abuse with secondary depressive symptoms and increased anxiety during withdrawal.
3. *Co-morbidities:* Patients with GAD may have episodes of panic disorder or depression superimposed on a chronic continuum of general anxiety. In such cases, both disorders may need to be treated simultaneously.
4. *Somatoform disorders:* Patients with GAD may focus on physical symptoms and make repeated medical visits for evaluation and/or reassurance. Some of these patients may appear to be hypochondriacal or present as persistent somatizers. There is sometimes not a clear distinction between somatization and GAD (see Chapter 12).

Prognosis

1. GAD usually is noted to emerge in the early 20s and tends to be a lifelong disorder. In some cases, GAD can be identified in childhood.
2. Since GAD tends to be a chronic, often lifelong disorder, it may need to be treated chronically. Unfortunately, as patients age and become demented, they have less ability to manage their anxiety.
3. It is unlikely that GAD can be abolished by treatment. It is more realistic to think of treatment as decreasing symptom intensity.

Treatments

1. *Psychopharmacology:* GAD symptoms can be reduced with benzodiazepines or azapirones (see Chapter 9 for more details).
   a. Benzodiazepines are generally helpful in low to moderate doses such as diazepam 2-5 mg tid or the equivalent (Table 9.1 lists benzodiazepine conversions).
   b. The azapirone buspirone (Buspar) is generally effective in doses of between 20 and 40 mg/day. A good starting dose would be 10 mg tid. (5 mg tid in older patients and those with brain damage). Since buspirone (in doses over 40 mg) also has some antidepressant effect, this drug may also be helpful in anxious patients with mixed depressive symptoms.

c. **Antidepressants** may be helpful in reducing symptoms of GAD and are a reasonable choice, especially if there is a significant component of depression. Side effects often limit treatment.

(1) *Duration of treatment:* GAD tends to be a long-standing disorder, which may require years of maintenance. It is worthwhile considering periodic tapering of medication to ensure that the patient still needs it.

(2) *Expected treatment response:* Response to medication is likely to be partial; nevertheless, "taking the edge off" can significantly improve the patient's quality of life.

2. *Relaxation (self-regulation) therapies:* If practiced sufficiently, these can decrease symptoms of generalized anxiety. However, this form of therapy may require professional training and continued "booster" sessions. See Chapter 9 for a review of relaxation therapies.

8.6   PHOBIAS

Definition and identification

1. A phobia is defined as an irrational fear that interferes with normal behavior.
2. The three major groups of phobias are as follows:
   a. Agoraphobia without panic disorder
   b. Social phobia
   c. Simple phobia.
3. **Agoraphobia**
   a. *Identification:* Agoraphobia is manifested as a fear of having distressful or embarrassing symptoms if one leaves home.
   b. *Onset:* The onset is usually between ages 20 and 40, more commonly in women.
   c. *Co-morbidity:* Agoraphobia often accompanies panic disorder and should be considered secondary to that disorder when they occur together. Agoraphobia should be considered as a possible diagnosis in any reclusive patients.
   d. *Differential diagnosis*
      (1) Major depression (withdrawn behavior)
      (2) Schizophrenia (reclusive behavior)
      (3) Social phobia (avoidant behavior)
      (4) Panic disorder (fear that going outside will precipitate an attack).
   e. *Treatment*
      (1) Combinations of behavioral treatment, supportive psychotherapy, and antianxiety medication are often helpful and need to be integrated.
4. **Social phobia**
   a. *Identification:* Social phobics have specific (e.g., public speaking) or general (embarrassment) fears of being with people, manifesting as extreme anxiety in those contexts.
   b. *Differential diagnosis*
      (1) Normative anxiety (e.g., some nondisabling anxiety of public speaking).

    (2) Avoidant personality disorder manifests as a generalized avoidance of social situations, not limited to particular circumstances.

    (3) Patients with delusions or hallucinations (e.g., schizophrenia, delirium, dementia) appear to show phobic behavior based on their psychotic determinants of behavior.

    (4) Depression (desire to avoid being with people).

  c. *Treatment*

    (1) Chapter 9 presents a review of the use of beta-blockers for "performance anxiety" as an aspect of social phobia. For example, 20-40 mg of propranolol about 45 minutes before the "performance" may abolish the autonomic symptoms of anxiety (e.g., tremulousness, sweating, tachycardia) that augment the person's fear and escalate the anxiety.

    (2) Social phobia symptoms may be helped by benzodiazepines in low doses, antidepressants, or MAOIs.

    (3) Desensitization through exposure and practice is often the preferred approach to treatment and can be quite successful.

5. Simple phobia

  a. *Identification:* Common simple phobias include fear of snakes, heights, crossing bridges, darkness, flying, and needles.

    (1) These phobias generally come to medical attention only when interfering with work or activity.

    (2) Two phobias that affect medical care include needle phobia and claustrophobia (in patients requiring MRIs or radiation therapy).

    (3) Simple phobias are almost ubiquitous in the general population. They may be persistent or have a limited course.

  b. *Differential diagnosis*

    (1) Major depression (with emergent phobia).

    (2) Psychosis: patients with delusions or hallucinations (e.g., schizophrenia, delirium, dementia) will appear to show phobic behavior based on their psychosis.

    (3) Posttraumatic stress disorder.

    (4) Obsessive compulsive disorder: fears of contamination may interfere with normal activities and appear as phobic behavior.

  c. *Treatment*

    (1) Behavioral therapy: involves a combination of relaxation and exposure desensitization.

      (a) In general, psychologists with special training in behavioral therapy are most effective at providing these treatments.

    (2) If the phobic behaviors occur as a component of another disorder (such as agoraphobia associated with panic disorder), the accompanying disorder should be treated simultaneously.

    (3) Needle phobia usually responds to a few sessions of behavioral therapy.

    (4) Claustrophobia for MRI usually responds to low dose benzodiazepines (e.g., 5-10 mg diazepam [Valium]) and/or behavioral therapy.

8.7   ADJUSTMENT DISORDER WITH ANXIETY

Definition and identification

1. An adjustment disorder with anxiety is defined as a reaction to an identifiable stressor. The period of difficulty is, by definition, shorter than 6 months.
2. No person goes through life without reactive anxiety. Most people find ways to either tolerate such anxiety or relieve it through personal formulas that reduce it or distract them from it.
3. Situational anxiety responses to psychosocial stress are among the leading precipitants of physician visits. It is for this reason that the medical evaluation should always include some questions about current life stresses (see Chapter 2).

Prevalence

1. Adjustment reactions are ubiquitous in the general population and especially in the medically ill, who are confronted with many new, frightening, and uncomfortable situations.

Differential Diagnosis

1. *Panic attacks:* Brief anxiety reactions may be confused with panic attacks but are not as extreme and do not have the full cluster of symptoms (see Box 8.4).
2. *Medical causes of acute anxiety*
   a. Anxiety may be the outcome of some underlying medical problem (See Boxes 8.2 and 8.3), such as an asthmatic attack, a cardiac dysrhythmia, or a drug or medication reaction.
   b. Repeated anxiety symptoms with no other apparent explanation should increase suspicion of some underlying medical cause.
3. *Psychosocial stress:* A minimal amount of interviewing is usually necessary to determine the psychosocial context underlying an anxiety reaction (see Chapter 2 on the psychosocial content of the psychiatry data base).
   a. Often it is only necessary to ask, "What do you think is making you so anxious?"
   b. Because of the increasing awareness of and willingness to discuss the problem, issues of sexual or physical abuse should be considered in patients with acute anxiety symptoms.
4. *Anxiety as an aspect of another psychiatric disorder*
   a. Repeated anxiety symptoms without an apparent cause should raise suspicion of some underlying psychiatric disorder including:
      (1) An affective disorder with accompanying anxiety.
      (2) An anxiety disorder such as OCD, posttraumatic stress disorder (PTSD).
      (3) Substance abuse.

Prognosis

1. Episodes of acute anxiety are self-limited, although they can be extremely uncomfortable for the patient.

Treatments

1. Reassuring patients that they are not medically ill or "losing their mind," along with some structured problem solving, are generally sufficient.
2. If the underlying cause is continuing and the patient is in extreme distress, short-term anxiolytic use may be helpful, such as:
   a. Diazepam (5-10) mg orally. If an intramuscular (IM) route is necessary, lorazepam 1-2 mg may be used.
   b. In the medically ill patient or in patients who should avoid benzodiazepines, low-dose neuroleptics can be helpful (such as perphenazine 2 mg PO or IM).
   c. Commonly employed anxiety reduction strategies are helpful and adaptive (e.g., exercise programs, social support).

8.8   POSTTRAUMATIC STRESS DISORDER (PTSD)

Definitions and identification

1. Posttraumatic Stress Disorder (PTSD) is recurrent anxiety precipitated by an exposure to or memory of some past traumatic situation. Stressors causing PTSD are severe and outside the range of normal experience (e.g., rape, combat, assault, traffic accidents).
2. Diagnostic criteria for PTSD are as follows:
   a. History of traumatic experience.
   b. Reexperience of the traumatic event by:
      (1) Intrusive memories.
      (2) Disturbing dreams.
      (3) "Flashbacks."
      (4) Psychological or physical distress as a result of reminders of the event.
   c. Avoidance of things associated with the trauma.
   d. Symptoms including:
      (1) Sleep problems.
      (2) Irritability.
      (3) Trouble concentrating.
      (4) Hypervigilence.
      (5) Startle responses.

Prevalence

1. PTSD has an estimated prevalence of about 1% of the general population but is obviously higher (up to 20%) in people who have been exposed to traumatic life events such as war, rape, catastrophes.
2. Unfortunately, as a consequence of our increasingly violent society, we may be seeing an increased incidence of PTSD.

Differential diagnosis

1. In psychotic disorders intrusive disturbing thoughts are not limited to a single traumatic event.
2. Cognitive deficits (of concentration and memory) in PTSD may resemble dementias.
3. Impulsive, irritable, or aggressive behaviors of personality disorders have a history that pre-dates the traumatic event.

4. Substance abuse should always be searched for because it is not uncommon for patients with PTSD to try to cope with their symptoms in this way.
5. The anxiety associated with PTSD may appear to be a panic attack.
6. The stressor and anxiety of an adjustment disorder are generally less severe.

Prognosis

1. Early intervention can help lessen the duration and severity of the resulting anxiety disorder.
2. Acute forms of PTSD, which come and go in 6 months or less, have a good prognosis for remaining in remission.
3. Chronic, remitting forms can be quite difficult to resolve and may require ongoing support and episodic interventions.

Treatments

1. Early intervention, with crisis counseling, can be an important preventive measure.
2. Support groups have been helpful for many patients.
3. Psychotherapeutic support can help decrease symptom frequency and severity. PTSD usually requires some form of psychotherapy (individual or group) designed for the specific trauma. It is probably best to seek out a therapist who has some experience dealing with the specific problem.
   a. Therapy often consists of a component of slowly coming into contact with the traumatic experience and reintegrating it into the present with some combination of support and desensitization.
4. Psychopharmacology.
   a. Most psychotropics have been tried to treat symptoms of PTSD. The groups showing the most promise are the antidepressants and buspirone.

References

Aronson TA, Craig TJ: Cocaine precipitation of panic disorder, *Am J Psychiatry* 143:643–645, 1986.

Brawman-Mintzer O, Lydiard RB, Emmanuel N et al: Psychiatric comorbidity in patients with generalized anxiety disorder, *Am J Psychiatry* 150(8):1216–1218, 1993.

Hoehn-Saric R, McLeod DR, eds: *Biology of anxiety disorders,* Washington DC, 1993, American Psychiatric Press.

Johnson J, Weissman MM, Klerman GL: Panic disorder, comorbidity, and suicide attempts, *Arch Gen Psychiatry* 47:805–808, 1990.

Katon WJ, ed: Panic disorder: somatization, medical utilization, and treatment. Proceedings of a symposium, January 24, 1992, *Am J Med* 1992.

Katerndahl DA, Pealini JP: Lifetime prevalence of panic states, *Am J Psychiatry* 150:246–249, 1993.

Maser JD, Cloninger CR, eds: *Comorbidity of mood and anxiety disorders,* Washington, DC, 1990, American Psychiatric Press.

Moreau D, Weissman MM: Panic disorder in children and adolescents: a review, *Am J Psychiatry* 149:1306–1314, 1992.

Nagy LM, Morgan CA, Southwick SM et al: Open prospective trial of fluoxetine for posttraumatic stress disorder, *J Clin Psychopharm* 13:107–113, 1993.

Noyes R, Reich J, Christiansen J: Outcome of panic disorder, *Arch Gen Psychiatry* 47:809–818, 1990.

Rapee RM, Barlow DH, eds: *Chronic anxiety,* New York, 1991, The Guilford Press.

Rickels K, Schweizer E: The treatment of generalized anxiety disorder in patients with depressive symptomatology, *J Clin Psychiatry* 54(suppl 1):20–23, 1993.

Solomon SD, Gerrity ET, Muff AM: Efficacy of treatment for posttraumatic stress disorder, *JAMA* 268(5):633–638, 1992.

Weissman MM, Klerman GL, Markowitz JS et al: Suicidal ideation and suicide attempts in panic disorder and attacks, *New Eng J Med* 321:1209–1214, 1989.

9 Treatment of Anxiety: Antianxiety Medications and Behavioral Therapies

The following are goals of this chapter:
1. To review the use of medications:
   a. Benzodiazepines
   b. Buspirone
   c. Other sedatives.
2. To provide instructions for teaching relaxation therapy.

9.1 BENZODIAZEPINES (BZ)

Introduction

1. **BZ indications for anxiety disorders**
   a. Panic disorder: Alprazolam and clonazepam have the most specific antipanic activity. For panic attacks, alprazolam in a dose as low as 0.25 mg tid is often helpful, though some patients may require 2 mg tid or more.
   b. Generalized anxiety: All BZ have a positive effect on generalized anxiety disorder (also see section on Azapirone in this chapter). A broad range of oral doses seem necessary for different patients (e.g., diazepam 2.5 mg tid to 10 mg tid).
   c. Acute anxiety: Benzodiazepines are appropriate for acute or short-term anxiety when the reason for the anxiety is one of the following:
      (1) Can be identified.
      (2) Will be time-limited.
      (3) Is not relieved by reassurance.
         (a) For example: a patient awaiting a cardiac catheterization is extremely anxious and cannot control anxiety despite reassurance. Prescribe, for example, lorazepam 0.5 mg, two to three times per day; or diazepam 2-5 mg, two to three times per day.

2. **Other indications for BZ**
   a. Short-term use as hypnotics (see Chapter 10).
   b. Musculoskeletal disorders (diazepam is approved for the treatment of muscle spasm).
   c. Seizure disorders (IV diazepam remains one of the drugs of choice for terminating repetitive grand mal seizures; lorazepam and clonazepam are also used as anticonvulsants).
   d. Treatment of sedative-withdrawal syndromes (see Chapter 14).
   e. Anesthesia (midazolam is commonly used as a preoperative adjunct).

Table 9.1 Summary of Benzodiazepines

Drug	Plasma Peak (hrs.)	Half-life (hrs.)	Active Metabolites	Half-life (hrs.)	Dose Equiv.	Duration
Alprazolam (Xanax)	1-2	12-15	Alphahydroxy-alprazolam	6	0.5	Short
Lorazepam (Ativan)	1-3 20 min IM	10-24	None		1.0	Short
Midazolam IM (Versed) IV		1-6	1-Hydroxy- Methylmidazolam		1-3	Short
Oxazepam (Serax)	1-4	3-24	None		15	Short
Chlordiazepoxide (Librium)	1-4	7-28	Desmethylchlordiazepoxide Demoxepam Desmethyldiazepam Oxazepam	5-30 14-95 25-100 3-24	12.5	Long
Clonzaepam (Klonopin)	1-2	18-56	None		0.25	Long
Clorazepate (Tranxene)	1-2	*	Desmethyldiazepam Oxazepam	25-100 3-24	7.5	Long
Diazepam (Valium)	0.5-2.0	20-50	Desmethyldiazepam Oxazepam	25-100 3-24	5	Long
Prazepam (Centrax)	4-6	*	Desmethyldiazepam Oxazepam	25-100 3-24	10	Long

3. Pharmacokinetics
   a. **Absorption**
      (1) The onset of action of orally administered BZ is mostly determined by GI absorption. Diazepam and clorazepate are the two most rapidly absorbed, although all BZ are well absorbed orally.
      (2) Lorazepam (and midazolam) are the only BZ reliably absorbed from IM sites. Diazepam and chlordiazepoxide intramuscular absorption is erratic.
      (3) Sublingual absorption: Lorazepam, alprazolam, and triazolam are compounded to allow sublingual absorption. Tablets should be placed under the tongue and allowed to dissolve passively. This may be a reasonable alternative for patients who are NPO. Absorption is slightly faster than oral rates.
      (4) Diazepam, lorazepam, and midazolam are used intravenously in some emergency situations, such as agitated delirium or laryngeal dystonia (from neuroleptics), which do not respond to anticholinergics. Lorazepam 1-2 mg given slowly IV would be a reasonable dose. IV BZ should be pushed very slowly to minimize the risk of respiratory depression and should not be used unless immediate resuscitation capability is available.
   b. **Distribution**
      (1) All BZ are highly lipophilic molecules that rapidly cross the blood-brain barrier and enter brain tissue.
      (2) Those BZ that are the most lipophilic (diazepam and clorazepate) have a shorter duration of clinical activity because they are rapidly redistributed to peripheral sites.
         (a) Therefore, even though diazepam has a lengthy plasma elimination half-life, it has a relatively short duration of clinical activity after a dose.
   c. **Metabolism**
      (1) All BZ are metabolized by the liver, involving either oxidation or glucuronide conjugation.
         (a) Oxidation can be impaired by conditions including old age, hepatic cirrhosis, or other drugs (e.g., cimetidine, estrogens, or isoniazid).
      (2) Benzodiazepines can be classified as long- or short-acting.
      (3) The long-acting drugs tend to have active metabolites with elimination half-lives of about 4 days.

Table 9.2   Benzodiazepine metabolism

Oxidative	Conjugative
Long-acting	**Short-acting**
Chlordiazepoxide	Alprazolam
Clorazepate	Lorazepam
Diazepam	Oxazepam
Prazepam	

(a) Long-acting drugs, if suddenly discontinued, do *not* have medically serious withdrawal symptoms and tend to self-taper. This reason is why you can "load" a patient in delirium tremens with chlordiazepoxide or diazepam and stop the BZ after a day (see Chapter 14).

(b) Long-acting drugs tend to accumulate with repeated doses, especially in the elderly or those with hepatic impairment.

(4) The short-acting drugs, which are quickly eliminated, have the potential for producing serious withdrawal reactions, including seizures. At moderate or high doses, clinically important withdrawal symptoms are common (see Box 9.1 for BZ withdrawal symptoms).

4. **Side effects**

a. Psychomotor impairment and drowsiness.

(1) Symptoms of muscle weakness, ataxia, dysarthria, vertigo, somnolence, confusion.

(2) Older patients are especially susceptible to psychomotor impairment and falls.

(3) Creates risk for car accidents, machinery accidents, or falls, especially if patients are also taking other sedative drugs or alcohol.

(4) While patients develop tolerance to these psychomotor side effects after 3 to 4 weeks, they apparently do not develop tolerance to the anxiolytic side effects.

b. BZ augment the sedative side effects of other sedatives, including the following:

(1) Narcotics

(2) Barbiturates

(3) Alcohol.

c. Cognitive impairment. BZ impair memory in two ways:

(1) Acute anterograde amnesia, usually associated with IV use but also reported with high-dose, high-potency benzodiazepines taken orally

(2) Impaired long-term memory from interference with memory consolidation, most often a problem in the elderly.

d. Depression of hypoxic respiratory drive

(1) The respiratory depressant effects of BZ is most marked in patients with CO_2 retention. Therefore, BZ should not be used in patients with pulmonary disease without checking a blood gas for elevated PCO_2.

(2) This problem is most marked when BZ are given intravenously with other respiratory depressants such as narcotics.

e. Depressive symptoms may be produced or increased.

f. Depersonalization, paranoia, confusion are reported with triazolam, generally at doses of 0.5 mg or more.

g. Paradoxical effects resulting in disinhibition, or agitation/aggression appear rarely, usually in patients with preexisting personality disorders, substance abusers, and underlying delirium or dementia. To manage BZ-induced dyscontrol, haloperidol 5 mg IM may be effective.

5. **Issues of abuse**
   a. Benzodiazepines are potentially drugs of abuse.
   b. It is extremely rare that the average person would become an abuser by a brief exposure to BZ.
   c. Addiction-prone personalities are more likely to become addicted to BZ. Other than for a medically indicated short-term use, BZ should be prescribed cautiously, if at all, for such individuals. See Chapter 14 for further discussion of medication and drug abuse issues.
   d. Course of action when the patient taking BZ asks for higher doses more frequently:
      (1) Some actually need higher doses than commonly prescribed. However, when a patient seems to require doses beyond the customary range, the physician should consider the potential of abuse.
      (2) Look for other signs of abuse:
         (a) Multiple prescribers
         (b) Lost pills
         (c) Emergency room visits for medication
         (d) A pattern of running out too soon
         (e) Concurrent abuse of other substances
         (f) Lack of legitimate diagnosis to warrant medication
         (g) Buying drugs on the street
         (h) Adverse behavioral consequences.
      (3) Eliminate multiple prescribers.
   e. Patients legitimately maintained on BZ for generalized anxiety should not be considered abusers.
6. **Discontinuing BZ and withdrawal issues**
   a. When to discontinue BZ:
      (1) If the patient is abusing the drug.
      (2) If the drug is causing significant side effects.
      (3) If the underlying disorder may no longer be present.
         (a) For example, panic disorder is likely to be episodic; therefore, after about 4 to 6 months of stability, consider a gradual taper.
   b. How to discontinue BZ:
      (1) The long-acting drugs will "self-taper." While a patient taking diazepam 30 mg/day might feel anxious or somewhat uncomfortable about stopping "cold-turkey," there will be no serious medical consequences.
      (2) The short-acting drugs need to be tapered to avoid sedative withdrawal symptoms.
   c. For symptoms of BZ withdrawal, see Box 9.1.
   d. Risk for withdrawal symptoms increases with:
      (1) Higher doses.
      (2) Duration of use (risk for withdrawal may be present within 1 week of continuous use).
      (3) Shorter plasma elimination half-life.
   e. Treatment of withdrawal:
      (1) Typical treatment involves giving a BZ or a cross-tolerant sedative in sufficient amount to eliminate the withdrawal symptoms. Then the patient is gradually withdrawn on a more controlled schedule.

Box 9.1   Benzodiazepine withdrawal symptoms

Anxiety	Insomnia
Dizziness	Headache
Anorexia	Hypotension
Hyperthermia	Muscle irritability
Tinnitus	Blurred vision
Tremor	Psychosis

    (2) Details of treatment of BZ and sedative withdrawal are described in Chapter 14.

    (3) Autonomic symptoms, if intense, can be controlled with beta-blockers.

7. **Drug interactions**

  a. The BZ have relatively few drug interactions. Relevant interactions include the following:

    (1) Augmentation of other CNS sedatives (e.g., alcohol, narcotics, antihistamines).

    (2) Drugs that increase BZ levels:

      (a) Fluoxetine

      (b) Cimetidine

      (c) Low-dose estrogen containing oral contraceptives

      (d) There is a report that erythromycin inhibits triazolam metabolism

      (e) Disulfiram

      (f) Isoniazid

    (3) Drugs whose levels may be increased by BZ:

      (a) Phenytoin

      (b) Coumadin

      (c) Digoxin

    (4) Drugs that may impair/delay BZ absorption:

      (a) Antacids

      (b) Anticholinergics

    (5) Drugs that decrease BZ levels:

      (a) Carbamazepine (and possibly other anticonvulsants).

8. **Overdose**

  a. Patients can ingest extremely large doses of BZ without dying.

  b. Deaths from BZ alone are extremely rare; however, deaths occur when BZ are mixed with other sedatives such as alcohol or barbiturates.

  c. Flumazenil (Mazicon), a benzodiazepine receptor antagonist that can reverse excessive sedation and psychomotor impairment, should be used in patients with cyclic antidepressant overdoses because of exacerbation of seizures.

9. **Use during pregnancy**

  a. Reports that use of diazepam during the first trimester is associated with increased risk of cleft palate and dysmorphism have not been fully substantiated. However, there is not adequate evidence to establish the safety of BZ during pregnancy.

  b. For treating agitation and anxiety after the second trimester, tricyclic antidepressants and diazepam both appear relatively safe and preferable to neuroleptics.

10. **Differences among the benzodiazepines**

  a. *Alprazolam (Xanax)*

   (1) Antipanic properties are very good; often effective within 24 hours. Effective doses may be as little as 0.25 mg or 0.5 mg tid. If a patient does not respond, the dose can be doubled. Usually patients do not require more than 2 mg tid.

   (2) Alprazolam is somewhat unique BZ because of its antidepressant effects. While not indicated as a first-line antidepressant, it may be helpful in mixed anxiety-depression states.

   (3) It is often difficult to discontinue alprazolam. Tapering must be done slowly often decreasing by as little as 0.25 mg/week to avoid rebound anxiety or withdrawal.

   (4) Some patients request an increase in dose or frequency to maintain an effect. This may raise concern about potential abuse. In such cases, consider crossing the patient over to longer-acting clonazepam.

      (a) Add up the total alprazolam dose and convert to one half that amount of clonazepam. Give the clonazepam in a bid dose. During the first 7 days, small doses of alprazolam can be use prn if needed. If more medication is needed after 7 days, clonazepam can be increased by 0.25 to 0.5 mg per week.

   (5) Alprazolam XR may be of value in eliminating plasma level variability and increasing compliance in the management of panic disorder. It appears that bid or even once daily dosage may be effective.

  b. *Chlordiazepoxide (Librium)*

   (1) Available in generic form.

   (2) Often used to prevent or treat sedative withdrawal syndromes, such as delirium tremens, in doses of approximately 50 mg every 3 hours.

   (3) Should be given orally, since it is not well absorbed IM. Details on treating delirium tremens are presented in Chapter 14.

  c. *Clonazepam (Klonopin)*

   (1) Indicated for the treatment of akinetic, myoclonic, and absence-type seizures.

   (2) An effective antipanic drug, often in doses as low as 0.25 mg bid. Some patients require about 1 mg tid.

   (3) Sedation is the most problematic side effect.

   (4) An effective antimanic drug, will slow down and sedate manic-agitated patients. Unfortunately, it is only available in oral form.

   (5) Active manic patients may require doses of 2 mg tid or qid. (Chapter 13 presents a review of the treatment of behavioral emergencies.)

d. *Diazepam (Valium)*
   (1) Available in generic form.
   (2) Indicated for treatment of status epilepticus and recurrent convulsive seizures.
   (3) Effective anxiolytic for short-term and acute use. The patient who needs to be calmed down might do well by taking diazepam 5 mg PO prn.
   (4) Diazepam is often preferred by sedative abusers, possibly because of its rapid brain uptake.
   (5) Not well absorbed from IM sites.

e. *Lorazepam (Ativan) and Oxazepam (Serax)*
   (1) Short-acting BZ with no active metabolites.
   (2) Metabolism does not depend on hepatic P 450 system; therefore, plasma levels are not altered by other medications, aging, or liver disease.
   (3) Lorazepam is well absorbed IM, a useful property in the medically ill and delirium tremens (2 mg lorazepam IM can substitute for 50 mg of chlordiazepoxide or 10 mg of diazepam). See Chapter 13 for more details on its use in emergency situations.

9.2 AZAPIRONES

1. This group of nonsedating anxiolytics is represented by **buspirone** (Buspar).
   a. *Indications*
      (1) Generalized anxiety disorder
      (2) General anxiety with accompanying depressive symptoms.
   b. *Other clinical applications*
      (1) Augments response of antidepressants.
      (2) Augments response of drugs that treat OCD.
      (3) Reduces the frequency and severity of episodic aggression in some populations with brain damage (such as those developmentally disabled and demented).
      (4) Case reports indicate potential usefulness in a variety of disorders including irritable bowel syndrome, premenstrual syndrome, PTSD, and tardive dyskinesia.
   c. *Clinical use*
      (1) Dose: The antianxiety dose range is between 20-40 mg/day, with a usual starting dose of 10 mg tid.
         (a) In patients with brain damage (e.g., post-stroke, Parkinson's disease, Alzheimer's disease, developmental disabilities) the starting dose should be 5 mg tid because of increased likelihood of side effects.
      (2) An adequate clinical trial requires about 1 month. If response is inadequate, increase the dose by increments of 5-10 mg every few weeks until 20 mg tid.
      (3) Antidepressant effects are generally seen at 40-80 mg/day. When used as an augmenter, start at 10 mg tid.

(4) Response lag time of several weeks is usual. Patients need to be educated and supported through the first few weeks.

    (a) For the patient who does not want to wait several weeks, try reasoning that their disorder has been present for a long time. If this does not work, two drugs can be started at one time. For example, 0.5 mg lorazepam tid. and buspirone 10 mg tid; or for the CO_2 retainer, a low dose neuroleptic (such as perphenazine 2 mg tid) and buspirone 10 mg tid. After about 3 weeks, the benzodiazepine or neuroleptic can be stopped.

d. *Side Effects* (5% to 10% incidence):
    (1) Dizzy, light-headed feeling; often dose related, may be reduced by breaking up the dose
    (2) Dull headache
    (3) Nervousness (different from the underlying anxiety).

e. *Drug interactions:*
    (1) Do not use with MAOIs
    (2) May increase haloperidol levels.

9.3   COMPARISON OF BENZODIAZEPINES AND AZAPIRONES

1. The basic differences between these two drug groups are as follows:

a. Indications: azapirones are indicated only for generalized anxiety; and, unlike benzodiazepines, are not effective for acute anxiety or panic disorder.

b. The azapirones lack the sedative side effects of the benzodiazepines, such as:
    (1) Psychomotor impairment and drowsiness.
        (a) Patients will be less likely to have accidents.
        (b) Elderly patients will be less likely to fall.
    (2) Augmentation of other sedatives. As a nonsedating anxiolytic, buspirone may be useful in patients who need to avoid additional sedation, such as:

Table 9.3   Comparison of benzodiazepines and azapirones

	Benzodiazepines	Azapirones
Indications		
Used for acute anxiety	Yes	No
Used for panic attacks	Yes	No
Used for general anxiety	Yes	Yes
Sedative effects		
Psychomotor impairment	Yes	No
Drowsiness	Yes	No
Sedative augmentation	Yes	No
cognitive effects	Yes	No
Abuse potential	Yes	No
Respiratory depression	Yes	No

(a) Medical patients taking narcotics for chronic pain (e.g., cancer patients).
(b) Epileptics taking phenobarbital or a BZ.
(c) Patients at risk for abusing alcohol.

c. Because the azapirones lack cognitive impairment, they are preferable for elderly patients with generalized anxiety.

d. Azapirones lack abuse potential. This fact may be a consideration for patients with a history of addiction.

e. Azapirones do not cause respiratory depression and are safe in patients with CO_2 retention.

f. The azapirones are not "cross-tolerant" with other sedatives and cannot be used to cover the physiologic withdrawal symptoms from alcohol or other sedatives.

9.4 OTHER SEDATIVE-HYPNOTICS

1. *Antihistamines,* such as diphenhydramine (Benadryl) or hydroxazine (Vistaril), are sometimes used to treat anxiety; however, they have no specific antianxiety properties. Patients feel less anxious because of sedative effects. In addition, these drugs have significant anticholinergic activity.

2. *Barbiturates* have basically no role in treating anxiety because of rapid tolerance, need for increased doses, abuse potential, lack of safety at high doses, overdose lethality, and many drug interactions.

3. *Meprobamate* (Miltown, Equanil) was the anxiolytic of choice during the 1950s but has little place today because it is not as effective as the other choices.

4. *Neuroleptics* may be useful for the treatment of anxiety in medically ill patients requiring a rapid response and in those who cannot tolerate benzodiazepines because of respiratory disease. In the anxious delirious patient, low-dose neuroleptics (e.g., perphenazine [Trilafon] 2 mg bid or tid) may be helpful. Because of the risk of tardive dyskinesia, these drugs should be used for as short a time as possible.

5. *Beta-blockers*
   a. The best use of beta-blockers for anxiety involves their use to prevent performance anxiety; 20-40 mg of propranolol given 45 to 75 minutes before a "performance" can decrease symptoms of anxiety. Propranolol is well absorbed orally, with a half-life of about 3 hours.
   b. Nadolol and atenolol, although they do not cross the blood-brain barrier, also appear to be effective in these situations.
   c. These drugs are not indicated as maintenance treatment for anxiety disorders.
   d. They should not be used in patients with heart failure, depression, delirium, asthma, hypoglycemia.

9.5 BEHAVIORAL (RELAXATION) THERAPIES

1. Two widely used methods for promoting relaxation.
   a. Progressive muscle relaxation
   b. The relaxation response.
2. Before beginning a procedure:

a. Discuss the procedure beforehand to elicit any specific questions, misconceptions, or concerns.
b. A comfortable, quiet setting without interruptions is important.
c. While tape recorded or printed instructions can be used, the initial session with the physician can be important in establishing a positive alliance for future work.
d. The few contraindications for these techniques include the following:
   (1) Dementia or delirium (patients may not be able to concentrate adequately).

Box 9.2   Basic Instructions for Progressive Muscle Relaxation

1. Select a comfortable sitting or reclining position.
2. Loosen any tight clothing.
3. Take a deep breath, hold momentarily, and exhale as fully as possible.
4. Tense toes and feet (curl the toes, turn the feet in and out). Hold the tension, become aware of the tension, then relax toes and feet.
5. Tense lower legs, knees, and thighs. Hold the tension, become aware of the tension, and then relax legs.
6. Tense buttocks. Hold and become aware of the tension, then relax.
7. Tense fingers and hands. Hold the tension, become aware of the tension, then relax.
8. Tense lower arms, elbows, and upper arms. Hold the tension, become aware of it, then relax.
9. Tense abdomen. Hold the tension, become aware of it, then relax.
10. Tense chest. Hold the tension, relax. Take a deep breath, hold it momentarily, then slowly exhale.
11. Tense the lower back. Hold the tension, become aware of it, then relax.
12. Tense the upper back. Hold the tension, become aware of it, then relax.
13. Tense the shoulders. Hold and be aware of the tension, then relax and let your shoulders droop down.
14. Tense the neck in front and back. Hold the tension, become aware of it, then relax.
15. Now clench the teeth until tension in the facial muscles is felt. Become aware of it, then relax letting the jaw drop slightly.
16. Now wrinkle the forehead. Become aware of the tension on the top and back of the head then relax, and let the eyes relax.
17. Continue sitting for a few minutes, feeling the relaxation flowing throughout the body. Know the difference between muscles that are tense and muscles that are relaxed. Scan for any muscle groups that remain tense and first increase tension then relax them.
18. Now stretch, feeling renewed and refreshed, and continue usual activities.

Box 9.3   Basic Instruction for the Relaxation Response

The technique for eliciting the relaxation response consists of four basic elements:

1. **A mental device:** There needs to be some constant stimulus, for example, a sound, word (such as "one"), or a phrase repeated silently or audibly. Fixed gazing at an object is a suitable alternative. The purpose of this procedure is to focus attention away from the continuous flow of sensory distractions and intellectual preoccupations.

2. **A passive attitude:** During the aural or visual practice, distracting thoughts are to be disregarded. One should not be concerned with performance standards. When lapses are recognized, the practitioner should patiently return to the mental device without self-criticism or concern about success or failure.

3. **Decreased muscle tone:** The subject should be in a comfortable position to minimize any muscular strain or tension.

4. **A quiet environment:** A quiet environment with decreased stimuli should be chosen. A quiet room where there is no concern about unexpected interruptions is usually suitable. Most techniques instruct the practitioner to close the eyes.

    (2) Psychotic patients.
    (3) Some patients with an obsessive need for control (they may feel uncomfortable).
    (4) Borderline personality disorders (they may become disorganized).
  e. Explain that relaxation techniques require practice to master. Their effects on long-term anxiety may require months. However, some patients with more acute anxiety responses may benefit from only a few sessions of training.

3. **Progressive muscle relaxation**
  a. People are intuitively aware that muscle relaxation is associated with anxiety reduction.
  b. Unfortunately, many people are unaware of chronically tensed muscles or are unable to relax even when they become aware of their problem.
  c. Learning to specifically sense and control muscle tension forms the basis of a widely used and effective relaxation method.

4. **The relaxation response**
  a. Research in this area was pioneered by Dr. Herbert Benson at Harvard Medical School.
  b. His method for inducing a relaxed state is presented in Box 9.3.

References

Benson H, Beary JF, Carol MP: The relaxation response, *Psychiatry* 37:37–46, 1974.
Bixler EO, Kales A, Manfredi RL et al: Next-day memory impairment with triazolam use, *Lancet* 337:827–831, 1991.

Busto U, Sillers EM, Naranjo CA, et al: Withdrawal reaction after long-term therapeutic use of benzodiazepine, *N Engl J Med* 315:854–859, 1986.

Clark DM: A cognitive approach to panic, *Behav Res Ther* 24(4):461–470, 1986.

Cohn JB, Wilcox CS: Low-sedation potential of buspirone compared with alprazolam and lorazepam in the treatment of anxious patients: a double-blind study, *J Clin Psychiatry* 47:409–412, 1986.

Dietch JT, Jennings RK: Aggressive dyscontrol in patients treated with benzodiazepines, *J Clin Psychiatry* 49:184–188, 1988.

Dubovsky SL: Generalized anxiety disorder: new concepts and psychopharmacologic therapies, *J Clin Psychiatry* 51:3–10, 1990.

Garner SJ, Eldridge FL, Wagner PG et al: Buspirone, an anxiolytic drug that stimulates respiration, *Am Rev Respir Dis* 139:946–950, 1989.

Goff DC, Midha KK, Brotman AW et al: An open trial of buspirone added to neuroleptics in schizophrenic patients, *J Clin Psychopharm* 11(3):193–197, 1991.

Goldberg RJ: Anxiety reduction by self-regulation: theory, practice and evaluation, *Ann Intern Med* 96:483–487, 1982.

Greenblatt DJ, Harmatz JS, Engelhardt N et al: Sensitivity to triazolam in the elderly, *N Engl J Med* 324:1691–1698, 1991.

Kathol RG, Russell N, Slymen DJ: Propranolol in chronic anxiety disorders, *Arch Gen Psychiatry* 37:1361–1365, 1980.

Kirkwood CF: Flumazenil—a benzodiazepine receptor antagonist, *Pharmacol Ther* 243:252, 1991.

Patterson JF: Alprazolam dependency: use of clonazepam for withdrawal, *South Med J* 81:830–836, 1988.

Ray WA, Griffin MR, Downey W: Benzodiazepines of long and short elimination half-life and the risk of hip fracture, *JAMA* 262:3303–3307, 1989.

Rickels K, Freeman E, Sondheimer S: Buspirone in treatment of premenstrual syndrome, *Lancet* 1:777, 1989.

Salzman C: The APA task force report on benzodiazepine dependence, toxicity and abuse, *Am J Psychiatry* 148:151–152, 1991.

Schweizer E, Patterson W, Rickels K et al: Double-blind, placebo-controlled study of once-a-day sustained-release preparation of alprazolam for the treatment of panic disorder, *Am J Psychiatry* 150(8):1210–1215, 1993.

Sussman N: How to manage anxious patients who are depressed, *J Clin Psychiatry* 54(5):8–16, 1993.

Sleep Problems and the Use of Hypnotics

The following are goals of this chapter:
1. To review history pertinent to evaluating sleep disorders.
2. To present medical and psychiatric differential diagnoses of sleep problems.
3. To define the primary sleep disorders and their treatments.
4. To review the use of hypnotic medication.

Introduction

1. Approximately 20% to 40% of adult Americans complain of sleep disturbance during a one-year period.
   a. About 10% have a chronic sleep disorder.
2. In community samples at one point in time, about 10% have insomnia and 3% hypersomnia.
3. Having trouble sleeping is one of the most common problems of medical patients, especially the elderly.
4. The request for sleeping medication is one of the most common issues confronting the physician.

10.1 EVALUATION OF SLEEP PROBLEMS

1. History (see Fig. 10.1)(Table 10.1)
   a. Review longitudinal course and duration of sleep problem with investigation of possible precipitating events.
   b. Document the effects on daytime behavior.
   c. Ask patients their views of what constitutes normal sleep (for a disorder of sleep-state misperception).
      (1) Some people have a fixed number of hours in mind.
      (2) Insomnia severity should be judged only in terms of its impact on daytime functioning (mood, fatigue, muscle aches, impaired attention, or concentration).
   d. Describe the entire 24-hour period in terms of:
      (1) Regularity of bed-times and awakenings (to assess sleep hygiene, insufficient sleep, and circadian rhythm sleep disorders)
      (2) Review possible symptoms with patient and bed partner (if possible):
         (a) Snoring (may be related to sleep apnea)
         (b) Bed-wetting (REM period eneuresis)

Patient's description of sleep problem:_____

1. Duration of sleep problem:_____

2. Possible precipitating events:_____

3. Effects on daytime behavior:_____

4. Sleep features:
       Irregular bed-times and awakenings
       Snoring
       Bed-wetting
       Myoclonus or restless legs
       Breathing problems
       Nightmares
       Panic attacks
5. Psychiatric history:
       Affective disorder
       Anxiety disorder
       Psychotic disorder
       Delirium
       Dementia
6. Medical history:
    a. Medication use:_____
    b. Alcohol and drug use:_____
    c. Medical problems, including:
       incontinence or polyurea   orthopnea
       headaches   paroxysmal nocturnal dyspnea
       jaw pain from teeth clenching or grinding
other pain:_____

Figure 10.1.
Sleep history chart.

       (c) Myoclonus and restless legs
       (d) Breathing problems (may be related to sleep apnea or cardiop-
          ulmonary disease)
       (e) Nightmares (related to possible PTSD, parasomnias, or stress)
       (f) Pain (primary medical problem needing treatment)
       (g) Panic attacks (panic disorder may manifest as nighttime
          attacks).
   e. Review depression, anxiety, psychosis and psychiatric history as the
     possible primary disorder.
   f. Review medication use (See Table 10.2).
   g. Review alcohol and drug use.
   h. Review medical issues that impair sleep, such as:

Table 10-1   Classification of sleep disorders

International Classification	DSM Classification
I: Intrinsic Sleep Disorders	
Psychophysiologic insomnia	Primary insomnia
Sleep-state misperception	Primary insomnia
Idiopathic insomnia	
Narcolepsy	
Recurrent hypersomnia	
Posttraumatic hypersomnia	
Obstructive sleep apnea syndrome	Hypersomnias related to a physical condition
Central sleep apnea syndrome	
Central alveolar hypoventilation syndrome	
Periodic limb movement disorder	Myoclonic sleep disorder
Restless legs syndrome	
II: Extrinsic Sleep Disorders	
Inadequate sleep hygiene	
Environmental sleep disorder	
Altitude insomnia	
Adjustment sleep disorder	
Insufficient sleep syndrome	
Limit-setting sleep disorder	
Sleep-onset association disorder	
Food allergy insomnia	
Nocturnal eating (drinking) syndrome	
Hypnotic-dependent sleep disorder	
Stimulant-dependent sleep disorder	
Alcohol-dependent sleep disorder	
Toxin-induced sleep disorder	
III: Circadian Rhythm Sleep Disorders	
Time zone change (jet lag) syndrome	
Shift work sleep disorder	
Irregular sleep-wake pattern	
Delayed sleep phase syndrome	Sleep-wake schedule disorders
Advanced sleep phase syndrome	
Non-24–hour sleep-wake disorder	

      (1) Incontinence or polyurea
      (2) Orthopnea
      (3) Paroxysmal nocturnal dyspnea
      (4) Headaches
      (5) Jaw pain from teeth clenching or grinding
      (6) Any other pain.
2. Ask the patient to keep a 2-week log of sleep-wake times, medication and substance use, eating, activity, and symptoms.
3. Objective sleep studies:
   a. Guidelines for referral include
      (1) Failure to respond to treatment
      (2) Suspicion of, without confirmation, of primary sleep disorder such as sleep apnea or nocturnal myoclonus
      (3) Sorting out etiology in complex or refractory cases.

10.2   CLASSIFICATION OF SLEEP DISORDERS

For international and DSM classifications of sleep disorders, see Table 10-1.

10.3   INTRINSIC SLEEP DISORDERS

1. **Psychophysiologic insomnia**
   a. Also called *learned* or *conditioned* insomnia.
   b. Often starts with some increased arousal or anxiety and then becomes conditioned.
   c. Maintained by bad habits and sleep-incompatible behaviors such as:
      (1) Worrying before bedtime
      (2) Working in bed
      (3) Arguing in bed
      (4) Exercising too late
      (5) Eating too late
   d. Treatment.
      (1) See approaches to improving sleep hygiene (See Box 10.1).
2. **Sleep-state misperception**
   a. Patient may have a fixed and inaccurate or unrealistic idea of the amount of sleep is necessary.
   b. Education may help, especially by pointing out the minimal effects on daytime behavior. Sleep hygiene interventions may also help.
3. **Idiopathic insomnia**
   a. A trait, often life-long phenomenon, usually beginning in childhood.
   b. Sleep hygiene interventions may help.
   c. Chronic low-dose hypnotics, used intermittently may help.
4. **Narcolepsy**
   a. Can be a serious, life-long disabling disorder.
   b. Onset usually during teens.
   c. Has a genetic component—chances of offspring to have the disorder are about 1:20.
   d. Prevalence estimates range between 0.02% to 0.1%.
      (1) Often remains undiagnosed
   e. Symptoms (may be widely variable, only 10% have all):
      (1) Excessive daytime sleepiness with sleep attacks (in 100%).

Box 10.1   Improving Sleep Hygiene

1. Go to sleep and get up at the same time daily.
2. Discontinue possibly offending drugs.
3. Maintain regular mealtimes with a small dinner; avoid eating after dinner.
4. A predictable evening routine.
5. Avoid overstimulation from exercise, disturbing reading, television, arguing with family, work projects, etc.
6. Exercise daily, but not too late at night.
7. Avoid daytime naps.
8. Learn some relaxation method (see Chapter 9) and practice it near bedtime.
9. Create a sleep-promoting environment by cutting down on noise, light, etc.

---

(2) Cataplexy (sudden muscle weakness in response to intense emotional stimulus) (in 70%).

(3) Disrupted nighttime sleep with multiple awakenings.

(4) Sleep paralysis: awareness of inability to move despite wanting to, usually occurs upon waking up (hypnopompic) or falling asleep (hypnogogic) (in 50%).

(5) Hypnogogic hallucinations (in 25%).

(6) Automatic behavior (doing things with reduced awareness, often resulting in a period of little recollection of activity.

(7) *Note:* Sleep apnea, though not a symptom of narcolepsy, occurs more often in narcoleptics than the general population.

f. Social impact.

(1) Impaired school or work performance.

(2) Often a pattern of self-prescribed stimulants.

g. Objective confirmation.

(1) Multiple Sleep Latency Test: In narcolepsy, sleep onset is usually in the range of only 5 minutes (usually longer than 10 minutes is normal).

(2) There are reports of the presence of a leukocyte antigen, DR-2 in almost all patients with narcolepsy.

h. Treatment.

(1) Stimulants (e.g., methylphenidate) can help the sleep attacks and sleepiness.

(2) Cataplexy may be reduced by tricyclic antidepressants.

(3) Patient and family education is important.

5. **Idiopathic hypersomnia**

a. A diagnosis of exclusion made by history of a lifelong pattern of prolonged sleep, napping from youth.

b. The Multiple Sleep Latency Test shows these patients to take longer than narcoleptics to fall asleep but less than normals.

6. **Obstructive sleep apnea syndrome**
   a. Identification and definition.
      (1) Repeated apneas for 10 seconds or longer, resulting in multiple episodes of hypoxemia (oxygen saturation often below 80%).
      (2) Multiple brief awakenings (of which patient is not aware).
      (3) Excessive daytime sleepiness.
      (4) Impaired daytime function often with cognitive impairment, depressive symptoms, personality change.
      (5) An age-related disorder. Prevalence is about 9% in women and 24% for men; may be present in up to 50% of older men. About one third of adult male hypertensives are likely to have undiagnosed sleep apnea.
      (6) If untreated, is associated with pulmonary hypertension, increased risk of cardiac arrhythmia, and death.
   b. A specific diagnostic investigation (sleep laboratory study) should be ordered in patients with suggestive symptoms such as loud snoring, lung disease, or heart failure.
   c. Treatment.
      (1) Avoid sleeping on back.
      (2) Weight loss.
      (3) Avoid hypnotics and alcohol.
      (4) Nasal continuous positive airway pressure (CPAP) can keep the pharynx open and reverse snoring and sleep disturbance in many patients. Unfortunately, many patients find the mask uncomfortable and will not use it. In such cases, low-flow nasal oxygen may help both apnea and hypoxia, if the obstruction is not major.
      (5) Surgery to reduce upper airway obstruction may be helpful.

7. **Central sleep apnea syndrome**
   a. Sleep apnea caused by impaired central respiratory drive.
   b. Can occur in combination with obstructive apnea.

8. **Periodic limb movement disorders**
   a. *Nocturnal myoclonus.*
      (1) Consists of 1-3 second muscle twitches in the legs and feet, which appear every 20-40 seconds during sleep (usually in non-REM phase).
      (2) Frequent history of kicking off the bed covers.
      (3) Some myoclonic movements are normal in early childhood, disappear in late childhood and often reemerge in old age.
      (4) Often seen in conjunction with sleep apnea, narcolepsy, uremia, diabetes.
      (5) Treatment.
         (a) Clonazepam (1-2 mg/h), clorazepate, diazepam, or baclofen have been used with some success
         (b) Other drugs reported to be helpful in some patients include opioids, *l*-dopa.
   b. *Restless legs syndrome*
      (1) A sleep onset disorder.
      (2) Patients shift legs because of feelings of vague discomfort.
      (3) Associated with uremia, anemia, pregnancy, and nocturnal myoclonus.

(4) Treatment trials include opioids, carbamazepine, clonidine, benzodiazepines, baclofen, and *l*-dopa.

10.4 EXTRINSIC SLEEP DISORDERS

1. **Inadequate sleep hygiene**
   a. Bad habits create and/or maintain ongoing sleep problems.
2. **Environmental sleep disorder**
   a. External disruptions include:
      (1) Being awakened (by nursing or medical staff or newborns)
      (2) Noise and lights on medical units
      (3) Attached equipment, uncomfortable beds
3. **Adjustment sleep disorder**
   a. Temporary life stress is an extremely common cause of sleep disturbance.
      (1) The nature of the stress will usually be apparent (there should not be a history of continuous sleep problem).
4. **Stimulant-dependent sleep disorder**
   a. Stimulants produce sleep-onset insomnia and rebound hypersomnia.
5. **Alcohol- and hypnotic-dependent sleep disorders**
   a. Involves development of tolerance to sleep-inducing properties of these drugs.
   b. Increased withdrawal-arousals also produce sleep problems.

10.5 CIRCADIAN RHYTHM SLEEP DISORDERS

These disorders involve misalignment between biological circadian rhythms and external conditions influencing waking behavior. Treatment usually involves some manipulation of cues to reregulate sleep timing.

1. **Irregular sleep-wake pattern**
   a. Daytime napping and/or irregular sleep schedule interfere with normal sleep patterns (often seen in institutionalized patients).
   b. Treatment
      (1) Exercise programs may help
      (2) Keep patients from napping
      (3) Maintain consistent time of getting out of bed.
2. **Delayed sleep phase syndrome**
   a. People (often young adults) known as "night owls" who have sleep-onset insomnia and morning hypersomnia.
3. **Advanced sleep phase syndrome**
   a. People (usually older patients) who have hypersomnolence in early evening and middle-of-night arousal.

10.6 PARASOMNIAS

Parasomnias refers to events that occur during sleep. They usually occur during childhood and are considered pathologic only if they persist into adulthood. They usually involve a partial arousal.

1. **Sleepwalking and sleep terrors**
   a. Occur during the first third of the night during NREM sleep.
   b. Stress, anxiety, and sleep deprivation may worsen these.

   c. Somnambulism (sleep walking) rarely occurs in adults (episodes
      estimated in 2% to 5%).
   d. Night terrors consist of a powerful autonomic discharge often accom-
      panied by a scream.
      (1) A stage 4 phenomenon, usually occurring early in the night.
   e. Unlike nightmares, the patient does not recall any content.
2. **Sleep starts**
   a. Sudden muscle contractions, clinically insignificant.
3. **Sleepwalking**
   a. Usually indicates psychopathology in adults.
   b. Intervention: assure safety; avoid any related alcohol or drug use.
4. **Parasomnias usually associated with REM sleep** (see Box 10.2)
   a. *Nightmares*
      (1) Occur in about 5% to 10% of adults, most likely during REM
         sleep.
      (2) Patients awake and are frightened with recall of the nightmare.
      (3) May be precipitated by withdrawal from drugs that suppress REM
         activity (many antidepressants).
      (4) Associated with certain drugs (e.g. propranolol, reserpine, thior-
         idazine).

Box 10.2   Parasomnias*

Arousal disorders
Confusional arousals
Sleepwalking
Sleep terrors

Sleep-wake transition disorders
Rhythmic movement disorders
Sleep starts
Sleepwalking
Nocturnal leg cramps

Usually associated with REM sleep
Nightmares
Sleep paralysis
Impaired sleep-related penile erections
Sleep-related painful erections
REM related sinus arrest
REM sleep behavior disorder

Others
Sleep bruxism
Sleep eneuresis
*Similar terms are used in International and DSM classifications.

(5) Most common in personality disorders or during stressful periods; may accompany severe PMS and PTSD.

(6) Treatment: REM reduction may occur with low dose amitriptyline (50-75 mg/h).

b. *REM sleep behavior disorder*

(1) REM sleep motor paralysis is absent and patients may act out their dreams, occasionally causing injury.

(2) Treatment: usually responds to clonazepam 1-2 mg/h.

5. **Sleep eneuresis**

a. Rare in adults. Treated with behavioral conditioning, withholding fluids at night; imipramine 25-75 mg/h.

10.7 SLEEP DISORDERS RELATED TO ANOTHER MENTAL DISORDER

1. Major depression and dysthymia: Insomnia is a common presentation of affective disorder.

a. Sleep disturbance is a component of 90% of major depression, with sleep fragmentation, redistribution of REM sleep into the first part of the night. Bipolar patients are usually hypersomnolent during depression.

2. Schizophrenia (during acute phase)

3. Panic disorder (nighttime panic attacks occur)

4. Generalized anxiety (interferes with sleep onset)

5. Obsessive-compulsive patients (ruminate or nighttime rituals)

6. Posttraumatic stress disorder (repetitive dreams)

7. Delirium (sundowning and sleep-wake dysregulation)

8. Dementia (increased awakenings, daytime napping)

9. Parkinson's disease (sleep disturbance in 75% with increased awakenings and decreased REM and delta sleep)

10. Klein-Levin syndrome (a rare form of periodic hypersomnolence) accompanied by hyperphagia, hypersexuality, mood disturbance and hallucinations. Most frequently occurs in males in late adolescence.

10.8 SLEEP DISORDERS RELATED TO MEDICAL CONDITIONS

1. Congestive heart failure

2. Pain

3. Asthma

4. Headache

5. Pulmonary disease with dyspnea

6. Incontinence (including diuretic induced)

7. Hiatal hernia and esophagitis

8. Fibrositis or fibromyalgia (associated with sleep disturbance in 60% to 90% of cases)

9. Uremia and chronic renal failure

10. Estrogen deficiency

11. Hyperthyroidism

12. Parkinson's disease

13. Epilepsy

14. Obesity.

10.9   SLEEP DISORDERS ASSOCIATED WITH MEDICATIONS

1. All stimulants:
   a. Caffeine
   b. Theophylline
   c. Amphetamines
   d. Cocaine
   e. Methylphenidate
   f. Pseudoephedrine
   g. Phenylpropanolamine
   h. Nicotine
   i. Over-the-counter nasal decongestants and appetite suppressants
   j. Albuterol and beta-adrenergic agonists.
2. Dopamine agonists:
   a. Amantadine
   b. *l*-dopa (Sinemet)
   c. Bromocriptine.
3. All sedatives (because of withdrawal arousal):
   a. alcohol (when used to initiate sleep, there is often rebound alerting after 4 to 5 hours)
   b. Short-acting barbiturates
   c. Short-acting benzodiazepines
4. Other drugs:
   a. Steroids
   b. Alpha-methyldopa
   c. Propranolol
   d. Oral contraceptives
   e. Thyroid hormone
   f. Neuroleptics (produce akathisia)
   g. Metoclopramide (akathisia)
   h. Reserpine
   i. Tricyclic antidepressants (during withdrawal because of REM rebound)
   j. Stimulating antidepressants (e.g., bupropion, fluoxetine, desipramine, MAOIs, protriptyline).

10.10   HYPNOTIC DRUGS

For a list of hypnotic agents, see Table 10.2.
1. Benzodiazepines (BZ): A number of BZ are used primarily for sleep.
   a. They are all indicated only for short-term use.
   b. BZ prolong the first 2 stages of sleep and shorten stages 3 and 4 and REM sleep.
   c. *Diazepam* is rapidly absorbed, with rapid onset. Its long half-life makes it a poor choice for continued use, especially in the elderly.
   d. *Oxazepam* and *temazepam* (Restoril) are intermediate-acting agents, with a fairly slow onset of action. This can be speeded up by using the powder from the capsules or taking the medication an hour before bedtime.
   e. *Lorazepam* is a short-acting agent, which has a disadvantage in the elderly of having relatively greater amnestic effects.

Table 10.2 Hypnotic agents

Drug	Plasma Peak (hr)	Half-life (hr)	Active Metabolites	Half-life (hr)	Dose Equiv.	Duration
Estazolam (ProSom)	2	10-24	None		1	Short
Flurazepam (Dalmane)		—	N-desalkylflurazepam	32-100	15	Long
Quazepam (Doral)	1-3	39	2-oxoquazepam N-desalkyl-2-oxoquazepam	75 190	7.5	Long
Temazepam (Restoril)	2.5	7-14	None	—	15	Short
Triazolam (Halcion)	1.0-1.5	2-5	None	—	0.25	Short
Zolpidem (Ambien)	1-2	2-5	None	—	10	Short

    f. ***Flurazepam*** (Dalmane) is a long-acting agent, which often shows more of an effect on the second night. Its buildup can have negative effects on memory and psychomotor function.

    g. ***Triazolam*** (Halcion) has a rapid elimination, which may provoke a middle of the night rebound wakefulness. It has also been reported to cause agitation, amnesia, paranoia.

    h. ***Quazepam*** (Doral) is highly lipophilic and rapidly absorbed. It has a long-acting metabolite. The parent compound is selective for BZ-1 benzodiazepine receptor, and it may be less likely to cause cognitive and motor side effects. The active metabolite is the same as that of flurazepam.

    i. ***Estazolam*** (ProSom) has a relatively fast onset of action and an elimination half-life, which is sensible for a night's sleep (about 10-14 hours).

2. Other drugs used as hypnotics:

    a. ***Zolpidem*** (Ambien) is chemically unrelated to the benzodiazepines but binds to BZ receptors (mainly the BZ-1 receptor).

        (1) Peak plasma level in 1 to 2 hours.

        (2) Half-life of about 2.5 hours (longer in elderly and patients with liver disease).

        (3) Side effects are dose related: up to 10 mg side effects are dizziness, headache, nausea, diarrhea, next day drowsiness.

        (4) The BZ receptor antagonist flumazenil (Mazicon) is an effective antidote for overdose.

        (5) Usual dose is 10 mg (5 mg for elderly or debilitated).

    b. ***Trazodone:*** In doses of 50-100 mg, trazodone can be an effective hypnotic. It appears to increase stages 3 and 4 sleep (restorative sleep) and does not interfere with REM stage sleep. Some patients may become slightly orthostatic.

    c. ***Amitriptyline*** (Elavil) and other tricyclic antidepressants are sometimes used as hypnotics. They have some sedative properties, but they carry a number of liabilities including anticholinergic activity, orthostasis, P cardiac conduction delays.

    d. ***Chloral hydrate:*** can be effective for several nights as a hypnotic. It is available in syrup form for those with difficulty swallowing pills.

        (1) Disadvantages: Chloral hydrate can displace other protein-bound drugs. Tolerance develops rather quickly and the dose often needs to be escalated if this drug is used for more than 3-4 days. The lethal dose may be as low as 5-10 g (only 20 times the typical nightly dose).

    e. ***Alcohol*** is a favorite self-prescribed hypnotic. Some people experience a rebound alerting effect about 4 hours after a drink and find themselves awake again during the night. Nevertheless, a bedtime drink can be used in some geriatric settings as an effective agent.

    f. ***Barbiturates*** such as secobarbital (Seconal) or Nembutol in doses of 100 mg can effectively put someone to sleep. The disadvantages are they may be lethal in overdose and that tolerance develops fairly quickly.

    g. ***Diphenhydramine*** (Benadryl) is often used because it is sedative and seems innocuous. The major drawback is its anticholinergic activity. The same can be said for other OTC agents, which often have scopolamine.

References

Akpinar S: Restless legs syndrome treatment with dopaminergic drugs, *Clin Neuropharmacol* 10:69-79, 1987.

Aldrich MS: Narcolepsy, *N Engl J Med* 323:389-394, 1990.

Aldrich M, Eisler A, Lee M et al: Effects of continuous, positive airway pressure on phasic events of REM sleep in patients with obstructive sleep apnea, *Sleep* 12:413-419, 1989a.

Association of sleep disorders clinics steering committee: *International Classification of sleep disorders,* Rochester, MN, 1990, American Sleep Disorders Association, 1990.

Baker MI, Oleen MA: The use of benzodiazepine hypnotics in the elderly, *Pharmacotherapy* 8:241-247, 1988.

Boivin DG, Montplaisir J, Poirier G: The effects of *L*-dopa on periodic leg movements and sleep organization in narcolepsy, *Clin Neuropharmacol* 12:339-345, 1989.

Czeisler CA, Allan JR, Strogatz SH et al: Bright light resets the human circadian pace-maker independent of the timing of the sleep-wake cycle, *Science* 233:667-671, 1986.

Fletcher E, DeBehnke R, Lovoi S et al: Undiagnosed sleep apnea in patients with essential hypertension, *Ann Intern Med* 103:190-195, 1985.

Ford DE, Kamerow PB: Epidemiologic study of sleep disturbances and psychiatric disorders, *JAMA* 262: 1479-1484, 1989.

Globus GG: A syndrome associated with sleeping late, *Psychosom Med* 31:528-535, 1969.

Goldenberg DL: Fibromyalgia syndrome, *JAMA* 257: 2782-2787, 1987.

Hauri P: Primary sleep disorders and insomnia. In TL Riley, ed, *Clinical aspects of sleep and sleep disturbance,* Boston, Butterworth.

Healey ES, Kales A, Monroe LJ et al: Onset of insomnia: role of life-stress, *Psychosom Med* 43:439, 451, 1981.

Mendelson WB: Pharmacotherapy of insomnia, *Psychiatr Clin North Am* 10:555-563, 1987.

Millman RP, Fogel BS, McNamara ME et al: Depression as a manifestation of obstructive sleep apnea: reversal with nasal continuous positive airway pressure, *J Clin Psychiatry* 50:348-351, 1989.

Moran MG, Stoudemire A: Sleep disorders in the medically ill patients, *J Clin Psychiatry* 53:29-36, 1992.

Mouret J, Lemoire P, Minuit MP et al: Effects of trazodone on the sleep of depressed subjects, *Psychopharmacology* 95:537-543, 1988.

Prinz PN, Vitiello MV, Raskind MA et al: Geriatrics: sleep disorders and aging, *N Eng J Med* 323(8):520-526, 1990.

Reynolds CF, Hoch CC, Stack J et al: The nature and management of sleep/wake disturbance in Alzheimer's dementia, *Psychopharmacol Bull* 24:43-48, 1988.

11 Psychotic Symptoms, Schizophrenia, and Neuroleptics

The following are goals of this chapter:
1. To define psychotic symptoms.
2. To review mental status questions pertinent to psychotic symptoms.
3. To provide a differential diagnosis for psychotic symptoms.
4. To define schizophrenia as a major disorder characterized by psychotic symptoms.
5. To review the indications and details for using neuroleptics.

11.1 IDENTIFICATION OF PSYCHOTIC SYMPTOMS

1. Every mental status examination must include questions about psychotic symptoms.
2. Patients may not reveal psychotic symptoms without specific questions.
3. Mental Status Examination for psychotic symptoms (see Box 11.1):
   a. *Delusions:* False beliefs that continue despite disconfirming evidence. Typical delusions include:
      (1) Somatic delusions (common in major depression in the elderly). Screening questions:
         (a) "Do you believe something is wrong with your body?" or,
         (b) If the patient complains of a somatic symptom, "What do you think may be causing that problem?"
      (2) Paranoid (and persecutory) delusions: Beliefs of being followed, persecuted, poisoned, or in some way singled out as special.
         (a) Typical of many schizophrenics.
         (b) Common secondary to stimulant (e.g., amphetamine) abuse.
         (c) Screening questions may include:
            (*i*) "Do you feel that people are out to get you or that they might have something to do with your problems?"
         (d) Denial of paranoid delusions does not mean they are absent. It may be important to record that the patient seems guarded and appears paranoid.
         (e) Other common paranoid delusions (especially in the elderly) include:
            (*i*) Someone is stealing things
            (*ii*) A dead person is present
            (*iii*) Family members are impostors

Box 11.1   Psychosis Questions for Mental Status Examination

Psychosis

Delusions: None   Somatic   Paranoid
Hallucinations: None   Auditory   Visual
    Command   Other
Disorganized: Behavior   Verbal behavior
                Content   Process
                Thought

        (*iv*) Spouse infidelity
        (*v*) Abandonment.
    (f) Before deciding that someone is delusional, consider whether the alleged events are actually taking place.
b. *Hallucinations*
    (1) Auditory hallucinations.
        (a) Often present in schizophrenics.
        (b) Also common in major depression (see Chapter 5).
        (c) Screening questions:
            (*i*) "Are you hearing voices?" may be too abrupt for patients to reveal their symptoms.
            (*ii*) An alternate question would be: "It is not unusual for someone who is very depressed/distressed, to hear voices saying disturbing things . . . such as you are a bad person, or a person who does not deserve to live. Are you experiencing anything like that?"
        (d) If the patient acknowledges auditory hallucinations, try to elicit more details.
        (e) Command hallucinations, which tell patients to hurt themselves or others, are very dangerous.
        (f) As psychotic patients improve, "voices" become more voices, then no longer bother the person, then become indistinct sounds.
    (2) Visual hallucinations.
        (a) A hallmark of delirium, most common secondary to a medical disorder.
        (b) Screening questions:
            (*i*) "Are you sometimes having difficulty telling whether you are awake or dreaming?"
            (*ii*) "It is not unusual for someone withdrawing from medication to have strange visions of things not really there. Are you having any symptoms like that?"
        (c) As with delusions, it may be necessary to infer the presence of visual hallucinations from behavior.
    (3) Olfactory hallucinations.
        (a) Warrant consideration of a temporal lobe abnormality.

(b) Olfactory hallucinations of depressed or schizophrenic patients are generally bizarre.

(4) Tactile hallucinations:

(a) May involve sensations of something crawling on the skin.

(b) Most commonly seen during drug withdrawal or as a symptom of complex partial seizures.

(c) Rare in other primary psychiatric diagnoses.

c. *Disorganized behavior, language, or thinking*

(1) Grossly disordered behavior (agitated or withdrawn),

(2) Disordered language (unintelligible speech), or

(3) Disordered thinking (illogical reasoning).

11.2   DIFFERENTIAL DIAGNOSIS OF PSYCHOTIC SYMPTOMS

1. **Medical disorders:** Many underlying medical disorders can create psychotic symptoms (see Box 3.1 and 3.2).

   a. This category should always be the first consideration. Chapter 13 reviews the history and physical examination relevant to identifying these underlying medical problems.

2. **Psychotic depression** is sometimes misdiagnosed as schizophrenia but has a different treatment and prognosis. Depressed mood may be noted in schizophrenics (or schizoaffective patients); but in the patient with affective disorder, the psychotic symptoms occur *only* in the context of the severe depression and *not* at other times.

3. **Schizoaffective disorder** presents itself with symptoms that meet criteria for major depression and schizophrenia. When doubt exists, the patient should be treated for both the mood and schizophrenic disorder to avoid the risk of neglecting one treatable component.

4. **Mania** as part of bipolar disorder (see Chapter 7) or secondary to some medical problem can be difficult to distinguish from schizophrenia, especially during an acute presentation. When in doubt, it is worth erring on the side of mania because it is more treatable.

5. **Brief reactive psychosis** patients can look like schizophrenics, except that it usually occurs in relation to some traumatic event and its duration is between 1 day and 1 month.

6. **Schizophreniform disorder** consists of psychotic symptoms lasting longer than 1 month but less than 6 months.

7. **Delusional disorder** consists of an isolated delusional belief. This disorder usually emerges in middle or late life and is usually not very responsive to neuroleptics (or other treatments).

8. **Personality disorder (schizotypal):** Some people have a personality characterized by odd beliefs and interpersonal difficulties, which together appear schizophrenic. However, they never have the psychotic or disorganized behavioral criteria for schizophrenia.

9. **Obsessive compulsive disorder (OCD)** may manifest as bizarre behavior and/or obsessions. OCD patients may be misdiagnosed as schizophrenic and treated with neuroleptics instead of anti-OCD drugs such as clomipramine or fluoxetine (see Chapter 8).

10. **Autism** has an onset before age 12 and involves disorders of multiple psychological functions but is not characterized by delusions or hallucinations.

11. **Mental retardation** patients may behave strangely and talk in ways that seem psychotic. It can be difficult to distinguish these patients from schizophrenics.
12. **Malingering** with psychotic symptoms usually involves personality disordered patients seeking some secondary gain (see Chapter 12).
13. **Schizophrenia:** Finally, after considering these other possibilities, psychotic symptoms may be a result of schizophrenia.

11.3   SCHIZOPHRENIA

Definitions and Identification

1. There must be an active phase of disease during which the patient has two of the following psychotic symptoms:
   a. Delusions
   b. Hallucinations
   c. Incoherence or loosening of associations
   d. Catatonic behavior
   e. Flat or grossly inappropriate affect.
2. There must be a marked negative effect of these symptoms on functioning (e.g. work, social relations, self-care).
3. Other diagnostic possibilities must be ruled out.
4. The active phase must last at least 1 week, and there must be some continuous disturbance for at least 6 months. This 6-month period can be made up of prodromal symptoms that occurred before the active phase, and/or residual symptoms such as:
   a. Social withdrawal or isolation
   b. Impaired role functioning
   c. Peculiar behaviors
   d. Impaired self-care
   e. Blunted or inappropriate affect
   f. Speech content abnormality
   g. Odd beliefs
   h. Unusual perceptual experiences
   i. Loss of initiative and energy.

Epidemiology and Risk Factors

1. Peak incidence of onset is between ages 15-24. However, onset may occur in succeeding decades, including into the 70s.
2. Lifetime risk is 1:100, but increases about tenfold if a parent, sibling, or child is affected.
3. Other risk factors:
   a. Lower socioeconomic status
   b. Pre-morbid schizoid, paranoid, or eccentric personality
   c. A family setting characterized by high expression of criticism, hostility, and emotional overinvolvement.

Clinical Features

1. Abnormalities of thought content:
   a. Being controlled by outside forces
   b. Thoughts can be overheard
   c. Thoughts are being inserted.

2. Abnormalities of thought process:
   a. Loss of abstraction ability
   b. Loose associations
   c. Extreme vagueness
   d. Thought blocking.
3. Abnormalities of verbal behavior:
   a. Preservation
   b. Mutism
   c. Neologisms (made up words)
   d. Echolalia (repeating heard words).
4. Abnormalities of motor behavior:
   a. Repetitive behaviors
   b. Negativism
   c. Echopraxia (imitating movements)
   d. Waxy flexibility
   e. Prolonged motor hyperactivation
   f. Deterioration of grooming and manners
   g. Catatonia (withdrawn stupor).
5. Abnormalities of perception:
   a. Hallucinations (usually auditory)
   b. Illusions (distorted perceptions).
6. Abnormalities of affect:
   a. Flat/blunt affect (indifference)
   b. Inappropriate affect
   c. Anhedonia
   d. Unusual fears.
7. Abnormalities of ego function:
   a. Lack of reality testing
   b. Lack of behavior self-control
   c. Distorted interpersonal behaviors.
8. *Note:* Intelligence and cognitive functions such as memory, orientation, and attention are usually intact, except in the active psychotic, disorganized phase.

Course

1. The most common course involves acute exacerbations of psychosis, with increasing residual dysfunction between episodes.
2. Good outcome is associated with the following (poor outcome with the opposites):
   a. Family history of affective disorders
   b. Good premorbid functioning
   c. Acute onset, in mid-life
   d. Presence of affective component
   e. Intact family function.
3. While a return to full premorbid functioning is possible, residual impairment often increases with repeated acute episodes.
   a. Residual symptoms may become attentuated late in the course of the disease.
4. Neuroleptic medications (with the exception of clozapine and perhaps thioridazine) reduce the so-called "positive" symptoms (such as delu-

sions and hallucinations) more than the "negative" symptoms (such as social withdrawal and reduction of affect).

11.4 TREATMENT OF PSYCHOTIC DISORDERS—NEUROLEPTICS

Identification

Table 11.1 provides a summary of the neuroleptics in general use.

1. **Mechanisms of action:** Although the chemical structures of neuroleptics are different, they share the property of blocking postsynaptic dopamine receptors.
2. **Predicting response:** No patient characteristics predict response to a particular neuroleptic. The choice of medication is made primarily on the basis of side effect profiles.
3. **Pharmacokinetics**
   a. Absorption: Oral absorption is somewhat variable (30-60 minutes) and may be impaired by antacids and food.
      (1) Oral elixers are better absorbed than capsules or tablets and offer a good alternative to IM injections, with comparable onset of action (15-30 minutes).
   b. Metabolism: Neuroleptics undergo heaptic metabolism. With the exception of haloperidol, they have many active metabolites.
      (1) Haloperidol has a plasma elimination half-life of about 16 hours.
4. **Side effects**
   a. The **major neurologic side effects** involve the extrapyramidal system (EPS). EPS side effects include the following:
      (1) *Dystonia,* or abnormal muscle tone.
         (a) Torticollis (neck rotation)
         (b) Oculogyric crisis (eyes turn upwards)

Table 11.1 Neuroleptics

Agent	Dose Equiv. (mg)	Sedative	Anticholinergic	Extrapyramidal	Hypotensive
Clozapine (Clozaril)	100	5	3	1	4
Haloperidol (Haldol)	2	1	1	4	1
Loxapine (Loxitane)	10	2	1	4	1
Molindone (Moban)	10	1	2	4	2
Rivperidone (Rivperdal)	*	1	0	1	2
Thiothixene (Navane)	5	1	1	4	1
PHENOTHIAZINES					
Chlorpromazine (Thorazine)	100	3	3	2	3
Fluphenazine (Prolixin)	2	2	2	4	2
Mesoridzine (Serentil)	50	2	4	1	2
Perphenazine (Trilafon)	8	2	2	3	3
Thioridazine (Mellaril)	100	4	4	1	3
Trifluoperazine (Stelazine)	5	1	2	4	2

    (c) Opisthotonus (back arching)

    (d) Lingual

    (e) Laryngeal (very rare).

(2) *Acute dystonia* may result from one dose of any neuroleptic, including prochlorperazine (Compazine).

    (a) Treatment (IM or IV dose):

        (*i*) 2 mg of benztropine (Cogentin)

        (*ii*) 50 mg diphenhydramine (Benadryl)

        (*iii*) Repeat doses in about 20 minutes if needed

        (*iv*) If no response, try lorazepam 1 mg IM (or IV)

        (*v*) With laryngeal symptoms, give doses closer together. Very rarely, tracheotomy may be required.

    (b) Prevention:

        (*i*) Young muscular males are at highest risk of acute dystonia (with an incidence of about 40%) and should be treated prophylactically.

        (*ii*) Add 2 mg of benztropine to the initial neuroleptic dose (compatible in the same syringe if given IM).

        (*iii*) It is usually sufficient to repeat the benztropine only once every 24 hours.

(3) *Dyskinesia* involves abnormal muscle movements, typically pseudo-Parkinsonian, which may occur any time during treatment.

    (a) Any muscle group can be involved including the extremities, the trunk, the head and neck, or diaphragm.

    (b) Treatment.

        (*i*) Decrease the neuroleptic or add an anticholinergic (such as benztropine 1-2 mg qd) or a dopamine agonist (such as amantadine 50-100 mg bid), see Table 11.2.

(4) *Akinesia:* The akinetic patient is often mistakenly identified as being depressed.

Table 11.2 Antiparkinson medications

Agent	Half-life (hours)	Dopamine	Histamine	Acetylcholine	Daily dose (mg)
Amantadine (Symmetrel)	24	3+ Agonist			50-150 bid
Benztropine (Cogentin)	24	2+ Agonist		3+ Antagonist	1-4
Biperiden (Akineton)				2+ Antagonist	2-8
Diphen-hydramine (Benadryl)	3-5		Strong antagonist	1+ Antagonist	50-200
Trihexy-phenidyl (Artane)	Short	1+ Agonist		4+ Antagonist	1-8

(a) Treatment:
- (*i*) Reduce neuroleptic if possible
- (*ii*) Use anticholinergic or dopamine agonist as for treating dyskinesia.

(5) *Akathisia*
- (a) Identification:
  - (*i*) Incidence of about 40% for patients taking neuroleptics.
  - (*ii*) May be subjective only, with the patient complaining only of an uncomfortable inner feeling (like a motor running).
  - (*iii*) More often, patients are restless.
  - (*iv*) Akathisia can be so distressing that patients may jump out a window to try to escape the terrible feelings.
  - (*v*) Remember that metoclopramide (Reglan) blocks dopamine receptors and can cause this side effect in cancer patients or diabetics.
- (b) Treatment:
  - (*i*) Lower the neuroleptic dose (if possible), or
  - (*ii*) Administer low dose beta-blockers (such as propranolol 5-30 mg tid), or a
  - (*iii*) Low dose diazepam (2-5 mg tid).
  - (*iv*) Anticholinergics (benztropine 2 mg bid) are often not as effective.

(6) *Tardive dyskinesia, (TD)* means late onset movement disorder.
- (a) Incidence:
  - (*i*) A patient needs exposure of at least 3 to 6 months to be at risk for developing TD.
  - (*ii*) The incidence is about 25% in patients taking neuroleptics for 2 years. Half of those cases are irreversible.
  - (*iii*) Because of the significant risk, document informed consent for patients exposed to neuroleptics for more than 3 months.
- (b) Identification:
  - (*i*) TD can look like a regular dyskinesia but responds to opposite treatment. Interventions that improve a regular dyskinesia (e.g., lowering the neuroleptic or adding an anticholinergic or dopamine agonist) make TD worse.
  - (*ii*) TD typically involves oral-buccal-lingual muscles but may involve limbs or trunk.
- (c) Differential diagnosis:
  - (*i*) Other neurologic diagnoses may appear as TD (see Box 11.2).
- (d) Monitoring:
  - (*i*) Examine for abnormal movements before starting on neuroleptics and at regular 6-month intervals.
  - (*ii*) Consider using the Abnormal Involuntary Movement Scale (AIMS) (see Fig. 11.1).
- (e) Prevention:
  - (*i*) Because of the lack of effective treatment, prevention is key. The lowest neuroleptic dose for the shortest time period should be the guiding principle.

Box 11.2   Differential Diagnosis of Tardive Dyskinesia

Neurologic Disorders	**Drugs**
Brain neoplasms	Amphetamines
Fahr's syndrome	Anticholinergics
Huntington's disease	Antidepressants
Idiopathic dystonias	Heavy metals
(tics, blepharospasm, aging)	*L*-dopa
Ill-fitting dentures	Lithium
Meige's syndrome	Magnesium
(spontaneous oral dyskinesia)	Phenytoin
Postanoxic EPS	
Postencephalitic EPS	
Torsion dystonia	
Wilson's disease	

(f) Treatment:

    (*i*) There is no consistently successful treatment for TD.

    (*ii*) Lowering the dose (or discontinuing the neuroleptic) if possible may remove the TD symptoms, usually after a period of weeks of exacerbation.

    (*iii*) Drugs that may be tried:

        (*a*) Lithium

        (*b*) Buspirone (in high doses)

        (*c*) Lecithin

        (*d*) Physostigmine

        (*e*) Benzodiazepines

        (*f*) Vitamin E (1600 IU/day) has been demonstrated to have some significant positive effects.

    (*iv*) Patients with bad TD are best referred to a specialty program.

b. **Other neuroleptic side effects** include (refer to Table 11.1):

    (1) *Sedation* may be helpful in the agitated patient but often creates problems.

      (a) Treatment:

        (*i*) Lower the dose, if possible

        (*ii*) Give the dose at bedtime

        (*iii*) Switch to a less sedating drug.

    (2) *Anticholinergic activity* (which varies inversely with the tendency to cause EPS) can be dangerous, especially in the elderly and medically ill.

      (a) Treatment:

        (*i*) Switch to a neuroleptic with lower anticholinergic effects

        (*ii*) Suggest sugarless mints or gum to help dry mouth

        (*iii*) Prescribe bulk agents or stool softeners

        (*iv*) For urinary retention, bethanecol may be helpful (for details, see Chapter 6).

- At some point, observe the patient unobtrusively.
- Use a firm chair, without arms.
- Remove anything (e.g., gum, candy) from the patient's mouth.
- Inquire about dentures and their condition.
- Ask if patient notices any movements and if they bother or interfere with activities.
- Rate the following as:

0 = None
1 = Minimal
2 = Mild
3 = Moderate
4 = Severe

___ Have patient sit in chair with hands on knees, legs slightly apart and feet flat on floor. (Look at entire body for movements in this position.)

___ Ask patient to sit with hands hanging unsupported. If male, hands between legs. If female and wearing a dress, hands hanging over knees. (Observe hands and other body areas.)

___ Ask patient to open mouth. (Observe tongue at rest within mouth.) Do this twice.

___ Ask patient to protrude tongue. (Observe abnormalities of tongue movement.) Do this twice.

___ Ask patient to tap thumb, with each finger, as rapidly as possible for 10 to 15 seconds; separately with right hand, then with left hand. (Observe facial and leg movements.)

___ Flex and extend patient's left and right arms, one at a time.

___ Ask patient to stand up. (Observe in profile. Observe all body areas again, hips included.)

___ *Ask patient to extend both arms outstretched in front with palms down. (Observe trunk, legs, mouth.)

___ *Have patient walk a few paces, turn, and walk back to chair. (Observe hands and gait.) Do this twice.

*Activated movements.

Figure 11.1.
Abnormal Involuntary Movement Scale (AIMS).

(3) *Orthostatic hypotension:*
    (a) As with the tricylic antidepressants, orthostasis can be a problem for patients with:
        (*i*) Intravascular volume depletion
        (*ii*) Patients who have been on bed rest
        (*iii*) The elderly, who can fall and become injured.
    (b) Document lying/standing blood pressure/pulse with associated symptoms.
    (c) Treatment:
        (*i*) Make sure the patient is hydrated
        (*ii*) Suggest that support stockings may help
        (*iii*) Switch to another medication.
(4) *Jaundice* of a cholestatic hypersensitivity type is an uncommon side effect.

(a) Usually seen with the phenothiazines within the first few months of treatment.

(b) Patients may be switched to another class of neuroleptic (e.g., from chlorpromazine to haloperidol).

(5) *Increased Prolactin* occurs because prolactin-inhibiting factor is dopamine.

(a) May cause galactorrhea or reduced testosterone production.

(b) Symptoms usually resolve over weeks to 1 month after lowering or stopping the drug.

(6) *Lowering seizure threshold:* All neuroleptics lower seizure threshold to some degree.

(a) This is not a reason to avoid neuroleptics in an epileptic as long as the patient is taking adequate anticonvulsants.

(7) *Prolongation of HIS bundle conduction:*

(a) A property of the phenothiazines (along with quinidine-like effects) shared with the tricyclic antidepressants.

(b) Pretreatment ECGs should be checked in patients over 40 and those with a cardiac history.

(8) *Weight gain* seems to be associated with increased appetite.

(a) Appetite suppressants should not be used.

(b) Calorie restriction is appropriate.

(c) Weight gain does not usually occur with molindone.

(9) *Agranulocytosis* is a rare side effect associated with phenothiazines and clozapine, usually early in treatment.

(a) Clozapine requires weekly WBC monitoring.

(b) Reports of chills, fever, or sore throat should raise suspicion of this problem.

(10) *Neuroleptic malignant syndrome (NMS)* is a life-threatening side effect of neuroleptics.

(a) Incidence (in some form) may be as high as 2%, though life-threatening cases are rarer.

(b) Identification: NMS should be considered in any patient receiving neuroleptics who appears to be getting worse, rather than getting better. Clinical features include:

(*i*) Fever

(*ii*) Extreme muscle rigidity (unrelieved by anticholinergics)

(*iii*) Delirium

(*iv*) Elevated creatinine phosphokinase (CPK) levels: patients may get CPK elevation of up to 800 by having IM injections and physical restraints. However, elevations over this level are caused by some other pathologic process.

(c) Course and treatment:

(*i*) Patients with mild NMS may resolve spontaneously with discontinuation of neuroleptics.

(*ii*) Amantadine (100 mg bid) is often used in milder cases.

(*iii*) Daily CPKs should be followed in patients with suspected NMS.

(*iv*) More serious cases can die from shock, renal failure (with myoglobinuria), respiratory failure, or disseminated intravascular coagulation (DIC). Patients may need medical intensive care monitoring with supportive treatment. Pharmacological treatments that are often used include dantrolene or bromocriptine.

(11) *Retinitis pigmentosa* is a potential complication seen in patients receiving daily doses of 800 mg or more of thioridazine.

5. Neuroleptic dosing and duration

a. For schizophrenia:

  (1) An adequate neuroleptic trial for schizophrenic psychosis is a minimum of 4 weeks at a dose of a minimum of 400 mg/day of chlorpromazine or its equivalent.

    (a) While some symptoms, such as physical agitation, may respond rapidly, other psychotic symptoms may take 4 to 6 weeks to improve.

    (b) Response cannot be shortened by increasing to very high dose levels, although agitation can be controlled quickly (see Chapter 13).

    (c) Use the lowest effective dose.

  (2) 20% to 40% of schizophrenics will not respond to neuroleptics.

    (a) Some nonresponders may respond to clozapine.

  (3) For a first episode of schizophrenia, neuroleptic taper should be attempted after 6 to 12 months of stability.

    (a) In more chronic cases where drug tapering has always led to relapse, continuous medication is indicated.

b. For delirium:

  (1) To treat "sundowning" in elderly or medically ill patients:

    (a) Low dose neuroleptics, such as haloperidol 0.5 mg (or equivalent) may effectively decrease agitation and confusion.

    (b) Such an approach should not become a "standing" order.

  (2) Delirium with significant physical agitation may require larger doses of neuroleptics (see Chapter 13) such as haloperidol 25 mg over 4 hours, along with a 1-2 mg lorazepam every few hours.

c. For psychotic depression:

  (1) Small adjunctive doses of neuroleptics, such as haloperidol 2 mg/day added to antidepressant medication may be effective. Larger doses may also be necessary.

d. For dementia:

  (1) 20% to 40% of Alzheimer's patients have a psychotic component, and many of these patients warrant judicious use of neuroleptics.

  (2) The limiting factor is usually EPS. An approach to using neuroleptics in these patients is described in Chapter 17.

e. For psychotic patients that do not respond to neuroleptics, consider:

  (1) Is the diagnosis correct? Could there be, for example, an underlying sedative withdrawal syndrome, which is not responsive to neuroleptics?

  (2) Has the patient developed akathisia, with increased restlessness and agitation?

  (3) Has the patient developed NMS, with increased delirium?

  (4) Has the patient been receiving an adequate dose for a long enough time period?

  (5) Is the patient actually taking the medication?

6. **Depot neuroleptics**
   a. Available for treatment of chronic schizophrenics and other psychotic conditions where compliance is a problem.
   b. Approximately 12.5 mg (0.5 ml) of depot Prolixin decanoate every 2 to 3 weeks (a typical starting dose) is the equivalent of 10 mg of oral Prolixin hydrochloride per day. There is no simple formula to establish the necessary depot dose.
   c. For Haldol decanoate:
      (1) Available as 50 or 100 mg/ml.
      (2) 10 to 20 times patient's daily dose of oral haloperidol is the initial month's dose of haloperidol decanoate.
      (3) For patients who are elderly, debilitated, or stabilized on oral doses ≤10 mg/day of oral Haldol, use the decanoate form at 10 to 15 times that dose.
      (4) The initial dose should not exceed 100 mg.
      (5) Doses are usually given on monthly intervals, but may need greater frequency. After the first month, the maintenance dose may only require one third to one half the amount.
      (6) Total doses over 300 mg are rarely needed, and a monthly maintenance dose of 200 mg is most often effective for preventing relapse in chronic schizophrenics.
   d. Before starting a depot preparation, the patient should try the oral form of the drug to be sure it is tolerated and effective.

7. **Clozapine—the "novel" neuroleptic**
   a. Clozapine differs from the other neuroleptics insofar as it has a relatively low affinity for D2 receptors. It is more active at D1 and D4 receptors (in the mesolimbic area, not the nigrostriatal region) in addition to prominent serotonergic (5HT-2) and alpha-adrenergic receptors.
      (1) Therefore, clozapine does not cause extrapyramidal side effects or risk of tardive dyskinesia (except in rare case reports).
      (2) Some poorly responsive, paranoid schizophrenics may be helped by this drug.
      (3) Negative symptoms of schizophrenia may improve on this medication.
      (4) Unfortunately, there is a 1% to 2% incidence of agranulocytosis, which has the potential to be fatal. Clozapine use must be monitored by weekly CBCs.
      (5) Indications:
         (a) Failure to respond to trials of two neuroleptics.
         (b) Inability to tolerate other neuroleptics, usually because of severe EPS. Patients such as psychotic Parkinson's disease may require this approach.
      (6) Contraindications:
         (a) Previous granulocytopenia
         (b) Severe hepatic or renal impairment
         (c) Pregnancy
         (d) History of poor compliance (unless close monitoring can be assured).
      (7) Clozapine is generally started at low doses such as 25 mg bid and slowly over several weeks increased to about 300 mg/day. Elderly patients may be started on doses half that amount.

Table 11.3   Neuroleptic drug interactions

Agent	Effect
Antihypertensives	Worsen orthostasis
Antacids	Impair absorption
Epinephrine	Worsens hypotension
Anticholinergics	Augmented
Anticonvulsants	Decrease neuroleptic levels
Tricyclics/SSRIs	Increase neuroleptic levels
Lithium	May increase toxicity
Nicotine	Decreases levels

8. **Risperidone**
   a. This new drug is indicated for treatment of psychotic symptoms. It differs from conventional antipsychotics because it is a combined serotonin-dopamine antagonist.
   b. It may be superior to typical neuroleptics in overall efficacy, in effectiveness for both "positive" and "negative" symptoms of schizophrenia, a low rate of EPS, and a potential therapeutic effect on TD.
9. **Neuroleptic use in pregnancy**
   a. No specific teratogenic deformity is associated with neuroleptics; however, they should be used only if absolutely necessary during pregnancy, especially during the first trimester.
   b. If exposed to neuroleptics during the last trimester, the newborn may manifest extrapyramidal symptoms during the first weeks of life.
   c. Chlorpromazine has been associated with neonatal jaundice.
   d. Neuroleptics are secreted in breast milk.
10. **Overdose**
   a. Patients can survive extremely high doses of neuroleptics.
   b. Problems encountered with overdose (depending on the drug's side effects) could include the following:
      (1) Seizures
      (2) Anticholinergic syndrome
      (3) Extra-pyramidal side effects
      (4) NMS
      (5) Hypotension
      (6) Cardiac arrhythmias
      (7) Coma.
11. **Drug interactions:**
   a. For neuroleptic drug interactions, see Table 11.3.
   b. Because neuroleptics are highly protein bound, they may displace other protein-bound medications such as warfarin or digoxin.

11.5   NONNEUROLEPTIC TREATMENTS FOR PSYCHOTIC SYMPTOMS OF SCHIZOPHRENIA

1. ECT is generally not effective in schizophrenia but is occasionally tried to treat nonresponsive patients with severe symptoms.

2. Lithium may be helpful in augmenting neuroleptics (especially if the patient is actually bipolar). Patients receiving this combination should be observed carefully for signs of increased lithium or neuroleptic toxicity.

3. Antidepressants added to neuroleptics may help some of the accompanying depressive symptoms.

4. Benzodiazepines are occasionally helpful added to neuroleptics in controlling schizophrenic behaviors, but there are no predictive clinical symptoms.

5. Anticonvulsants are occasionally helpful in stabilizing behavior in patients diagnosed with schizophrenia.

6. Because many types of brain damage can lead to symptoms that resemble schizophrenia, patients should be carefully evaluated for the possibility of a (treatable) delirium or dysrhythmia.

11.6   NONMEDICATION ASPECTS OF TREATING SCHIZOPHRENIA

1. While medication plays a critical role, a number of other aspects of treatment are crucially important to rehabilitation and recovery:

   a. Psychosocial therapies are often best coordinated by a case manager, especially for patients with chronic illness. Aspects of therapy may include:

      (1) Assistance with problem solving
      (2) Crisis intervention as needed
      (3) Nonstressful socialization opportunities
      (4) Family education and support
      (5) Availability of structured day hospitals during times of potential relapse
      (6) Activity groups and opportunities for vocational training
      (7) Social skills training

   b. The chronic schizophrenic patient cannot usually be adequately treated unless these multidimensional, community-based needs are addressed in an integrated program.

References

Adler AA, Angrist B, Reiter S et al: Neuroleptic-induced akathisia: a review, *Psychopharmacology* 97:1-11, 1989.

Adler AA, Peselow E, Rotrosen J et al: Vitamin E treatment of tardive dyskinesia, *AM J Psychiatry* 150(9):1405-1407, 1993.

Alvir J, Lieberman JA, Safferman AZ et al: Clozapine-induced agranulocytosis, *N Eng J Med* 329(3):162-167, 1993.

Angrist B, Schulz SC, eds: *The neuroleptic-nonresponsive patient: characterization and treatment,* Washington DC, 1990, American Psychiatric Association Press.

Baldessarini RJ, Frankenburg FR: Clozapine: a novel antipsychotic agent, *N Engl J Med* 324:746-754, 1991.

Cummings JL: Organic psychosis, *Psychosom* 29:16-26, 1988.

Goff DC, Baldessarini RJ: Drug interactions with antipsychotic agents, *J Clin Psychopharmacology* 13(1):57-67, 1993.

Greden JF, Tandon R, eds: *Negative schizophrenic symptoms: pathophysiology and clinical implications,* Washington DC, 1991, American Psychiatric Press.

Herz MI et al: Intermittent vs maintenance medication in schizophrenia: two-year results, *Arch Gen Psychiatry* 48:333, 1991.

Kales A, Stefanis CN, Talbott J, eds: *Recent advances in schizophrenia,* New York 1990, Springer-Verlag.

Keck PE, McElroy SL, Pope HG: Epidemiology of neuroleptic malignant syndrome, *Psychiatr Ann* 21:148-151, 1991.

Lazarus A, Mann SC, Caroff SN: The neuroleptic malignant syndrome and related conditions, Washington DC, 1989, American Psychiatric Association Press.

Lindenmayer JP: Recent advances in pharmacotherapy of schizophrenia, *Psychiatric Annals* 23(4):201-208, 1993.

McGlashan TH: Predictors of shorter-, medium-, and longer-term outcome in schizophrenia, *Am J Psychiatry* 143:50, 1986.

Pearlman CA: Neuroleptic malignant syndrome: a review of the literature, *J Clin Psychopharmacol* 6:257-273, 1986.

Propping P, Friedl W: *Genetic studies of biochemical, pathophysiological, and pharmacological factors in schizophrenia.* In Tsuang MT, Simpson JC, eds: *Handbook of schizophrenia,* vol 3, *Nosology, epidemiology, and genetic schizophrenia,* Amsterdam, 1988, Elsevier.

12 Somatoform Disorders

The following are goals of this chapter:
1. To define somatoform disorders.
2. To provide a differential diagnosis of somatoform disorders.
3. To review the indications and procedure for amytal interviewing.
4. To provide treatment approaches for each somatoform disorder.

12.1 SOMATOFORM DISORDERS: OVERVIEW

The somatoform disorders are defined as a group disorder in which:
1. Physical symptoms suggest a physical disorder for which there is no demonstrable underlying physical basis, and
2. There is a strong presumption that the symptoms are linked to psychological factors.

The somatoform disorders include the following:
1. Somatization
2. Conversion disorder
3. Hypochondriasis
4. Body dysmorphic disorder
5. Somatoform pain disorder
6. Malingering
7. Factitious disorder.

12.2 SOMATIZATION DISORDER

Definition and identification

1. Somatization is defined as the manifestation of psychological stress in somatic symptoms.
2. Somatization is distressing to the patient and can often lead to repeated medical visits.
3. Because of research establishing the validity of somatization disorder, much of the literature has focused on this extreme form of somatization.
4. Some chronic forms of somatization may not meet the full diagnostic criteria for somatization disorder. For clinical purposes it is helpful to work with a category of "partial" somatization disorder.
5. Somatization disorder is defined as:
   a. A history of many physical complaints (or the belief that one is sick) beginning before age 30 and lasting for several years.

b. At least 13 symptoms involving the following systems, for which no other medical cause has been found:
   (1) Gastrointestinal
   (2) Cardiopulmonary
   (3) Central nervous system
   (4) Peripheral nervous system
   (5) Genitourinary system
   (6) Reproductive system
   (7) Pain.

Prevalence

1. Somatization disorder's lifetime prevalence is less than 2%, mostly in females.
2. Somatizers who do not meet full criteria for somatization disorder are much more common. Anyone in primary care practice will easily recognize chronic somatization as a common problem.

Differential diagnosis

1. **Medical disorders,** which present themselves with vague, multiple, and confusing chronic somatic symptoms, can be misdiagnosed as somatization. These disorders include:
   a. Hyperparathyroidism
   b. Porphyria
   c. Multiple sclerosis
   d. Systemic lupus erythematosis
   e. Fibromyalgia
   f. Endometriosis
   g. Myasthenia gravis.
2. **Psychiatric disorders:**
   a. Schizophrenia with multiple somatic delusions.
      (1) In schizophrenia somatic complaints are usually more bizarre, and other psychotic criteria exist (see Chapter 11).
   b. Panic disorder, in which the physical symptoms only occur during a panic attack.
   c. Malingering, in which symptoms are consciously produced for the purpose of clearly definable secondary gain. The presence of an unresolved lawsuit or disability claim can make assessment very complicated.
   d. Factitious disorder, in which the person fabricates symptoms for some secondary gain for reasons of which the patient may not be fully aware.
   e. Chronic depression, in which the patient may complain about physical symptoms as a component of the affective illness.
   f. Generalized anxiety, with multiple somatic manifestations (see Box 8.1).
   g. Substance abuse can account for many confusing symptoms, especially if surreptitious.

Prognosis

1. Somatization disorder tends to be chronic
2. With proper management (see next section) somatization disorder can be contained, but it is usually not cured.

Treatments

1. The following intervention is a generally accepted strategy based on assumptions about the underlying psychological needs of these patients.
   a. Patients do not want symptom relief but rather a relationship and understanding.
   b. Patients want the physician to acknowledge they are sick.
   c. Reassurance that nothing is physically wrong usually does not help.
   d. A positive organic diagnosis will not cure the patient.
   e. Avoid challenging the patient.
   f. Agree there is a problem and show a willingness to help.
   g. Little is gained by a premature explanation that symptoms are based on emotions.
      (1) When such an explanation is (eventually) offered, it should be done gradually and not in a way that makes the patient feel rejected.
   h. The emphasis should be on function, not symptoms.
      (1) Try to understand the patient's stresses and coping resources and to set targets for more adaptive behaviors.
      (2) Reinforce non-illness behaviors and communications. Whenever possible, talk about anything other than symptoms.
   i. Regularly scheduled appointments are required so the patient does not have to manifest symptoms to seek help.
   j. Diagnostic tests should be limited. Some focused physical examination and occasional laboratory tests may be helpful (for both physician and patient), with more reliance on signs than symptoms.

12.3   ACUTE SOMATIZED SYMPTOMS

Definition

1. Most people have transient physical manifestations of stress.
   a. Such somatized distress is a frequent reason underlying medical visits.

Prevalence

Acute somatized symptoms are ubiquitous and are likely to account for a high percentage of symptoms in primary care.

Differential diagnosis

1. **Medical disorders:** In addition to the chronic, recurrent medical disorders (see previous section), any acute medical problem can coincide with a difficult emotional situation.
   a. For example, patients under intense stress may develop cardiac ischemia, myocardial infarction, stroke, asthma, etc.
   b. No matter what the emotional context, acute symptoms must always be medically evaluated.
2. **Psychiatric disorders:**
   a. The psychiatric differential is the same as for chronic somatization, possibly with some extra emphasis on panic disorder (see Box 8.4 for symptoms of a panic attack).

Prognosis

1. Acute somatized symptoms generally respond to brief interventions.
2. Some patients develop somatization as a chronic behavior.

Treatment

1. Identify the relevant psychosocial distress issues by a "psychosocial review of systems" (see Chapter 2).
2. Do a brief physical evaluation to assure the patient that a medical problem is not being overlooked.
3. Explain that the physical symptom is linked to the underlying distress.
   a. For example, you might say, "When people get very stressed, they often start to feel tightness in their chest."
4. Reassure the patient that there is no illness requiring medical treatment.
5. Follow-up with some treatment that addresses the underlying distress (e.g., office counseling, brief therapy).

12.4   CONVERSION DISORDER

Definition and identification

1. A conversion disorder is a loss of physical function that *suggests* a physical disorder but is instead, a manifestation of an unconscious conflict or problem.
2. Criteria for conversion disorder are:
   a. Loss or alteration of physical functioning that suggests a physical disorder
   b. Psychological stressor exists in some temporal relationship to symptom onset
   c. Symptoms are not consciously produced
   d. Symptoms limited to pain are called *psychogenic pain disorder*
   e. Careful physical diagnosis may reveal symptoms that are anatomically impossible (such as a midline sensory change or unilateral frontal bone vibration defect).

Prevalence

1. No good data on the prevalence of conversion disorders exist.
2. Classic pseudoneurologic symptoms, such as loss of function of a limb, are unusual but are still seen.
3. Less dramatic conversion symptoms, such as chest pain developing after the loss of a loved one who died of a heart attack, are probably quite common.

Differential diagnosis

1. **Medical disorders:**
   a. The same list of "obscure" medical disorders presented in the section on somatization may masquerade as "conversion."
   b. In follow-up studies of conversion disorder, many cases are eventually identified as a medical problem, such as multiple sclerosis.
2. **Psychiatric disorders:**
   a. Refer to the list of diagnoses in the somatization section.

Prognosis

1. Conversion disorders generally resolve over time, with or without interventions.
2. Some may continue with chronic symptoms.

Treatments

1. Before starting treatment, keep in mind that:
   a. A conversion disorder exists for some reason.
      (1) Its purpose is to protect the patient from some intolerable psychological situation.
   b. Removing this defense, by use of hypnosis for example, may leave the patient feeling overwhelmed and vulnerable.
   c. Any specific treatments must include a component that addresses the underlying distress, not just the symptom itself.
2. Hypnosis and amytal interviewing: Use of these methods requires special training and experience.
   a. Either of these methods can facilitate uncovering the underlying conflict.
   b. Under the altered state, the symptom may temporarily or permanently disappear.
      (1) For many physical symptoms, the nonspecific effects of relaxation can account for symptom improvement (e.g., decreased pain, tremors, or autonomic symptoms).
      (2) The "reversal" of a major symptom, such as inability to use a limb, generally indicates a psychological basis for the symptom.
      (3) Sodium amytal, a barbiturate with anticonvulsant effects, can decrease symptoms secondary to underlying seizures.
   c. Sequential clinical interview may be required.
   d. It is not clear that amytal or hypnosis results in any faster resolution of the problem than sequential clinical interviews.
      (1) It may be helpful to "suggest" to these patients that their symptom is not permanent and will gradually resolve on its own. In the meantime, it may be important to look at other problems the person is facing.
   e. Indications for hypnosis or amytal interviews:
      (1) As an aid in the diagnosis of:
         (a) Mute or stuporous patient
         (b) Catatonia
         (c) Conversion disorder
         (d) Unexplained muteness
         (e) Differentiation of functional from organic stuporous/mute states
         (f) Functional disorders from malingering.
      (2) As a therapeutic interview aid for disorders of repression and dissociation:
         (a) Abreaction of posttraumatic stress disorder
         (b) Recovery of memory in psychogenic fugue and amnesia
         (c) Recovery of function in conversion disorder.
   f. Medical contraindications to amytal:
      (1) Absolute contraindications
         (a) Barbiturate allergy
         (b) History of porphyria.
      (2) Relative contraindications
         (a) Upper airway infection or inflammation encroaching on airway; laryngitis

- (b) Severe cardiac, liver, renal, or pulmonary impairment
- (c) Congestive heart failure
- (d) Pulmonary infection
- (e) Barbiturate addiction
- (f) Hypotension or severe hypertension, if more than 500 mg is to be used
- (g) Need to wait at least 12 hours after last drink if alcohol intoxication is suspected.

g. Psychiatric contraindications to hypnosis or amytal interview:
   - (1) Paranoid patients (e.g., patient may feel "doctor is attempting to read mind")
   - (2) Patients who refuse procedure
   - (3) Patients who are too hopeful with expectations of a magical cure
   - (4) Psychotic patients.

h. Risks of amytal interviewing:
   - (1) Primary risk is respiratory, usually associated with too rapid administration of the amytal solution (i.e., >50 mg/min) or too much total drug (>500 mg), leading to apnea or airway closure.
   - (2) Vasomotor collapse and laryngospasm, which are rare and generally a risk only for deeper level of anesthesia.
      - (a) Resuscitation equipment and staff should be available.
   - (3) Psychotic regression.
   - (4) Prolonged abreactive states mimicking a psychotic break.

i. Amytal interviewing procedure:
   - (1) The purpose of the procedure should be explained fully and the patient reassured.
   - (2) It should be emphasized that amytal is not a "truth serum."
   - (3) Patients should then be asked to state their understanding of the reason for the procedure and any questions.
   - (4) Patients should also be told that any remarks made will be held in confidence.
   - (5) A relative or trusted friend should be available to accompany the patient home if performed on an outpatient basis and to remain in attendance during the procedure if the patient wishes.
   - (6) Additional hospital personnel should be available if restraint is required for an untoward abreaction.
   - (7) The signing of a specific consent form is optional and depends on the policy of the institution. Recording the practice of informed consent in the charge is required.
   - (8) A quiet room should be used with resuscitation equipment and appropriate staff nearby.
   - (9) Patients should recline and be told that the medication will make them relax and feel like talking.
   - (10) Insert a 21-gauge scalp vein needle.
   - (11) Infuse a 5% solution of sodium amytal (500 mg of amytal dissolved in 10 ml of sterile water) at a rate of no faster than 1 ml/min (50 mg/min) to prevent respiratory depression and/or apnea (some use a 10% solution not to exceed 1 ml/min).
   - (12) Talk to the patient:
      - (a) Begin with neutral topics

(b) If the patient is mute, continue to suggest that the patient will soon feel like talking

(c) Prompt the patient with known facts about the patient's life.

(13) Infusion should be continued until:

    (a) Drowsiness, slurring of speech and sustained rapid lateral nystagmus, or

    (b) Patient counting backwards from 100 starts to skip numbers

    (c) Sedation threshold is usually between 150 mg-350 mg (3-7 ml); however, elderly or organically impaired patients may respond with as little as 75 mg (1.5 ml).

(14) Proceed gradually with questions toward more affect-laden topics.

(15) If the patient is mute or verbally inhibited, do not press too hard on potentially frightening topics to prevent panic during the interview.

(16) Respiratory rate should be monitored. Some suggest also monitoring blood pressure and pulse rate.

(17) To maintain the level of narcosis, infuse amytal at a rate of 0.5-1.0 ml every 5 minutes or so with the 5% solution.

(18) The interview may last from 15 minutes to 1 hour, with an average of 30 minutes.

(19) The interview may be concluded by:

    (a) Returning to some neutral topics

    (b) Giving supportive statements.

(20) The patient should lie down for a minimum of 15 minutes until able to walk without assistance. Others advise 2 to 5 hours of in-bed supervision.

12.5   HYPOCHONDRIASIS

Definition

1. Preoccupation or fear that one has a disease even though this belief cannot be supported by physical signs or symptoms.
2. The fear or preoccupation continues despite medical reassurance.
3. The duration is at least 6 months.

Prevalence

Little data on the true prevalence of this disorder exist, although it seems to be extremely common.

Differential diagnosis

1. **Medical disorders:** Refer to the list for somatization disorder.
2. **Psychiatric disorders:** Refer to the list for somatization disorder.
   a. Preoccupation with being physically ill may be a form of obsessive compulsive disorder.
   b. Hypochondriacal concerns are a common aspect of affective illness.
   c. Hypochondriacal concerns may also emerge in the early stages of dementing illness.
   d. Schizophrenics sometimes focus on a delusional belief in a physical disorder.

Prognosis

1. If hypochondriasis is part of some other primary psychiatric disorder (e.g., depression), it usually resolves when the primary disorder resolves.
2. Hypochondriasis, in general, tends to be chronic with some remissions and exacerbations, often depending on stress.

Treatment

1. Reassurance and patience are important.
2. For patients with monosymptomatic hypochondriasis, a number of medications have been helpful, including pimozide and MAOIs.
3. Patients with persistent hypochondriasis may be given trials of anti-OCD medication and, occasionally, neuroleptics. These medications are not usually effective.

12.6 BODY DYSMORPHIC DISORDER

Definition

1. This disorder usually begins between adolescence and midlife and consists of a pervasive feeling that some body part is ugly, distorted, or defective.
   a. Usually, the person can acknowledge some exaggeration but feels the problem is still significant.
2. The patients often consult dermatologists, primary physicians, and plastic surgeons.

Differential diagnosis

1. Depression with somatic preoccupations.
2. Obsessive-compulsive disorder (may be closely related and difficult to distinguish).
3. Anorexia nervosa (preoccupation is limited to being too fat and is accompanied by other symptoms, see Chapter 18).
4. Transsexualism (preoccupation limited to gender-related physical characteristics).
5. Schizophrenia with somatic delusions (patient has symptoms of the disorder).

Treatment

1. There is little evidence of the effectiveness of any interventions, which have included:
   a. Actually performing the requested surgery
   b. Psychotherapy
   c. Psychopharmacology
      (1) Drugs used to treat OCD
      (2) MAOIs
      (3) Pimozide (has produced some results).

12.7 FACTITIOUS DISORDER

Definition

1. Munchausen syndrome is considered a severe form of factitious disorder characterized by three features:

   a. Simulation of disease
      (1) Symptoms are produced voluntarily, but the motivations may not be conscious or clearly definable.
      (2) The psychological hypothesis is that developmental trauma leads to a need to be taken care of, although in a sometimes painful setting, and symptoms serve as a way of avoiding stressful situations.
   b. Pathological lying
   c. Wandering to new medical settings.
2. Factitious disorders usually fall into one of two categories:
   a. Young women, employed in the health professions.
   b. Men of lower socioeconomic class with a lifelong pattern of social maladjustment.
3. Common accompanying features include:
   a. Personality disorder
   b. Higher than expected knowledge of medicine
   c. Willingness to undergo uncomfortable procedures
   d. History of multiple hospitalizations
   e. Multiple surgical scars.
4. Making the diagnosis:
   a. Requires a high degree of suspicion
   b. Constant observation during an admission may be necessary.

Treatment

1. Approaches used with somatizing patients (see above) are helpful.
   a. Avoiding unnecessary procedures is an important goal.
2. Treating coexisting psychopathology (e.g., depression, anxiety, and psychotic symptoms) may be helpful.
3. Confrontation usually prompts the patient to sign out of treatment.

References

Barsky AJ, Klerman GL: Overview: hypochondriasis, bodily complaints, and somatic styles, *Am J Psychiatry* 140(3):273–283, 1983.

Brown FW, Golding JM, Smith GR: Psychiatric co-morbidity in primary care somatization disorder, *Psychosom Med* 52:445–451, 1990.

deGruy F, Columbia L, Dickinson P: Somatization disorder in a family practice, *J Family Practice* 25(1):45–51, 1987.

Fallon BA, Klein BW, Liebowitz MR: Hypochondriasis: treatment strategies, *Psychiatric Annals* 23(7):374–381, 1993.

Goldberg RJ, Novack DH, Gask L: The recognition and management of somatization: what is needed in primary care training, *Psychosom* 33(1):55–61, 1992.

Kaplan C, Lipkin M, Gordon GH: Somatization in primary care: patients with unexplained and vexing medical complaints, *J Gen Int Med* 3:177–90, 1988.

Kellner R: Functional somatic symptoms and hypochondriasis: a survey of empirical studies, *Arch Gen Psychiatry* 42:821–833, 1985.

Kirmayer LJ, Robbins JM, eds: Current concepts of somatization: research and clinical perspectives, Washington DC, 1991, American Psychiatric Association Press.

Smith GR, Monson RA, Ray DC: Patients with multiple unexplained symptoms: their characteristics, functional health, and health care utilization, *Arch Intern Med* 146:69-72, 1986.

Smith GR, Monson RA, Ray DC: Psychiatric consultation in somatization disorder: a randomized controlled study, *N Eng J Med* 314(22):1407–1413, 1986.

Spiro HR: Chronic factitious illness, *Arch Gen Psychiatry* 18:569–579, 1968.

Warwick HMC, Salkovskis P: Hypochondriasis, *Behav Res Ther* 28(2):105–117, 1990.

Behavioral Emergencies and Forensic Issues

13

The goals of this chapter are to review:
1. Management strategies for behavioral emergencies
2. Differential diagnosis for these emergencies
3. Pertinent history and physical examination
4. Medication management: benzodiazepines and neuroleptics
5. The assessment of suicidal and homicidal ideation
6. The appropriate use of physical restraints
7. The clinical evaluation of competence
8. Medico-legal issues pertinent to commitment.

13.1 THE BEHAVIORAL EMERGENCY

A behavioral emergency is defined as any agitated (or potentially threatening) physical behavior.
1. Step one: create a safe environment.
   a. The first priority is to create a safe environment for the patient, staff, and other patients.
      (1) Do not put yourself in danger where a patient could trap you in a closed room, or assault you.
      (2) Assess the patient in a room with no breakable or dangerous objects.
      (3) Separate patients from overstimulating situations.
      (4) Consider the use of security guards to:
         (a) Stand nearby if needed
         (b) Stay in the room to indicate that acting out will not be tolerated
         (c) Assist in applying physical restraints
         (d) Search for (or remove) weapons.
2. Step two: avoid escalating the situation.
   a. Skillful interviewing may avoid escalation of the behavior. Such techniques generally consist of:
      (1) Nonthreatening behaviors
      (2) Avoiding physical proximity

      (3) Avoiding threatening behaviors (e.g., clenching fists)
      (4) Remaining calm in voice and behavior
      (5) Using clear and simple communication that does not create ambiguity or stimulate paranoia
      (6) Helpful listening.

3. Step three: brief initial assessment.
  a. Should be done in the first 5 minutes.
  b. Items from a brief history, physical, and mental status provide data for initial diagnostic decisions.
  c. Differential diagnosis:
    (1) A behavioral emergency may result from a wide range of underlying etiologies. The medical history and sociodemographics influence the probability of which disorders are most likely.
    (2) **Delirium:** agitated behavior as a result of some underlying medical cause (see Boxes 3.1 and 3.2).
      (a) Because of the prevalence of substance abuse and alcoholism, withdrawal delirium is a common cause of agitated behavior.
    (3) **Manic disorder:** The patient often has a history of mood swings and previous manic episodes.
    (4) **Schizophrenia:** The patient often has a history of relapsing when completing neuroleptic medication.
    (5) **Personality Disorder:** Some antisocial or borderline personalities have aggressive-destructive behavior tendencies, especially if depressed or using drugs.
  d. **History**
    (1) **Onset**
      (a) Acute onset usually implies delirium.
      (b) Mania may have a sudden onset but usually builds up over time, and often follows a depressive episode.
      (c) Schizophrenic decompensation often follows increasing withdrawal, paranoia, or other psychotic symptoms.
    (2) **Past psychiatric history**
      (a) Mania, schizophrenic agitation, or antisocial/borderline behavior all have high rates of recurrence.
      (b) A thorough assessment is always needed because of frequent medical comorbidity (and substance abuse) in psychiatric patients.
    (3) **Medical problem list**
      (a) The longer the list of active medical problems, the more likely is delirium (see Box 3.1).
    (4) **Drugs and medication**
      (a) Are a common cause of behavioral emergencies (see Box 3.2)
      (b) Establish a complete drug list
      (c) Obtain additional history from people who are with the patient
      (d) Obtain a toxicology screen.
    (5) **History of head injury**
      (a) Patients, especially the elderly, may forget or overlook a minor head injury that may result in a subdural.
  e. **Mental status:**
    (1) Delirium is characterized by:

- (a) **disorientation**
- (b) **Impaired** (or fluctuating) level of **consciousness**
- (c) **Visual hallucinations,** and/or sensory illusions.
- (2) However, acute manics and schizophrenics also may be disoriented and may have disorganized attention.

f. **Physical examination:**

- (1) **Vital signs** should be obtained as soon as possible.
  - (a) Elevated temperature with altered mental status or behavior should raise suspicion of central nervous system infection, especially in patients with AIDS, cancer, diabetes, and those on immunosuppressive drugs and steroids.
  - (b) Elevated blood pressure: if extreme may indicate intracranial bleeding or stroke.
  - (c) Rapid respiratory rate may indicate pulmonary embolism, salicylate intoxication, acid-base abnormalities.
  - (d) Pulse irregularities, tachyarrhythmias, and bradyarrhythmias may indicate myocardial infarction, or other cardiac disorders.
- (2) **Head injury:** Always examine for signs of head injury because alcoholics or schizophrenics are at high risk for accidents and assaults.
- (3) **Screening neurologic exam:** Minimal observations should include:
  - (a) Movement of extremities
  - (b) Extraocular movements
  - (c) Pupillary function
  - (d) Facial asymmetry.

4. **Medication strategies:**

a. **Prevention:**

- (1) With the escalating or mildly agitated patient, offer some oral medication with the following suggestion: "You might find this medication will help you feel calmer."
- (2) Once medicated, the patient may feel in enough control to decrease further confrontation.

b. **Rapid tranquilization:**

- (1) Refers to rapidly loading medication to decrease behavioral agitation. It does not refer to any misguided attempt to rapidly "cure" schizophrenia.
- (2) Once the patient is physically calm, a more thorough physical examination and interview can take place.
- (3) Benzodiazepines vs. neuroleptics (see Table 13.1):
  - (a) For agitation resulting from sedative withdrawal, benzodiazepines are definitely more effective.
  - (b) There are not sufficient studies to determine which medication is preferable in other behavioral emergencies.
  - (c) There is increasing combined use of these two drug groups.

c. **Rapid neuroleptization:**

- (1) One standard approach is to administer dose every 30 to 60 minutes until the patient is calm.
  - (a) Typical IM doses are haloperidol 5 mg, thiothixene 10 mg, or loxapine 25 mg.

Target symptoms:
- ☐ Hallucinations   ☐ Suicidal   ☐ Delirium
- ☐ Delusions   ☐ Violence   ☐ Agitation
- ☐ Bizarre behavior   ☐ Homicidal   ☐ Incoherent
- ☐ Mute   ☐ Other:

History:
- ☐ Head injury   ☐ Seizures   ☐ Headache
- ☐ Alcohol   ☐ Narcotics   ☐ Cocaine
- ☐ Sedatives   ☐ Hallucinogens

Psychiatric diagnoses:

Surgery:

Medical diagnoses:

Physical examination:
- ☐ Head trauma   ☐ Cranial nerve abn.
- ☐ Motor abn.   ☐ Meningeal signs

Temp_____   Heart rate_____

BP_____   Resp. rate_____

Preliminary diagnosis:
- ☐ Delirium   ☐ Schizophrenia   ☐ Delirium tremens
- ☐ Mania   ☐ Depression   ☐ Paranoia
- ☐ Personality disorder

Management:
- ☐ Restraints   ☐ Constant observation   ☐ Security
- ☐ Transfer   ☐ Medication:

Figure 13.1

Data summary sheet for behavioral emergencies.

    (b) Most patients respond (i.e., become physically calm) with a few doses.

(2) Another option is to double the dose every 30 to 60 minutes until the patient responds.

(3) Oral elixir is usually well absorbed and can show a response in about 10 to 20 minutes.

(4) IM neuroleptics are well absorbed and generally show an effect within 10 to 15 minutes.

(5) Haloperidol is often used intravenously in the general hospital, although this is not an FDA approved route.

(6) A subset of delirious patients appear to require very high doses of neuroleptics. Psychiatric consultation should be sought if a patient does not respond to 3 or 4 doses of a neuroleptic.

(7) Haloperidol, loxitane, or thiothixene are generally used for rapid tranquilization because they lack anticholinergic, hypotensive, cardiac, or extreme sedative side effects (see Table 11.1).

(8) Potential adverse consequences of neuroleptization with haloperidol:

    (a) Cardiovascular, hemodynamic, or respiratory effects are rare.

    (b) Neuroleptic malignant syndrome (see Chapter 11) is extremely rare but should be considered if the patient appears to be getting worse instead of better.

Table 13.1   Psychotropic medication in physically agitated patients

Indications and Issues	Low Potency Neuroleptics*	High Potency Neuroleptics†	Benzodiazephines
Indications			
Schizophrenia	•	•	
Bipolar mania	•	•	•
Delirium tremens			•
Agitated delirium	•	•	•
Issues			
NMS	•	•	
EPS	•	•	
Sedation	•		•
Hypotension	•		
Anticholinergic	•		
Respiratory			•
Cardiac	•		
Ataxia			•
Withdrawal			•
Seizures	•	•	

*Chlorpromazine, thioridazine
†Haloperidol, thiothixene, loxitane

    (c) Akathisia (see Chapter 11), resulting in increased agitation, may occur in 10% to 40%.

    (d) Acute dystonia has an incidence as high as 40% in young muscular males.

       (i) Cogentin 2 mg can be added to the first dose to prevent dystonia (see Chapter 11).

       (ii) In patients with cervical traction or other spinal instability, a dystonia can be life-threatening. Therefore, do not use neuroleptics in such patients.

(9) Once the patient is calmed, the total amount of neuroleptic used can be added up and prescribed in divided doses over each of the following several days to avoid relapse.

d. **Rapid loading with benzodiazepines:**

(1) Benzodiazepines lack extrapyramidal side effects and there is no risk of neuroleptic malignant syndrome.

(2) Lorazepam (Ativan) is the only benzodiazepine reliably absorbed IM.

(3) Benzodiazepines will treat delirium tremens; neuroleptics will not.

(4) There is no standard formula for rapid loading with benzodiazepines.

    (a) A typical regimen might be lorazepam 0.5 to 2 mg IM every 1 to 2 hours until behavior is controlled.

    (b) Patients with sedative withdrawal syndromes often need higher total doses than other agitated patients.

(5) Issues with benzodiazepine use (also see Chapter 9):

    (a) Respiratory depression is a risk for CO_2 retainers and those on other respiratory depressants such as narcotics.

    (b) Psychomotor impairment can lead to falls if the patient is not monitored.

    (c) Excessive sedation: patients do not like to be "put to sleep."

    (d) Some personality disorders may become disinhibited and require haloperidol.

e. Contraindications to rapid loading with neuroleptics or benzodiazepines:

  (1) Do not give neuroleptics:

    (a) In possible neuroleptic malignant syndrome

    (b) When acute dystonia could be serious (i.e., patients in traction)

    (c) In cases of sedative withdrawal unless a sedative is also used.

  (2) Do not give benzodiazepines:

    (a) To a patient retaining CO_2.

  (3) Do not give either drug:

    (a) To a patient who may have an evolving intracranial process, such as subarachnoid hemorrhage, intracranial bleeding, or swelling following trauma.

      (i) Level of consciousness is important in determining the need for neurosurgical intervention.

      (ii) Medication may be given in conjunction with the attending trauma surgeon.

f. Other medication options:

  (1) **Narcotics:**

    (a) Morphine is commonly used to control agitation in postsurgical, trauma, or acute myocardial infarction patients.

    (b) In general, the calming effect is only temporary and the patient may require larger and more frequent doses.

  (2) **Trazodone:**

    (a) In doses between 25 to 100 mg PO, trazodone may calm acutely agitated patients.

    (b) Trazodone has no anticholinergic effects but can produce orthostatic hypotension (see Table 6.1).

  (3) **Beta-blockers** and **buspirone:**

    (a) Not useful in acute situation

    (b) Can decrease episodic aggression after head injury or other brain damage. (See Chapter 17 for additional details.)

13.2   SUICIDE EVALUATION

1. Suicide is completed by over 30,000 Americans each year and is the eighth leading overall cause of death (second among youth).

2. Evaluation and documentation of suicidal ideation is a core component of any psychiatric assessment (see Box 5.4 for mental status questions regarding suicide).

3. A high percentage of patients who commit suicide visit their primary care physicians in the prior few months.

Table 13.2   Mental status component of suicide, homicide, and violence evaluation

IDEAS	No	Indef	Def	Plans	No	Indef	Def
Suicide							
Homicide							
Violence							
What inhibits:				Reason to live:			

4. **Risk factors:**
   Risk factors provide a general context for an evaluation. The individual patient requires individual assessment, not just some "score" on a risk factors' scale.
   a. Chronic medical illness
      (1) Suicide risk is almost twice as high among cancer patients and significantly elevated among AIDS patients
      (2) Hemodialysis patients have a higher than expected suicide rate (as many as 5%), which is as high as in patients with chronic schizophrenia
      (3) Other medical patients with higher than expected risk include delirium tremens and respiratory diseases.
   b. Old age
      (1) White elderly males have a rapidly increasing incidence of suicide, 4 times higher than the national rate.
   c. Male sex (women try more often, men make more lethal attempts and succeed more often).
   d. Recent major mental illness accounts for a high percentage of suicides:
      (1) Major depression (50%)
      (2) Chronic alcoholism (20%)
      (3) Schizophrenia (10%)
      (4) Borderline personality (5% to 15%).
   e. Previous suicide attempts (present in 30% to 40%).
   f. Suicidal ideation (communicated in 60%).
   g. Visits to physicians (about 50% of completers had seen a physician in the previous month, usually with only moderate depression and mainly physical symptoms).
   h. Panic attacks (20% of those with panic disorder have a lifetime history of suicide attempts).
   i. Poor sleep.
   j. Unemployment.
   k. Unmarried.
5. **Clinical questions to evaluate suicide potential (see Table 13.2, suicide component of MSE):**
   a. The clinician is not expected to read the patient's mind or force the patient into a confession.

b. However, the clinician is expected to ask questions and document answers which allow a judgment to be made about suicide risk.
  (1) Box 5.4 provides an escalating series of questions leading up to direct questions about suicidal ideation and planning.
c. Every suicide evaluation should record (at least) the following:
  (1) Suicidal ideation and plan:
    (a) Patients with definite ideas and/or plan should be considered at high risk no matter what else is going on.
    (b) The presence of suicidal ideation or planning does not mean the patient has to be hospitalized; however, alternate treatment plans must be carefully worked out to protect the patient.
  (2) What would keep you from taking your life at this point?
    (a) Lack of a reason to live or lack of any future planning implies higher risk.
    (b) Reasons to live (e.g., children, religion, insurance money) or signs of future plans (not wanting to miss too much work) mitigate risk.
  (3) Presence or absence of significant cognitive impairment:
    (a) Delirium or other cognitive impairment make the interview less reliable.
    (b) Suicide risk evaluation should be deferred until the patient is clear from a drug-altered state or other delirium.
  (4) Presence or absence of psychosis:
    (a) Command hallucinations for suicide are ominous.
    (b) Any psychotic symptoms increase suicide risk.
  (5) Presence of a depressive prodrome:
    (a) Major depression with intensifying suicidal thoughts is a significant risk.
  (6) What the patient says it makes sense to do:
    (a) One of the best questions for clinical assessment of suicide risk is, "What do you think it makes sense to do now?"
    (b) Patients at high suicide risk often give answers like, "It really doesn't matter what happens to me anymore," or "I don't think anything can help."
    (c) Signs of future orientation can indicate that the suicidal planning is not imminent; e.g., if a patient shows concern about going back to work, being around for a child's birthday, or keeping an appointment with a therapist.
  (7) Confirmation by a third party:
    (a) When a story seems unclear, more information is often helpful. As described in Chapter 2, talking to another person can be helpful, as long as the patient gives consent.
    (b) In an emergency, it may be possible to bypass the patient's permission to talk to someone else.

6. **The chronically suicidal patient**
  a. Chronically suicidal patients are usually borderline personality disorders (see Chapter 16).
    (1) These patients are often angry and manipulative, making management decisions difficult.

      (2) These patients do have a high risk of eventual suicide, perhaps as high as 25%.

  b. Unfortunately, many borderline patients are not helped by hospitalization.

      (1) In fact, hospitalization may reinforce regressive behaviors.

      (2) A decision not to hospitalize such a patient must be accompanied by an alternate outpatient treatment plan and documentation of why hospitalization is not considered the best therapeutic approach.

  c. A number of psychotropics have been tried with borderlines with varying degrees of success (see Chapter 16).

  d. Consider concurrent diagnoses in the personality disordered patient.

      (1) For example, concurrent major depression, acute grief, or drug-induced delirium are treatable conditions, which might warrant a brief hospitalization.

7. **What to do if the patient is suicidal**

  a. If you believe the patient is at significant suicidal risk:

      (1) The patient should not be allowed to leave the interview setting without an appropriate treatment plan.

  b. Alternative plans include:

      (1) Referral and direct transport to a more experienced psychiatric clinician or emergency psychiatry setting.

      (2) Hospitalization, voluntary if possible, or by commitment if necessary.

      (3) If commitment is necessary, tell the patient that you feel there is significant suicide risk and that you must make decisions that will protect him or her at this time (see commitment section later in this chapter).

      (4) An outpatient alternative, if reliable and responsible supervision can be arranged.

      (5) Establishing a contract for safety with the patient may be appropriate for some patients with lower levels of suicidal ideation.

13.3   EVALUATION OF THE VIOLENT OR HOMICIDAL PATIENT

1. Because violence and murder are so prevalent, these behaviors are important to consider in the mental status.
2. Risk factors for violence:

  a. Previous history of violence

  b. Antisocial personality traits

  c. Substance abuse

  d. Brain impairment associated with disinhibition and episodic impulsiveness

  e. Signs of extreme anger or irritability.

3. Psychiatric disorders associated with violence

  a. Agitated schizophrenic patients may cause injury during attempts to control their behavior

  b. Paranoid disorders, including schizophrenia, have an increased risk of violent behaviors as responses to the delusions

  c. Mania with irritability can be provoked to violent behavior

    d. Severe personality disorders including borderline, narcissistic, and antisocial can be provoked to violence when they do not get what they want.

    e. Dementia (especially with delusions).

4. Medical disorders associated with violence

    a. Drug use including:

        (1) Phencyclidine (PCP)

        (2) Alcohol intoxication

        (3) Stimulant abuse

        (4) Sedative withdrawal.

    b. Epilepsy:

        (1) Prodromal irritability may lead to aggression.

        (2) Ictal aggression is rare.

        (3) Periictal aggression may result from:

            (a) Postictal automatisms

            (b) Postictal confusion or disinhibition.

5. Violence assessment:

    a. History (the best predictor of future behavior is past behavior):

        (1) Past episodes (number and means of violence)

        (2) Nature and number of arrests

        (3) Presence of premeditation or impulsiveness

        (4) Precipitants of violence.

    b. Mental status (see Table 13.2):

        (1) As with the suicide evaluation, use a series of questions such as:

            (a) "Have you been having thoughts of hurting anyone?"

            (b) "Have you gone so far as to have plans to harm someone?"

            (c) "You mentioned how angry you were with that guy. Have you been thinking about what you might do to get back at him?"

        (2) As with suicidal ideation and planning, it is possible to have a spectrum of responses from:

            (a) Indefinite (e.g., "I'm so mad I could kill someone") to

            (b) Definite (e.g., "When I get home, I'm really going to let her have it").

        (3) Define the degree of planning and the access to the means to carry out any plan.

            (a) For example, if a patient threatens to shoot someone, does he own or have access to a gun?

        (4) Delirium could impair impulse control or judgment.

        (5) Command hallucinations to harm someone are very dangerous symptoms.

        (6) Paranoia creates risk if there is a strong patient delusion focused on some individual.

        (7) Irritability raises risk of violent behavior.

    c. Physical examination: Issues relevant to violence potential include signs associated with drug intoxication or withdrawal (see Chapter 14) such as:

        (1) Ataxia, dysarthria, nystagmus, dilated pupils, sweating, tachycardia, increased blood pressure.

    d. Scales used to evaluate aggression:

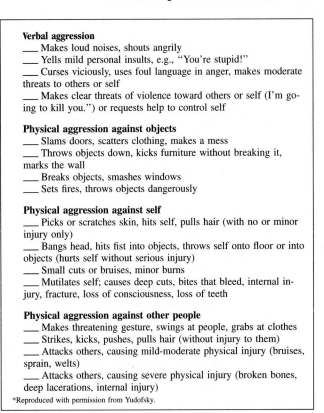

Verbal aggression
___ Makes loud noises, shouts angrily
___ Yells mild personal insults, e.g., "You're stupid!"
___ Curses viciously, uses foul language in anger, makes moderate threats to others or self
___ Makes clear threats of violence toward others or self (I'm going to kill you.") or requests help to control self

Physical aggression against objects
___ Slams doors, scatters clothing, makes a mess
___ Throws objects down, kicks furniture without breaking it, marks the wall
___ Breaks objects, smashes windows
___ Sets fires, throws objects dangerously

Physical aggression against self
___ Picks or scratches skin, hits self, pulls hair (with no or minor injury only)
___ Bangs head, hits fist into objects, throws self onto floor or into objects (hurts self without serious injury)
___ Small cuts or bruises, minor burns
___ Mutilates self; causes deep cuts, bites that bleed, internal injury, fracture, loss of consciousness, loss of teeth

Physical aggression against other people
___ Makes threatening gesture, swings at people, grabs at clothes
___ Strikes, kicks, pushes, pulls hair (without injury to them)
___ Attacks others, causing mild-moderate physical injury (bruises, sprain, welts)
___ Attacks others, causing severe physical injury (broken bones, deep lacerations, internal injury)

*Reproduced with permission from Yudofsky.

Figure 13.2.
Overt Aggression Scale.

    (1) Overt Aggression Scale (see Fig. 13-2).
  e. Management of homicidal ideation:
    (1) If a patient appears to pose a serious risk of harm to a specific person, the physician must do something appropriate.
    (2) Although law differs regionally, physicians are generally expected to:
      (a) Inform the intended victim of the risk and/or, inform the police
      (b) Detain the patient under mental health commitment (if necessary) and arrange for hospitalization.
    (3) When in doubt, obtain some guidance from a specialist in psychiatry or the law.

13.4   THE USE OF PHYSICAL RESTRAINTS

1. The use of physical restraints may be indicated for:
   a. Patients whose safety would otherwise be impaired or who might harm others.
   b. Intensely agitated patients (who often calm down when placed in restraints).
2. Patients placed in restraints usually have underlying diagnoses such as:
   a. Agitated delirium
   b. Schizophrenic agitation
   c. Manic agitation
   d. Patients with intense suicidal or homicidal behaviors
   e. Agitated drug intoxication/withdrawal.
3. Restraints should never be used as punishment or a substitute for staffing.
4. Restraints should be used only if there is no less restrictive alternative.
5. The use of restraints should be managed as follows:
   a. The specific indication should be clearly documented.
   b. There should be a signed physician's order (even if the procedure was initiated by some other staff).
   c. The order should specify a time limit.
   d. Anyone impaired enough to require restraints should have continuous staff observation.
   e. Restraints should be properly designed.
      (1) Do not use bed sheets taped into a knot.
   f. Restraints should be applied by experienced staff.
      (1) Five staff are necessary to restrain a resistant patient.
      (2) Security should be called to assist.
      (3) Nursing and security staff should receive training in this procedure.
   g. During the procedure the patient should be told in calm, simple terms, what is happening.
      (1) Patients may be confused or psychotic and misperceive the situation.
      (2) Say something like, "You are in a hospital . . . these people are nurses and security staff . . . no one is going to hurt you . . . we are trying to help make things safe for you."
   h. The need for restraints must be reevaluated (at least every shift) with documentation supporting continued use.
   i. How soon can you remove restraints?
      (1) As soon as the patient has demonstrated a reasonable period of behavioral stability.
      (2) The patient's promise that there will be no dangerous behaviors may not be enough to warrant removal.

13.5   COMMITMENT UNDER MENTAL HEALTH STATUTES

1. Strictly speaking, commitment is a judicial rather than a medical procedure.
2. Physicians generally are involved in filling out papers that allow for a period of detention prior to a formal commitment proceeding.

3. In a formal commitment hearing, the patient is represented by an attorney or mental health advocate.
4. Laws vary in different states; therefore when in doubt, check with a psychiatrist or legal consultant regarding criteria and procedure for commitment. However, most states share features to meet criteria for commitment:
    a. Immediate dangerousness to oneself or others, by virtue of a mental disorder, and in need of immediate care and treatment, or
    b. Incapability of caring for oneself in terms of food, clothing, shelter.
5. In many states a psychiatrist's signature is not necessary to sign a commitment paper. Often, other physicians (or allied health professionals) may sign.
6. Qualifying for commitment does not mean that a patient is incompetent to make decisions about treatment.
    a. A committed patient is considered competent to refuse psychotropic medication or medical procedures.
        (1) Medication may be used against the patient's wishes in emergency situations.
7. In most states commitment allows for a short period of detention (usually several days) for an assessment before a formal legal proceeding to evaluate the need to commit the patient to a longer period of care.
8. How does commitment under mental health statutes apply to medical patients who want to leave the hospital against medical advice or refuse treatment?
    a. If the patient is judged to be in immediate danger because of a mental disorder and can be treated in a setting under the jurisdiction of their mental health statutes, the patient could be committed under the mental health statutes.
    b. Patients in need of medical treatment who are delirious and show dangerous judgment are generally not committed on the basis of the mental health statutes. Instead, they are detained on the basis of implied consent associated with their incompetence to make a decision about the need for immediate treatment.
    c. When in doubt about what to do, base the decision on clinical judgment for the patient's health and safety; then seek legal advice. Maintaining the safety and health of the patient should always be the guiding principle.

13.6 COMPETENCE EVALUATIONS

1. Psychiatrists are commonly asked to help decide if a patient is competent.
2. Technically, competence is a judicial decision, not a medical one.
    a. However, judges often rely on the opinions of psychiatrists who are considered experts in obtaining and evaluating interview information.
3. Questions of competence should refer to some specific aspect of competence, such as:
    a. Competence to refuse a medical procedure
    b. Competence to manage finances
    c. Competence to be at home without supervision, etc.

4. The competence evaluation should focus on the specific aspect of competence in question.
   a. To be considered competent, a patient must be able to demonstrate an understanding of the issues in question. For example:
      (1) To be competent to manage finances, patients would need to show that they know their assets, income, expenses, how to make a transaction, the consequences of not paying a bill, etc.
      (2) To be competent to refuse a medical treatment, patients would have to demonstrate that they know: their medical condition, the treatment being suggested, the consequences of refusing the treatment, the alternatives, the risks/benefits of the treatment.
5. Refusal of treatment does not always mean the patient is not competent. Reasons patients refuse treatment include:
   a. Lack of information necessary to decide what to do
   b. Anger at the medical system because of delays, disappointments, or perceived oversights, etc., which need to be identified and addressed
   c. Disagreements within the family about what to do
   d. Confusion or delirium
   e. Depression with undue pessimism. Since "nothing could help anyway," why agree to treatment.
6. Questions about a patient's wishes for treatment may involve documents (e.g., living wills, durable powers of attorney). When in doubt, consult with a hospital risk manager.

References

Allebeck P, Bolund C, Ringback G: Increased suicide rate in cancer patients: a cohort study based on the Swedish Cancer-Environment Register, *J Clin Epidemiol* 42:611–616, 1989.

Appelbaum PS, Grisso T: Assessing patients' capacities to consent to treatment, *N Engl J Med* 319:1635–1638, 1988.

Appelbaum PS: The right to refuse treatment with antipsychotic medications: retrospect and prospect, *Am J Psychiatry* 145:413–419, 1988.

Donlon PT, Hopkin J, Schaffer CB et al: Cardiovascular safety of rapid treatment with intramuscular haloperidol, *Am J Psychiatry* 136:233–234, 1979.

Fenwick P: The nature and management of aggression in epilepsy, *J Neuropsychiatry* 1(4):418–425, 1989.

Fogel BS, Mills MJ, Landen JE: Legal aspects of the treatment of delirium, *Hosp Community Psychiatry* 37:154–158, 1986.

Lion JR: Clinical assessment of violent patients. In LH Roth, ed: Clinical treatment of the violent person, Rockville, MD, 1987 NIMH.

Murphy GE, Wetzel RD: The lifetime risk of suicide in alcoholism, *Arch Gen Psychiatry* 47:383–392, 1990.

Poythress NG: Avoiding negligent release: contemporary clinical and risk management strategies, *Am J Psychiatry* 147:994–997, 1990.

Ratey JJ, Nikkelsen EJ, Smith GB et al: Beta-blockers in the severely and profoundly retarded, *J Clin Psycopharmacol* 6:103–107, 1986.

Ratey JJ, Sovner R, Nikkelsen EJ et al: Buspirone therapy for maladaptive behavior and anxiety in developmentally disabled persons, *J Clin Psychiatry* 50:382–384, 1989.

Simon RI: *Concise guide to psychiatry and law for clinicians,* Washington DC, 1992, American Psychiatric Association Press.

Tesar GE, Stearn TA: Rapid tranquilization of the agitated intensive care unit patient, *J Intens Care Med* 3:195–201, 1988.

Yudofsky SC, Silver JM, Jackson W et al: The Overt Aggression Scale for the objective rating of verbal and physical aggression, *Am J Psychiatry* 143:35–39, 1986.

Yudofsky S, Stevens L, Silver J: Propranolol in the treatment of rage and violent behavior associated with Korsakoff's psychosis, *Am J Psychiatry* 141:114–115, 1984.

14 Alcohol, Substance Abuse, and Narcotics

The following are goals of this chapter:
1. To review the recognition and treatment of alcohol-related disorders.
2. To present the treatment of alcohol withdrawal syndromes.
3. To understand the significance and clinical use of blood alcohol levels.
4. To describe clinical issues in narcotic use for pain.
5. To present the management specifics for narcotic withdrawal.
6. To review the use of psychotropics as analgesic augmenters.

14.1 ALCOHOL ABUSE

1. Definition:
   a. The American Medical Association defines alcoholism as an illness characterized by significant impairment that is directly associated with persistent and excessive use of alcohol. Impairment may involve physiological, psychological, or social dysfunction.
2. Prevalence:
   a. Estimated prevalence in the U.S. is 7% to 10%
   b. Prevalence in medically hospitalized patients is 20% to 40%.
3. Morbidity and mortality:
   a. Alcohol is involved in about 30% of suicides and 60% of homicides.
   b. Alcohol is a major factor in accidents and domestic violence.
   c. Alcohol use is associated with:
      (1) Intoxication
      (2) Withdrawal
      (3) Wernicke-Korsakoff syndrome
      (4) Cerebral cortical atrophy (dementia)
      (5) Cerebellar degeneration
      (6) Polyneuropathy
      (7) Myopathy
      (8) Pellagra
      (9) GI disorders and bleeding: esophagitis, gastritis, hepatitis, pancreatitis, cirrhosis, GI cancers
      (10) Cardiovascular disorders: hypertension, cardiomyopathy
      (11) Hematologic disorders: thrombocytopenia, anemia, leukopenia
      (12) Infections
      (13) Dehydration

(14) Trauma
(15) Seizures.
4. Recognition:
   a. Alcoholism is poorly recognized. Casual interviewing of a patient is not sufficient.
   b. Several brief screening questionnaires can be useful, including:
      (1) **The CAGE questionnaire:** A simple four-item test with high sensitivity. An affirmative answer to more than one question is considered a basis for suspicion of alcoholism.
         (a) Have you ever felt the need to **C**ut down on drinking?
         (b) Have you ever felt **A**nnoyed by criticisms of drinking?
         (c) Have you ever had **G**uilty feelings about drinking?
         (d) Have you ever taken a morning **E**ye opener?
      (2) The **Michigan Alcohol Screening Test (MAST)** is composed of an original 25-item form and a shortened 10-item form. (see Box 14.1).
5. Treatment: Alcoholism is a chronic medical illness.
   a. Detoxification is the first step in treatment
   b. Maintenance of sobriety requires a maintenance program consisting of:
      (1) A support program, such as Alcoholics Anonymous
      (2) Treatment of psychiatric co-morbidities, such as depression or anxiety
      (3) Family treatment, to address enabling behaviors and support adaptive behaviors.

Box 14.1   Michigan Alcohol Screening Test*

Scoring Yes to 3 or more indicates alcoholism.
1. Do you feel you are a normal drinker?
2. Do friends or relatives think you are a normal drinker?
3. Have you ever attended a meeting of Alcoholics Anonymous?
4. Have you ever lost friends or girlfriends/boyfriends because of drinking?
5. Have you ever gotten in trouble at work because of drinking?
6. Have you ever neglected your obligations, your family, or your work for 2 or more days in a row because of your drinking?
7. Have you ever had DTs, severe shaking, or heard voices or seen things that were not there after heavy drinking?
8. Have you ever gone to anyone for help about your drinking?
9. Have you ever been in a hospital because of your drinking?
10. Have you ever been arrested for drunken driving or driving after drinking?

Brief version.
*From Pokorny AD, Miller BA, Kaplan HB: The brief MAST: a shortened version of the Michigan Alcohol Screening Test, *Am J Psychiatry* 129:342–345, 1972.

14.2   ALCOHOL INTOXICATION

1. Intoxication is the most common problem associated with alcohol use.
2. Intoxication is associated with serious potential for dangerous behavior, with violence directed toward self or others.
3. When dealing with the intoxicated patient, the following principles may be helpful:
   a. Security: If there is potential for aggressive behavior or if the patient could be armed, call security or police.
   b. Minimize threatening behaviors: Some principles in managing the aggressive patient are presented in Chapter 13. It is important to avoid making the patient feel more paranoid or threatened (i.e., by challenging or yelling back at the patient).
   c. Create a sociable environment: For example, offering food or coffee helps channel behavior into a social context.
4. Consider the need for transfer to a detoxification site for patients with a history of continuous ingestion of large amounts of alcohol.
5. Medical differential diagnosis of the intoxicated patient:
   a. Hepatic encephalopathy
   b. Hypoglycemia
   c. Postictal state
   d. Head trauma
   e. Central nervous system infection
   f. Intoxication by other drugs
   g. Confusion from Wernicke-Korsakoff syndrome.
6. Laboratory tests that may help in diagnosis:
   a. Blood alcohol level (see section below)
   b. Glucose level (may reveal alcohol-related hypoglycemia)
   c. Electrolytes and BUN levels (may reveal alcoholic ketoacidosis as well as dehydration)
   d. Toxicology screen (may reveal other substances)
   e. CBC (may reveal blood loss or infection)
   f. In a patient with hemorrhage or symptomatic liver disease, a PT, PTT, and platelet count.
7. Treatment:
   a. Protect the patient and others from physical harm
   b. Thiamine 100 mg IM, then orally tid for 2 weeks
   c. Multivitamins, daily
   d. For agitation, lorazepam 1-2 mg PO, with repeats if needed
   e. For severe agitation, haloperidol 5 mg IM
   f. Treat alcohol-related medical problems
   g. Constantly reevaluate for other problems.

14.3   ALCOHOLIC PARANOIA

1. Patients with this disorder become intensely jealous, hostile, and paranoid while on alcohol.
2. This disorder is very difficult to treat.
   a. Try small amounts of neuroleptics (usually of little help).
   b. Referral to an alcohol program that can help with abstinence.
3. Increased potential for violence during this state (often with a history of aggressive behaviors).

14.4 PATHOLOGIC INTOXICATION

1. Intoxication on small amounts of alcohol (often only 2-4 oz).
2. The intoxicated state may consist of aggressive, impulsive behaviors, with paranoia, which the patient does not remember afterward.
3. Managed with medication as described in Chapter 13.
4. Personality disorders often coexist.

14.5 WERNICKE-KORSAKOFF SYNDROME:

The full syndrome consists of the mnemonic COMA:
*C*onfusion
*O*phthalmoplegia
*M*emory impairment
*A*taxia

1. Patients may not show the complete syndrome.
2. Confabulation is not typical and is a consequence of the memory impairment.
3. Treatment is a medical emergency. When suspected, give:
   a. 100 mg thiamine and 1 mg folate IV followed by 100 mg thiamine daily for several weeks
   b. Clonidine (0.3 mg bid) has been reported to improve recent memory
   c. Propranolol has been reported to reduce rage attacks.

14.6 ALCOHOLIC HALLUCINOSIS

1. Vivid auditory hallucinations without other cognitive impairment.
2. Other sensory hallucinations may also occur.
3. The patient remains oriented and may be aware the voices are hallucinations.
   a. Voices are often accusatory and threatening.
      (1) Because of the nature of the hallucinations, these patients are at some risk for harming themselves or others.
   b. Hallucinations may occur while drinking, during withdrawal, or between episodes.
4. Less common than delirium tremens and not associated with delirium, tremor, disorientation, and agitation.
5. May be difficult to differentiate from intoxication in paranoid schizophrenia.
6. Treatment:
   a. If warranted, detain the patient in a protected setting.
   b. If the behavior creates immediate danger, treat as a behavioral emergency (see Chapter 13).
   c. The hallucinations generally clear within 30 days after cessation of drinking.

14.7 ALCOHOLIC DEMENTIA

1. Cognitive testing is abnormal in a high percentage of sober alcoholics.
2. Among the causes of impaired cognition in alcoholics are the following:

    a. Direct ethanol neurotoxicity
    b. Premorbid intellectual deficits
    c. Thiamine deficiency (dementia in alcoholics is usually nutritional)
    d. Recurrent head trauma
    e. Hepatocerebral degeneration
    f. Marchiafava disease (necrosis of corpus callosum).

14.8 HEPATIC ENCEPHALOPATHY

1. Usually of rapid onset, with delirium progressing to stupor and coma
2. Asterixis or tremor is present
3. Occurs in about 5% of patients with cirrhosis
4. Bromocriptine has been used with some success
5. Benzodiazepine antagonists are being tested as a treatment.

14.9 FETAL ALCOHOL SYNDROME

1. About 4 to 12 ounces of 100-proof alcohol must be consumed daily during pregnancy to produce this disorder
2. Defects in CNS include:
    a. Mental retardation
    b. Poor coordination
    c. Hyperactivity
    d. Growth deficiencies
    e. Facial abnormalities.

14.10 ALCOHOL CO–MORBIDITIES

1. Depression:
    a. Approximately 33% of alcoholics have a co-morbid affective disorder.
       (1) Depressive symptoms may be secondary to alcohol, or alcohol use may be a result of underlying depression.
          (a) History may reveal which came first.
          (b) Patient may need to be detoxed and alcohol free for at least 6 weeks to sort out diagnosis.
       (2) Antidepressants may be helpful in treating depression and helping to prevent relapse of drinking in some alcoholics.
2. Anxiety:
    a. Approximately 25% of alcoholics have a co-morbid anxiety disorder.
       (1) Anxiety may be secondary to alcohol withdrawal, or alcohol use may be a result of underlying anxiety.
    b. Generalized anxiety is a common co-morbidity: if identified and treated, it may decrease some of the patient's motivating tendency to drink.
       (1) Buspirone 10 mg tid may be useful because it is not potentially addicting and will not augment the sedative properties of alcohol if the patient relapses (see Chapter 9).
3. Chronic mentally ill:
    a. At least 25% of the chronically mentally ill have some complicating alcohol use.
4. Borderline personality disorder:

a. Substance abuse is a common co-morbidity and adds significantly to suicide risk.

14.11 ALCOHOL (AND SEDATIVE) WITHDRAWAL

Minor Abstinence and Major Abstinence (Delirium Tremens)

1. Introduction:
   a. Patients who discontinue sedatives too quickly are at risk for sedative withdrawal.
      (1) The severity of sedative withdrawal ranges from mild discomfort requiring no treatment (minor abstinence) to life-threatening symptoms requiring acute hospitalization (delirium tremens [DTs]).
2. Prevalence:
   a. Given the significant prevalence of alcohol and sedative use, it is not surprising that sedative withdrawal is also common.
   b. In a general medical hospital, about 40% of patients have been using sedatives; anxiety and behavioral agitation often represent sedative withdrawal.
      (1) When a medical patient suddenly becomes agitated, confused, or psychotic, delirium tremens should be at the top of the differential diagnosis list.
3. Significance:
   a. If untreated, DTs have a 10% mortality, which may increase to 25% with other acute medical disorders.

Minor abstinence syndrome

1. Symptoms (see Box 14.2) that may appear within 8 hours of the last drink and usually peak between 24 to 36 hours consist of:
   a. Morning hangover
   b. Morning shakiness
   c. Craving for alcohol
   d. Insomnia, vivid dreams
   e. Anxiety, irritability
   f. Nausea, vomiting
   g. Sweating, weakness, myalgias
   h. Tachycardia, hypertension
   i. Coarse tremor of hands and tongue.
2. Repeated episodes of minor withdrawal may appear to be a chronic anxiety disorder.
3. Minor withdrawal can be managed effectively in an outpatient settting, often with no medication.

Major abstinence syndrome (delirium tremens)

1. Risk factors for DTs include:
   a. A long, intense history of alcohol exposure
   b. A recent binge followed by abrupt cessation
   c. Previous history of DTs
   d. Presence of infection, head trauma, or poor nutrition.

Box 14.2   Abstinence signs in alcohol withdrawal

Minor Withdrawal

Appears within a few hours after alcohol discontinuance and generally disappears within 48 hours.

Symptoms

Hyperreflexia
Irritability
Nausea
Sleeplessness
Sweating
Tremor
Weakness

Major Withdrawal

Usually appears from 48 to 72 hours after discontinuance (or lowering of dose).

Symptoms

Confusion
Hallucinations
Hypertension
Seizures
Tachycardia
Tachypnea
Temperature
Tremulousness
Weakness

---

2. Timing:
   a. The onset and severity of withdrawal symptoms is determined by the half-life of the sedative.
      (1) Long-acting sedatives have a delayed onset of moderate withdrawal symptoms.
         (a) Major abstinence is unlikely to follow use of long-acting sedatives such as diazepam or chlordiazepoxide, whose active metabolites have a half-life of about 100 hours (see Chapter 9).
      (2) Short-acting sedatives have a rapid onset of severe withdrawal symptoms.
   b. With alcohol, DTs may begin as early as 24 hours after cessation or significant cutting back of drinking.
      (1) Loss of appetite, tremulousness, and irritability are early features.
      (2) Hallucinations usually, but not always, follow other symptoms of autonomic arousal.
      (3) The modal onset of DTs is about 72 hours but can be delayed as long as 7 days.

    (4) Shorter-acting sedatives, such as butalbital (in Fiorinal) may have
        earlier onset.
    (5) Abusers of very short-acting sedatives, such as triazolam (Hal-
        cion), may have onset of DTs within 24 hours of drug cessation.
3. Symptoms: (see Box 14.2).
    a. Symptoms may be obscured by concurrent medications or medical
        conditions. For example:
        (1) Beta-blockers can mask tachycardia
        (2) Narcotics can mask mydriasis
        (3) Antipyretics can mask fever.
4. Treatment:
    a. Sedative withdrawal syndromes can be effectively managed with
        cross-tolerant sedatives.
        (1) Alcohol is cross-tolerant but has a short half-life, causes gastric
            irritation, excessive sedation, and provides a confusing message
            for the patient
        (2) Antihistamines, chloral hydrate, and buspirone are not cross-
            tolerant
        (3) Beta-blockers may decrease autonomic symptoms but do not
            prevent or treat DTs
        (4) Neuroleptics are not cross-tolerant sedatives
        (5) Carbamazepine has shown some potential in treating DTs.
    b. DTs requires medical management capabilities.
        (1) Patients at risk for DTs should be closely monitored for changes
            in pulse, respiration, temperature, and heart rate
        (2) Increases in autonomic discharge are usually the first symptoms,
            followed by the delirium, hallucinations, and physical agitation.
            Occasionally, behavioral symptoms will precede.
    c. Modal treatment involves the use of a benzodiazepine. Because
        observing the patient on a regular basis (every 3 hours) is important to
        adjust dose according to response, 24-hour orders should *not* be
        written. Drug options include:
        (1) Chlordiazepoxide 25-100 mg PO every 3 to 6 hours on the first
            day; 20% decrease/day over 5 days
        (2) Diazepam 2-20 mg PO every 3 to 6 hours on the first day; 20%
            decrease/day over 5 days
        (3) Lorazepam 2 mg IM can be substituted for 10 mg PO diazepam or
            50 mg PO chlordiazepoxide
        (4) Diazepam 10–20 mg pulses PO or IV every 1 to 2 hours until
            symptoms improve, then discontinue.
    d. Once "loaded" with a long-acting benzodiazepine for 24 hours and no
        withdrawal symptoms are evident, the medication can be stopped
        (based on its long half-life) or at least decreased 25 to 50% each
        subsequent day to avoid oversedation. However, shorter-acting drugs,
        such as lorazepam, must be tapered.
    e. Because of the shorter half-life and lack of age-related hepatic
        metabolism, lorazepam is preferable in the elderly and those with liver
        impairment.
    f. Thiamine: Remember to treat alcoholics with 100 mg IV thiamine
        immediately and to continue thiamine orally for at least 3 more days.
    g. Magnesium: Hypomagnesemia is frequent in chronic alcoholics.

(1) Magnesium sulfate 1 g, IM or IV, every 6 to 12 hours for 48 hours
(2) Magnesium oxide, orally, 250-500 mg 4/time/day for 48 hours (diarrhea is the most common side effect).

h. Neuroleptics: While neuroleptics are not helpful in preventing or treating DTs, they may play an adjunctive role in reducing severe psychotic symptoms.

Alcohol withdrawal seizures

1. Withdrawal seizures may occur in one fourth to one third of continuous, heavy drinkers, more commonly in those with a history of epilepsy.
2. Seizures usually occur within 8 to 24 hours after cessation of drinking (and therefore almost always precede withdrawal delirium).
3. Check for and correct low magnesium.
4. Anticonvulsants are not helpful prophylactically and should be reserved for use in patients with a history of nonalcohol–related seizures.
   a. For those patients, phenytoin can be given in a loading dose of 15 mg/kg dissolved in 250-500 ml of 5% D5W over 4 hours, followed by 100 mg, PO every 8 hours for 3 to 4 days, or chronically if the EEG is abnormal.
5. An etiology other than an "alcohol withdrawal seizure" should be sought in patients whose seizures:
   a. Occur after the onset of delirium
   b. Are focal or multiple
   c. Are accompanied by elevated temperature
   d. Occur in the context of head trauma.

14.12   THE PENTOBARBITAL CHALLENGE TEST IN SEDATIVE USERS

1. Sedative abusers often use multiple sedatives, including benzodiazepines, barbiturates, and alcohol.
   a. When detoxing such a patient, establishing the correct initial treatment dose may be difficult. The patient's own history may be unreliable.
   b. The pentobarbital challenge test is a more objective way to determine the amount of sedative tolerance and serves as a method to determine a cross-over treatment dose. This test is performed as demonstrated in Box 14.3.

14.13   THE BLOOD ALCOHOL LEVEL

1. Blood alcohol levels (BALs) are fairly reliable indicators of ethanol in the blood and a reflection of brain ethanol levels.
2. BAL is reported as percent or mg% (to obtain mg%, multiply % by 1000).
3. BAL is influenced by a person's weight, rapidity of drinking, time elapsed since last drink, ability to metabolize alcohol, and presence of food.
4. On average, a person can decrease their BAL by 15 mg%/hour; a person with a history of drinking and activated enzymes can metabolize 30 mg%/hour.
   a. A heavy drinker with a BAL of 300, will have a BAL of 0 in only about 10 hours.

Box 14.3 Pentobarbital Method for Determining
Sedative Habit

1. This test must be performed in a patient who is not intoxicated.
2. If suspected daily sedative dose is 400-1200 mg day
   a. Give a dose of 200 mg of pentobarbital PO, and observe the
      patient in 1 hour. Interpret findings as follows:

Signs of intoxication at 1 hour	Habit level mg day
None	800
Nystagmus only	700-800
Nystagmus, ataxia, dysarthria	500-600
Coarse nystagmus, gross ataxia, somnolence	Below 500
Asleep but responsive	No tolerance

3. If no symptoms of intoxication develop, give an additional 100 mg
   PO every 2 hours until symptoms develop *or* a maximum total dose
   of 500 mg in 6 hours.
4. The total dose needed to produce intoxication is the patient's 6-hour
   pentobarbital requirement; multiply by 4 to obtain the 24-hour
   requirement.
5. After 2 days of pentobarbital treatment, substitute 30 mg phenobarbital for each 100 mg of pentobarbital; give this amount in three
   divided doses for 2 days, then decrease phenobarbital daily dose by
   30 mg/day.

---

5. On average:
   a. One drink gives a BAL of 30 mg%
   b. Two drinks give a BAL of 50-60 mg%
   c. Four to five drinks in an hour gives a BAL of 100 mg%, with some
      psychomotor impairment
   d. BALs between 150-300 are associated with staggering gait, passing
      out, blacking out (a period of amnesia following drinking), and
      irrational behavior.
6. A patient showing no symptoms at a high BAL has a high tolerance from
   chronic significant alcohol use
   a. A BAL of 150 mg% with no symptoms of intoxication is indicative of
      alcoholism
   b. A BAL of 350-400 mg% is considered a lethal dose for 50% of the
      population (LD50) (see Table 14.1).

14.14 COCAINE (AND STIMULANTS INCLUDING AMPHETAMINE) ABUSE:

1. Prevalence: After alcohol, cocaine is the most frequently abused drug
   with significant medical consequences.
2. Symptoms:

Table 14.1 Blood alcohol levels

| Blood Alcohol Level | | Clinical Findings |
%	mg/dl	(in nontolerant patients)*
0.05	50	Inattention, unsteadiness
0.10	100	Impaired memory, + Romberg (eyes closed)
0.15	150	Slurred speech, + Romberg (eyes open)
0.20	200	Stupor
0.25	250	Anesthesia
>0.35	>350	Respiratory arrest

*Patients with significant alcohol consumption develop tolerance and may have minimal findings even with BALs of >250.

a. Onset: Typical intranasal dose onset in minutes. Inhaled cocaine (crack) has faster onset and more intense autonomic and psychic effect, along with increased addicting reinforcement.
b. Common acute medical effects:
   (1) Anorexia
   (2) Insomnia
   (3) Hyperactivity
   (4) Pressured speech
   (5) Rapid thoughts
   (6) Hyperreflexia
   (7) Tachycardia
   (8) Diaphoresis.
c. Less common serious consequences:
   (1) Hyperpyrexia
   (2) Hypertension
   (3) Seizures
   (4) Myocardial infarction
   (5) Brain hemorrhage.
d. Acute psychiatric effects:
   (1) Similar to a panic attack, including palpitations and hyperventilation; however, unlike the fear and dysphoria of a panic attack, cocaine often produces euphoria.
   (2) Chronic effects:
      (a) Auditory and visual hallucinations
      (b) Paranoid delusions
      (c) Tendency to violent behavior
      (d) Tactile hallucinations
      (e) Autonomous panic attacks.
3. Recognition:
   a. Patients may be reluctant to admit their habit and instead report related symptoms (e.g., panic attacks or chest pain).
   b. Patients need to be asked directly; when in doubt, a toxicology urine screen may be helpful.

       (1) While the plasma half-life elimination of cocaine is quite brief, measured in hours, cocaine's metabolite (benzoyl ecognine) may be detected in the urine for up to several days.

  c. Physical symptoms of cocaine use:

       (1) Frequent intranasal use may cause abnormal nasal septum, rhinitis, and sinusitis

       (2) Freebase inhalers may develop bronchitis

       (3) Seizures

       (4) "Snowlights" (flashes of lights in the periphery of the visual fields)

       (5) Overdoses are associated with stroke, ventricular fibrillation, or cardiac arrest.

4. Selected medical treatment aspects of cocaine abuser:

  a. The cocaine habit is powerful. Rats given an opportunity to self-inject with cocaine may continue until they die of hyperthermia, seizures, or cardiac arrhythmias.

  b. Extreme autonomic hyperactivity can be counteracted to some extent with beta-blockers.

  c. Neuroleptics help associated psychosis.

  d. Chronic cocaine can "kindle" abnormal brain activity, leading to seizures and panic attacks, even after stopping cocaine.

  e. Withdrawal can lead to profound depression with increased suicide risk.

  f. Treatment must address both behavioral and physical habits.

       (1) In general, solo physicians will not be successful in treating cocaine (or other substance) addiction because a comprehensive behavioral program, including peer feedback and support, is necessary.

  g. Antidepressants and dopamine agonists have some potential in decreasing the drug craving associated with relapse.

  h. Treatment of associated psychiatric co-morbidity (e.g., depression or anxiety) is important.

14.15 HALLUCINOGENS

1. LSD, mescaline, psilocybin, dimethyltryptamine (DMT), methylenedioxymethamphetamine (MDMA, also known as "ecstasy"), phencyclidine (PCP) can all produce hallucinations, delusions, and intense affective symptoms.

2. PCP use is associated with violence.

  a. Physical symptoms of PCP intoxication include nystagmus, myoclonus, and ataxia.

3. Treatment:

  a. Create a safe setting

  b. Decrease sensory stimulation

  c. Use verbal reassurance

  d. Autonomic symptoms can be lessened with beta-blockers

  e. Benzodiazepines or neuroleptics may be helpful for agitation or psychosis

  f. Avoid use of drugs with anticholinergic side effects, which could increase the confusion.

14.16 ISSUES IN NARCOTIC USE

1. Respiratory depression is the major medical concern with acute narcotic use. In general, this is a problem for:
   a. Patients who have not had time to develop tolerance to this effect
   b. Patients receiving large IV doses
   c. Patients taking other sedatives (e.g. parenteral benzodiazepines), which depress respiratory function.
2. Common problems in pain management:
   a. The major reason for continued pain in medical/surgical patients is underuse of narcotic analgesics. The underdosing may take the form of:
      (1) Inadequate amount of narcotic per dose, or
      (2) Excessive time duration between doses.
   b. One method to establish the problem in pain control is to ask the patient to rate pain on a scale from "0 to 10," where "0" represents "no pain," and "10" represents "the worst pain he/she has experienced."
      (1) The first rating should be done about one-half hour after the narcotic dose, to see if the dose amount is adequate. If the rating is high at that point, a larger dose needs to be given.
      (2) The patient should be rated again just before the next dose is given. If that rating is high, the duration between doses may be too long.
   c. Scheduled vs. as needed (prn) dosing:
      (1) In general, a schedule is better.
      (2) Pain can often be managed on lower overall doses if it is kept from reemerging.
      (3) Drawbacks of prn schedule include:
         (a) Low nursing staffing may result in delays.
         (b) It "rewards" the patient for reporting pain.
      (4) A "reverse prn" schedule gives the patient the option, on a schedule, of refusing a dose of medication.
3. Patient controlled analgesia (PCA):
   a. Patients can control the release of small amounts of parenteral narcotics as they feel they need them.
   b. A "lock out" period keeps the patient from using too much too quickly.
   c. Overall, studies of PCA in the context of acute, usually postoperative, pain indicate better pain control using less narcotic.
4. Constipation:
   a. Occurs acutely and remains a serious problem during narcotic use.
      (1) May progress to paralytic ileus and obstruction.
   b. Patients requiring continuous narcotics should be placed on a prophylactic bowel regimen.
   c. Made worse by concurrent anticholinergic drugs.
5. Psychiatric effects of narcotics:
   a. Narcotics have been used for centuries for psychoactive properties, which can relieve symptoms of psychosis, anxiety, or depression.
   b. Many narcotics users seek narcotics as a means to treat underlying psychiatric disorders.
      (1) Psychiatric disorders often reemerge after chronic users discontinue narcotics.

6. Dose conversion:
   a. It is helpful to be able to inter-convert doses of narcotics, when:
      (1) Simplifying drug orders,
      (2) Detoxing a patient, or
      (3) Converting any narcotic
      (4) Converting from one narcotic to another.
   b. Box 14.4 lists a formula for inter-converting narcotics.
7. Tolerance, dependence, and addiction:
   a. *Tolerance:* refers to nervous system adaptation to continued exposure.
      (1) Over a few weeks tolerance develops to the respiratory depressant, analgesic, and some psychotropic effects.
      (2) After about 3 weeks, patients may require a higher dose to achieve the same pain relief.
         (a) This does escalation does not mean the patient is addicted or abusing the medication.
   b. *Dependence:* refers to a state resulting in the emergence of withdrawal symptoms if the drug is stopped.

Box 14.4   Narcotic Dose Conversions*

To convert an oral dose of any narcotic to an equivalent oral dose of morphine, multiply by:

0.15 for propoxyphene
0.2 for meperidine
0.33 for codeine
0.5 for pentazocine
2 for oxycodone
3 for methadone
8 for hydromorphone

To convert an IM dose of any narcotic to an equivalent oral dose of morphine, multiply by:

1.5 for pentazocine
6.0 for methadone
40 for hydromorphone
3.0 for morphine
0.8 for meperidine
30 for butorphanol

Another alternative for acute pain would be intranasal butorphanol (Stadol NS). A 2 mg dose is equivalent to 75 mg IM meperidine. Because this drug is a mixed agonist-antagonist, it should not be used in a patient already taking narcotic agonists, since withdrawal could be precipitated.

---

*Equivalent doses are approximate and may need to be adjusted, especially early in treatment.

Table 14.2   Narcotic half-lives

Narcotic	Duration of action (hr)
Codeine	4-7
Hydromorphone	4-6
Meperidine	2-4
Methadone	4-7
Morphine	2.5-7.0
Oxycodone	3-5
Pentazocine	3-4
Propoxyphene	4-7

     (1) Every patient who has continued exposure to narcotics for a few weeks and then stops will have typical withdrawal symptoms (see Table 14.3, which can be used as a rating sheet).

     (2) The time of onset and severity of symptoms is proportional to the half-life of the drug (see Table 14.2).

     (3) This physiologic dependence is related to, but not equivalent to, the psychological/behavioral dependence that patients also may develop.

  c. *Addiction:* refers to a state of tolerance and dependence, with a behavioral component consisting of a preoccupation with obtaining and using the drug in question.

     (1) Cancer patients with chronic malignant pain, maintained on morphine, are not addicts.

     (2) Paradoxically, physicians who withhold narcotics from patients who legitimately need them can create addicts by forcing them to become preoccupied with obtaining the drugs they need.

8. Narcotic withdrawal:

  a. Onset and duration:

     (1) Proportional to duration of action (see Table 14.2).

     (2) Starts within a half day for short-acting narcotics (e.g., heroin) and usually ends after several days.

     (3) Starts after a few days for longer-acting drugs (e.g., methadone) and continues in some drawn-out form for a number of weeks.

  b. Severity:

     (1) Patients rarely, if ever, die from narcotic withdrawal.

     (2) Sedative withdrawal, with seizures and autonomic dysfunction, is much more dangerous.

     (3) In cases of multiple drug addictions, it is prudent to withdraw the patient from one drug at a time.

     (4) Because of the physiologic stress, maintain narcotics until other medical problems are stabilized.

  c. Recognition: (see Table 14.3).

  d. Treatment:

     (1) Should be based on observation of symptoms rather than history.

       (a) Some addicts make up their dose to obtain a supply from a naive physician

Table 14.3   Narcotic withdrawal symptoms rating sheet

Patient name:

Date/Time:
Vital Signs:
BP
Temperature
Respirations
Pulse rate

Symptoms:
Drug craving
Anxiety
Yawning
Sweating
Lacrimation
Rhinorrhea
Insomnia
Mydriasis
Goose flesh
Tremors
Hot/cold
Aching bones
Anorexia
Restlessness
Nausea
Vomiting
Diarrhea
Orgasm

Dose:
Comments:

      (b) The composition and identification of street drugs is uncertain.
  (2) The principle is to achieve a narcotic level comparable to habitual level of use, and then decrease the daily dose in increments that balance withdrawal symptoms with time.
      (a) The taper can be 10% to 33%/day.
      (b) There is no way to eliminate all withdrawal symptoms.
  (3) For most street addicts, 5 mg of methadone PO qid will usually suffice.
  (4) Whatever dose is selected, observe and adjust on the basis of toxicity or withdrawal.
  (5) Clonidine as an alternative or adjunct.

Box 14.5 Clonidine Withdrawal Method*

Day 1:   0.4 mg test dose in the morning;
                      repeat test dose 0.4 mg at bedtime.
                      If tolerated, continue.
Day 2-10:   0.5 mg every morning;
                      0.2 mg every afternoon;
                      0.5 mg every evening.
Day 11-14:   Reduce dose daily by 50% of previous dose;
                      stop on day 14.

---

*(Sample for a 70 kg man). Major side effects are hypotension, sedation, dry mouth.

      (a) An alpha adrenergic agonist, which blocks autonomic discharge, can be used alone or with a narcotic taper to reduce withdrawal symptoms.

      (b) Box 14.5 provides a method for clonidine use

      (c) About one third of patients will not tolerate clonidine resulting from hypotension.

9. Methadone maintenance:

   a. Methadone maintenance programs provide treatment for narcotics addicts unable to succeed at abstinence.

   b. Physicians or hospitals without a license cannot provide methadone for this purpose.

   c. If a methadone maintenance patient is admitted to the medical hospital for some other problem, call the program to confirm the methadone dose and maintain the patient on that dose during the admission.

10. When the narcotics addict requires analgesics:

   a. Narcotics addicts should not be deprived of adequate analgesia.

   b. Remember that the patient will have tolerance. Therefore, addicts often need somewhat higher doses to achieve the expected effects.

11. Chronic malignant pain:

   a. Pain secondary to a malignancy (or other "malignant" medical condition) should be treated without prejudice about potential "addiction."

      (1) Fortunately, there is increasing consensus about providing terminal patients with adequate analgesia.

      (2) Oral morphine is the standard drug for chronic malignant pain. It does not require injections and can be titrated easily.

         (a) Oral morphine elixir is used on an every 3-hour basis.

         (b) Oral morphine can provide relief equivalent to parenteral doses.

         (c) Box 14-4 shows the inter-conversions of different narcotics to the "oral morphine equivalent."

         (d) Once a daily dose has been established, it can be converted to a sustained release form (such as MS Contin), which becomes more convenient for the patient.

        (i) Give one half the daily oral morphine elixer dose on an every 12-hour basis, as MS Contin, or one third on an every 8-hours basis.

        (ii) Oral or parenteral morphine can be used as necessary for breakthrough pain.

    (3) Fentanyl patches are another alternative for the chronic malignant (and postsurgical) pain.

       (a) Once the patient's narcotic requirement has been established, convert to the equivalent patch dose as follows:

Oral 24-hour Morphine dose (mg)	Fentanyl patch Dose (µ/h)
45-134	25
135-224	50
225-314	75
315-404	100
405-494	125
495-584	150
585-674	175
675-764	200
765-854	225
855-944	250
945-1034	275
1035-1124	300

       (b) Oral (or parenteral) narcotic doses can be used to supplement "breakthrough" pain, if necessary.

    (4) Butorphanol (Stadol) nasal spray is available as an alternative to the IM route, with comparable acute pain relief. Dose is usually 1 mg (1 spray) in each nostril, with a repeat if needed.

       (a) Because butorphanol is a mixed agonist-antagonist, it cannot be used in patients already taking narcotics because it can precipitate withdrawal.

12. Nonmalignant chronic pain (e.g., chronic low back pain/chronic headache) creates significant treatment dilemmas and problems.

    a. Some patients with chronic pain seem to be able to maintain fairly low, consistent doses of narcotic.

    b. Many patients with chronic pain show addictive behaviors, which contribute to management problems:

      (1) Using multiple providers to prescribe analgesics

      (2) Using multiple medications

      (3) Running out of prescriptions early

      (4) Losing their supply of medication

      (5) Using the emergency room for refills.

    c. The "correct" medication is rarely the cure for chronic pain, even though these patients feel some medical treatment will cure them. Chronic pain represents a complex behavioral problem more than a limited medical symptom.

    d. Treatment:

      (1) Convert the patient from the acute to the chronic pain paradigm:

     (a) In the acute paradigm, pain is seen as a symptom of an underlying, treatable medical problem. Therefore, acute pain is evaluated aggressively and treated with surgery when possible or medication if needed.

     (b) The acute paradigm does not apply very well to chronic pain.

     (c) In the chronic pain paradigm, there is no simple surgical cure; and narcotics do not solve the problem. Treatment involves a program combining:
       (i) Behavioral elements (stressing adaptive functions and positive behaviors),
       (ii) Physical therapy and exercise components, and
       (iii) Attention to underlying psychosocial stresses and psychiatric co-morbidities.

13. Psychotropics as analgesic augmentors:
   a. Nonnarcotics analgesics (e.g., the nonsteroidal antiinflammatory drugs [NSAIDs]):
     (1) Work by different mechanisms and may significantly augment pain relief for patients already taking narcotics
     (2) Antiinflammatory properties may be effective in inflammatory conditions where narcotics are more nonspecific.
   b. Antidepressants:
     (1) Most patients with chronic pain should have a trial of some antidepressant, because of the prevalence of coexisting depression, which leads to symptom amplification.
     (2) Anti-depressants have some analgesic-augmenting properties demonstrated in:
       (a) Diabetic neuropathy
       (b) Postherpetic neuralgia
       (c) Tension and migraine headache
       (d) Myofascial pain.
     (3) Amitriptyline or imipramine are used in starting doses of 25-50 mg/day, increasing every 4 to 7 days by 25 mg increments.
     (4) Pain conditions are heterogeneous and some may be helped by noradrenergic, rather than serotonergic, augmentation.
   c. Antihistamines:
     (1) Hydroxyzine (Vistaril) is often used as a coanalgesic. Its mechanism of analgesic action is unknown; 25 mg of hydroxyzine alone appears to have the analgesic potency of about 2 mg of IM morphine.
   d. Stimulants: Dextroamphetamine in oral doses of 5-10 mg has been demonstrated to augment narcotic analgesia.
   e. Cocaine: Despite its use in Brompton's mixture, no study has ever documented analgesic potency of cocaine.
   f. Steroids: Important in a number of pain conditions including metastatic bone disease, epidural cord compression, headache as a result of increased intracranial pressure, and tumor infiltration of nerves.
   g. Neuroleptics: Most neuroleptics do not have significant analgesic properties and are more often used for their anxiolytic and antiemetic properties.

(1) Methotrimeperazine (Levoprome) is a unique phenothiazine reported to have analgesic potency and may be considered in patients who cannot tolerate narcotics. Begin with a test dose of 5 mg IM to assess effects on blood pressure and sedation. In general, doses of 10-20 mg IM every 6 hours are used.

h. Anticonvulsants: May act as "membrane stabilizers," which help exert some analgesic effect. Low doses of carbamazepine (e.g., 50 mg tid) and phenytoin have been used in neuropathic pain syndromes.

References

Charness ME, Simon RP, Greenberg DA: Ethanol and the nervous system, *N Engl J Med* 321(7):442-454, 1989.

Ewing JA: Detecting alcoholism: the CAGE questionnaire, *JAMA* 252:1905-1907, 1984.

Foy A, March S, Drinkwater V: Use of an objective clinical scale in the assessment and management of alcohol withdrawal in a large general hospital, *Alcoholism Clin Exp Res* 12:360-364, 1988.

Getto CJ, Sorkness CA, Howell T: Antidepressants and chronic nonmalignant pain: a review, *J Pain Symptom Manage* 2:9-18, 1987.

Giannini A: *Phencyclidine.* In Giannini A, Slaby A, eds: *Drugs of abuse,* Montvale, NJ 1989, Medical Economics Books.

Gold M, Giannini A: *Cocaine and cocaine addiction.* In Giannini A, Slaby A, eds: *Drugs of abuse,* Montvale, NJ 1989, Medical Economics Books.

Gold MS, Pottash AC, Sweeney DR et al: Opiate withdrawal using clonidine: a safe, effective and rapid nonopiate treatment, *JAMA* 234:343-346, 1979.

Hoffmann NG, DeHart SS, Fulkerson JA: Medical care utilization as a function of recovery status following chemical addictions treatment, *J Addictive Diseases* 12(1):97-108, 1993.

Holder HD, Blose JO: The reduction of health care costs associated with alcoholism treatment: a 14-year longitudinal study, *J Studies on Alcohol* 53(4):293-302, 1992.

Hoskin PJ, Hanks GW: Opioid agonist-antagonist drugs in acute and chronic pain states, *Drugs* 41(3):326-344, 1991.

Lange DE, Schacter B: Prevalence of alcohol-related admissions to general medical units, *Intl J Psychiatry in Med* 19(4):371-384, 1989.

Leggett BA, Powell LW, Halliday JW: Laboratory markers of alcoholism, *Dig Dis* 7:125-134, 1989.

Liskow BI, Goodwin DW: Pharmacological treatment of alcohol intoxication, withdrawal and dependence: a critical review, *J Stud Alcohol* 48:356-370, 1987.

Max MB. Lynch SA, Muir J et al: Effects of desipramine, amitriptyline and fluoxetine on pain in diabetic neuropathy, *N Engl J Med* 326:1250-1256, 1992.

McEvoy J: *The chronic neuropsychiatric disorders associated with alcoholism.* In Pattison E, Kaufman E, eds: *Encyclopedic handbook of alcoholism,* New York, 1982, Gardner.

Moertel CG: Treatment of cancer pain with orally administered medications, *JAMA* 244:2448-2450, 1980.

Moscovitz H, Brookoff D, Nelson L: A randomized trial of bromocriptine for cocaine users presenting to the emergency department, *J Gen Intern Med* 8:1-4, 1993.

Porter J, Jick H: Addiction rare in patients treatment with narcotics, *N Engl J Med* 302:123, 1980.

Sellers EM, Narango CA, Harrison M et al: Diazepam loading: simplified treatment for alcohol withdrawal, *Clin Pharmacol Ther* 6:822, 1983.

Selzer ML: The Michigan Alcoholism Screening Test: the quest for a new diagnostic instrument, *Am J Psychiatry* 127:89-94, 1971.

Stine SM, Kosten TR: Use of drug combinations in treatment of opioid withdrawal, *J Clin Psychopharm* 12(3):203-209, 1992.

Surawicz F: Alcoholic hallucinosis: a missed diagnosis: differential diagnoses and management, *Can J Psychiatry* 1:57-63, 1980.

Turner RC, Lichstein PR, Peden JG et al: Alcohol withdrawal syndromes: a review of pathophysiology, clinical presentation and treatment, *J Gen Int Med* 4:432-435, 1989.

Victor M, Adams RD, Collins GH: The Wernicke-Korsakoff syndrome, ed, 2 Contemporary Neurology Series, vol. 30, 1989.

Electroconvulsive Therapy

15

The following are goals of this chapter:
1. To review the indications for electroconvulsive therapy (ECT)
2. To review the side effects associated with ECT
3. To review the pre-ECT assessment and orders
4. To review ECT technical issues.

15.1 INTRODUCTION AND INDICATIONS

1. ECT is often neglected as a treatment option by nonpsychiatrists because of the lack of knowledge of its modern applications and technology.
2. ECT is a medical procedure in which a brief electrical stimulus is used to induce a seizure under controlled conditions, to treat certain major mental disorders.
3. ECT is generally not a first line treatment. ECT *should be considered* for the following disorders *when:*
   a. A patient has failed trials of medication because of nonresponsiveness
   b. A patient cannot tolerate the risks or side effects of medication
   c. There is a need for an immediate response (e.g., severe suicidal behaviors, severe nutrition problems).
4. ECT should be considered for:
   a. Major depression
   b. Bipolar disorder (depressed, manic, or mixed phases)
   c. Nonchronic schizophrenia (especially with prominent affective or catatonic symptoms)
   d. Schizoaffective disorder.
5. ECT may also be effective in:
   a. Some severe organic psychoses
   b. Delirium
   c. Refractory epilepsy
   d. Neuroleptic malignant syndrome
   e. Parkinson's disease.

15.2 CONTRAINDICATIONS

1. The following situations have a substantially increased risk associated with ECT:
   a. Space occupying intracranial lesions or other conditions associated with increased intracranial pressure

b. Recent myocardial infarction (standard practice is to wait 3 months after an MI to give ECT)
c. Recent intracerebral hemorrhage
d. Bleeding, or unstable vascular aneurysm or malformation
e. Retinal detachment
f. Pheochromocytoma
g. Anesthetic risk rated at ASA level 4 or 5
h. Ventricular arrhythmias
i. NOTE: Pregnancy is not a contraindication; ECT may be used in all trimesters, in consultation with the obstetrician.

15.3   ADVERSE EFFECTS

1. **Overall mortality:**
   a. Contemporary ECT including preoxygenation, brief anesthesia, muscle relaxation, and careful physiologic and cardiac monitoring is associated with a very low rate of morbidity and mortality.
   b. Mortality associated with ECT is comparable to (if not lower than) anesthesia mortality among surgical patients (about 0.9 deaths per 10,000 cases).
   c. The majority of deaths are cardiorespiratory complications.
2. **Cognitive effects:**
   a. Memory impairment has been considered the principle adverse effect of ECT.
   b. ECT is associated with four types of short-term memory impairment:
      (1) Postictal confusion immediately following treatment.
      (2) Retrograde amnesia for a variable period of minutes to hours before the treatment.
      (3) Anterograde amnesia for a variable period of minutes to hours to days.
      (4) Longer lasting subjective complaints of memory impairment, which are difficult to evaluate. Possible explanations include:
         (a) Some genuine neuropsychological impairment too subtle for standard testing to detect
         (b) Patients use this complaint for secondary gain
         (c) Patients become more aware of memory problems that preceded treatment
         (d) Memory difficulty may be part of residual psychopathology such as depression.
   c. Acquisition and retention of new memories and longer term memory are not impaired.
   d. The incidence and severity of cognitive effects depends to some extent on technical variables. The following variables are associated with increased chance of cognitive impairment:
      (1) Bilateral electrode placement
      (2) Higher stimulus intensity
      (3) Sine wave stimulation (should not be used)
      (4) More frequent treatments
      (5) Concomitant psychotropic use
      (6) Higher anesthesia dose.

e. For most young healthy patients, posttreatment confusion is generally limited to a few hours. For the elderly or those with other risk factors for confusion, posttreatment confusion may last all day, several days, or in unusual cases, up to a few weeks.
   (1) If a patient does not recover cognitive function sufficiently, additional treatments may have to be delayed.
   (2) Recording cognitive mental status before treatments is important to assess changes from baseline.

3. **Cardiovascular effects:**
   a. The majority of deaths attributed to ECT are a result of cardiac complications.
      (1) Cardiac complications occur in about 10% of patients, although the majority are transient.
   b. ECT is associated with several significant physiologic events that contribute to cardiovascular risk. These include:
      (1) Increased parasympathetic tone within the first 15 seconds, with potential for bradycardia and/or asystole, as well as various arrhythmias.
      (2) Immediate sympathetic discharge with marked increase in circulating catecholamines (plasma epinephrine is released mainly from the adrenal medulla) creating potential for tachyarrhythmias and hypertension.
         (a) Associated increased myocardial oxygen consumption may cause myocardial ischemia in susceptible patients.
         (b) Patients within 6 months of myocardial infarction should be treated cautiously if at all.
   c. Attenuation of autonomic changes may decrease cardiovascular complications.
      (1) Patients with preexisting hypertension or hypertensive responses to ECT should be premedicated using 5-10 mg labetolol IV about 90 seconds before seizure induction.

4. **Pulmonary effects:**
   a. General anesthesia creates risk for patients with pulmonary disease.
   b. Mild hypoxia, hypercapnia, and respiratory acidosis are not uncommon.

5. **Cerebrovascular effects:**
   a. A brief but marked increase occurs in intracranial pressure associated with increased cerebral blood flow following the electrical stimulus.

6. **Intraocular effects:**
   a. Increases in intraocular pressure may be relevant for patients with poorly controlled glaucoma.

7. **Intragastric effects:**
   a. Increases in intragastric pressure may lead to regurgitation or pulmonary aspiration, especially for patients with hiatal hernia.

8. **Other complications:**
   a. Estimated rate of complications is about 1 per 1400 treatments. These complications include:
      (1) Laryngospasm
      (2) Prolonged apnea

(3) Prolonged seizures (many ECT devices now allow monitoring of seizure duration)

(4) Tooth damage

(5) Fractures or dislocations (risks are quite minor with proper use of muscle relaxants)

(6) Posttreatment nausea, headache, and muscle soreness are not uncommon but usually respond to symptomatic treatments.

15.4   DRUG INTERACTIONS

1. **Reserpine** and **chlorpromazine** are contraindicated because of reports of cardiovascular collapse and respiratory depression.

2. **Lithium** can prolong neuromuscular blockade of succinylcholine, as well as contribute to severe posttreatment delirium. In general, lithium should be discontinued before ECT.

3. No specific evidence exists for contraindications for giving ECT to a patient taking **MAOIs** or **tricyclic antidepressants**.

4. Patients receiving **coumadin** may continue on that medication, but they should have PT maintained at less than two times control.

15.5   THE ECT PROCEDURE

Consent

1. Patients must provide signed informed consent.

2. If the patient is not considered competent to provide consent, it may be possible to proceed with consent provided by a spouse or family member. When in doubt about the legality of a substituted decision maker, consult a risk manager.

Pre-ECT assessment

1. The minimal assessment prior to ECT should include:

   a. Psychiatric assessment to document appropriate diagnosis and history

   b. Mental status examination

   c. Physical and neurologic examination to establish presence of any risk factors

   d. Laboratory studies:

      (1) CBC

      (2) Electrolytes (especially for patients taking diuretics or on digitalis)

      (3) Renal function (BUN, creatinine)

      (4) EKG

   e. Consultation from specialists (including pre-ECT anesthesiology) should be obtained if there is concern about cardiac, pulmonary, or other special medical risk factors.

Pre-ECT orders

1. Patient is kept NPO for 8 hours before treatment.

2. Some practitioners use pretreatment atropine (0.4 mg IM) 30 to 40 minutes before ECT to dry secretions and provide anticholinergic blockade of the vagal bradycardias and/or asystole.

a. Other practitioners feel that atropine contributes to confusion and agitation after treatment.

b. Glycopyrrolate 0.2 to 0.4 mg IV (which does not cross the blood-brain barrier) is used as a substitute for atropine by some clinicians.

3. Important medications may be given prior to ECT with small sips of water.

   a. Diuretics may be held, because being NPO already lowered fluid levels.

   b. Rauwolfia alkaloids should have been discontinued several weeks before ECT to avoid potential apnea, hypotension, and cardiac dysrhythmias.

ECT techniques

1. Patients are given a short-acting IV barbiturate (e.g., methohexital 0.75 mg/kg).

2. Once asleep, patients receive a muscle relaxant (usually IV succinylcholine 0.6 mg/kg) to minimize muscle response to the seizure.

3. The anesthetist ventilates the patient, with 100% oxygen, along with oximetry monitoring.

4. Electrodes are applied by the psychiatrist (unilateral or bilateral placement) and an electrical stimulus is administered to induce a seizure.

   a. Parameters involved in stimulus dosing involve wave form, stimulus duration, and intensity.

   b. Nondominant unilateral electrode placement may be associated with less memory impairment than bilateral treatment but also may be ineffective if the stimulus intensity is too low, even if a seizure is induced.

   c. Pulse wave form is always used (with rare exceptions) instead of sine wave form because it can induce the seizure with a lower total amount of electricity; therefore, it is associated with less cognitive impairment.

5. Missed seizures:

   a. If a patient does not have a seizure induced, a higher intensity stimulus is applied (up to 4 times) after a 20 to 40 second delay.

   b. Causes of missed seizures include:

      (1) Excessively high dose of anesthesia

      (2) Concomitant use of anticonvulsants (including benzodiazepines)

      (3) Inadequate oxygenation

      (4) Inadequate hydration.

   c. Seizures can be enhanced with caffeine sodium benzoate (500-2000 mg) IV over 1 minute, given 2 to 3 minutes before anesthesia induction.

6. Prolonged seizures (greater than 180 seconds):

   a. Should be terminated pharmacologically.

7. Seizure duration:

   a. The seizure itself generally lasts 20 seconds (considered a minimum effective seizure duration) to 90 seconds.

8. Treatment conclusion:

   a. The patient begins to wake up within a minute and is monitored until fully alert.

   b. Many patients are able to resume normal activities in several hours.

(1) NOTE: ECT can be done as an outpatient procedure in patients without medical complications.

Number of treatments

1. A full course of ECT is generally six to nine treatments.
   a. Since treatments are usually given every other day, a full course may take 3 weeks.
2. Relapse is an important clinical problem.
   a. Antidepressant medication (re)started after successful ECT may help prevent relapse.
   b. Some patients require episodic continued ECT to maintain remission (maintenance ECT).

References

Alexopoulos GS, Young RC, Abrams RC: ECT in the high risk geriatric patient, *Convulsive Therapy* 5(1):75-87, 1989.

American Psychiatric Association: *The practice of electroconvulsive therapy: recommendations for treatment, training, and privileging,* task force report of the American Psychiatric Association, Washington DC, 1990. The Association.

Burke WJ, Rubin EH, Zorumski CF et al: The safety of ECT is geriatric psychiatry, *J Am Geriatr Soc* 35:516-521, 1987.

Coffey CE, Figiel GS, Weiner RD et al: Caffeine augmentation of ECT, *Am J Psychiatry* 147:579-585, 1990.

Coffey CE, Weiner RD, Djang WT et al: Brain anatomic effects of ECT: a prospective magnetic resonance imaging study, *Arch Gen Psychiatry* 48:1013-1021, 1991.

Coffey CE: *The clinical science of electroconvulsive therapy*, Washington DC 1993, American Psychiatric Association Press.

Drop LJ, Welch CA: Anesthesia for electroconvulsive therapy in patients with major cardiovascular risk factors, *Convulsive Ther* 5:88-101, 1989.

Enns MW, Reiss JP: Electroconvulsive therapy, *Can J Psychiatry* 37:671-678, 1992.

Knos GB, Sung YF, Cooper RC et al: Electroconvulsive therapy induced hemodynamic changes unmask unsuspected coronary artery disease, *J Clin Anesth* 2:37-41, 1990.

Price TRP, McAllister TW: Safety and efficacy of ECT in depressed patients with dementia: a review of clinical experience, *Convulsive Ther* 5:61-74, 1989.

Sackheim HA, Devanand DP, Prudic J: Stimulus intensity, seizure threshold, and seizure duration: impact on the efficacy and safety of electroconvulsive therapy, *Psychiatric Clin N Am* 14:803-843, 1991.

Stoudemire A, Knos G, Gladson M et al: Labetolol in the control of cardiovascular responses to electroconvulsive therapy in high risk depressed medical patients, *J Clin Psychiatry* 53:508-512, 1990.

Weiner RD, Coffee CE: *Electroconvulsive therapy in the medical and neurologic patient.* In Stoudemire A, Fogel BS, eds *Psychiatric care of the medical patient,* New York, 1993, Oxford University Press.

Welch CA, Drop LJ: Cardiovascular effects of ECT, *Convulsive Ther* 5:35-43, 1989.

Personality Disorders

The following are goals of this chapter:
1. To describe the features of the following personality types:
   a. Dependent
   b. Obsessive-compulsive
   c. Histrionic
   d. Paranoid
   e. Narcissistic
   f. Schizoid
   g. Antisocial
   h. Borderline
   i. Long-suffering
   j. Passive-aggressive.
2. For each type, to review the potential impact on medical practice
3. For each type, to review management guidelines.

16.1 INTRODUCTION

Prevalence

1. About 10% of the population has personality disorder.
2. The prevalence appears to be higher in medical and psychiatric populations, increasing to about one third of psychiatric patients seen in general hospital psychiatry to about one half of alcohol and substance abuse patients.

Co-morbidity

1. Both major depression and panic disorder have a high rate of co-morbidity of personality disorder, estimated to occur in about 25% to 50% of patients.
2. Co-morbid personality disorder is likely to be found in patients with somatization, eating disorder, chronic pain, recurrent suicide attempters, and patients with PTSD.

Definition

1. **Personality traits** are enduring patterns of behavior.
   a. Traits are *not* pathologic, nor are they mental disorder diagnoses.
   b. Recognition of traits can be helpful in understanding reaction to stresses, including illness.

2. **Personality disorders** are made up of personality traits, which show a maladaptive persistence and inflexibility.

Recognition

1. The purpose of recognizing personality disorder is to understand a patient's illness behaviors.
   a. For example, substance abuse cannot be treated in most cases without understanding accompanying personality features.
   b. Personality disorders often complicate the doctor-patient relationship.
2. Personality disorders are often overlooked, especially in the elderly.
3. Medical patients with problem behaviors are often labeled as personality disorders, when actually their problem is delirium.
4. Both personality traits and disorders tend to become exaggerated and more fixed with dementia.
5. Because personality tends to be enduring, a change in personality often indicates some underlying brain disorder.
   a. Frontal lobe disease, for example, often presents itself with a "change in personality."
6. Recognition is not easy except when the patient has an exaggerated form of behavior. Information helpful in describing personality may be obtained from:
   a. Observation of dress and interview participation. Is the patient meticulous, disorganized, sociable or guarded, etc.?
   b. Listening to how patients express their needs. Is the presentation overly dramatic or excessively complaining? Does the patient try to convey self-importance?
   c. Asking some specific questions:
      (1) How has the person interacted with significant people?
      (2) Does the patient feel close to or confide in anyone? You could ask, "How is your current problem affecting your closest relationship?" Listen for evidence of manipulation, exploitiveness, or overdependence.
      (3) What illness behavior has the patient shown in the past? You may inquire, "When you were in the hospital (or sick) before, what was that like for you?" Listen for feelings of helplessness or a pattern of conflict with caretakers. Ask about what was helpful or problematic with previous physicians.
      (4) "What sort of interests do you have and what do you do to enjoy yourself?" This question can reveal many personality features including mood, level of social involvement, and degree of maturity.
      (5) If possible, ask friends, family, and staff about what type of person the patient is. You may hear, for example, "Father never really trusts anyone," or "Mother has always been a complainer like this no matter what anyone does for her."
7. Use of Testing:
   a. The Minnesota Multiphasic Personality Inventory (MMPI) is the best known standardized test for evaluating personality. The test is self-administered, takes a few hours to complete, and for a small fee can be rapidly scored by computer. The MMPI can be useful when puzzled by a patient with possible factitious illness or chronic pain.

Specific personality disorders and their management

For personality types in medical management and appropriate interventions, see Table 16.1.

16.2 DEPENDENT PERSONALITY

1. Definition:
   a. The dependent personality often has a strong attachment and involvement with one or a series of medical providers. The dependent person is uncomfortable when separated from the provider and feels helpless.
2. Impact on medical care:
   a. Dependent patients:
      (1) Are concerned about getting enough care
      (2) Make frequent, often unnecessary office visits or phone calls or unwarranted requests for special attention
      (3) Insist on having everything done for them
      (4) May withdraw from treatment if they feel too deprived
      (5) May become angry from perceived inadequate care.
3. Intervention:
   a. Inquire about and help address current stresses.
   b. The physician might say, "I know your recent illness has you very worried and that accounts for your many attempts to call. Let's set up some regular times to talk. Of course, you can call me anytime if you feel there is a real emergency."
   c. Drawing boundaries must be done in a way the patient does not experience as punishment or withdrawal.

16.3 OBSESSIVE COMPULSIVE

1. Definition:
   a. The obsessive compulsive personality is perfectionistic, work-oriented, inflexible, rigid, and has a need to be in control.
2. Impact on medical care:
   a. Obsessive-compulsive patients are
      (1) Indecisive
      (2) Preoccupied with details to the extent that decision-making is often impaired
      (3) Frustrating because of trying to attain more opinions
      (4) Noncompliant as a way of keeping control.
3. Intervention:
   a. These patients are not comfortable simply being told what to do.
   b. Appropriate amounts of information must be provided to allow participation in management decisions.
      (1) Ways to return some control may include asking patients to monitor their own blood pressure or to initiate an exercise program.
   c. Benzodiazepines should be avoided if possible because sedative effects are perceived as a further interference with autonomy.
   d. Be responsive to concerns and complaints, but do not get embroiled in detailed descriptions of insignificant side effects.

Table 16.1 Personality types in medical management

Personality Type	Meaning of Illness	Response	Intervention
Dependent	Expects limitless care and interest	Demanding or withdrawn	Satisfy needs with limit setting
Obsessive-compulsive	Threatens control	Obstinate, uncooperative	Information; give control
Histrionic	Defect, punishment	Seductive	Reassure; avoid collusion
Paranoid	Confirms weakness, expects assault	Blames others, hostility	Clear plans, keep distance
Narcissistic	Threatens grandiosity	Grandiosity, disparaging	Confidence, professional
Schizoid	Anxiety with forced contact	Seclusive, uncooperative	Accept distance
Antisocial	A potential opportunity	Looks for an advantage	Set limits
Borderline	More anxiety	Increased disorganization	Set limits
Long-suffering	Love and care = suffering	Complaining, rejecting	Acknowledge difficulties
Passive-aggressive	Another frustration	Complains, blames	Avoid angry response

16.4 HISTRIONIC

1. Definition:
   a. The histrionic personality is very concerned about being attractive and often behaves in seductive or self-dramatizing fashion.
   b. This patient tends to be self-centered and histrionic and makes an impression as being emotionally shallow, capricious, and coquettish.
   c. The histrionic patient has been described as "hysterical" or the "dramatizing, captivating type."
   d. Their responses are generally out of proportion to the stimulus; for example, they may show signs of intense affection to a casual acquaintance.
2. Impact on medical care:
   a. The histrionic patient:
      (1) Creates problems not so much from the disorders they present, as from the way they present their disorders.
      (2) Provides vague, nonfactual, histories. They pay more attention to impressions and feelings than to logic and detail.
      (3) Often have a certain seductive appeal and may tempt the provider into an inappropriate personal relationship.
      (4) Experiences illness as a threat to attractiveness and leads to efforts to be desirable and be taken care of.
3. Intervention:
   a. Appreciate the threat that illness poses to a person to whom attractiveness is so important.
   b. Understand seductive behavior as a response to distress. Reassure the patient of an interest in taking care of the illness.
   c. Maintain a professional stance despite any temptation to collude with the patient in a flirtatious and misleading way.
   d. If the patient is especially seductive, tell the patient that such behavior makes treatment more difficult and that a special relationship is not necessary for the best medical treatment.

16.5 PARANOID

1. Definition:
   a. Has also been called the "guarded, querulous type" or the "guarded, suspicious" type.
   b. Continually vigilant and suspicious of others' motives.
   c. Guarding against some threat, they continually question reasons for events.
   d. Frequently blame other people for their illness.
   e. Have difficulty establishing close relationships, usually work alone, are cold and unemotional, and never share their thoughts.
   f. Have a litigious strain and easily take offense.
2. Impact on medical care:
   a. The paranoid patient:
      (1) Feels especially vulnerable in a weakened condition.
      (2) Is sensitive to the intrusions of history-taking and the ambiguities of the diagnostic process.
      (3) May suddenly flee (sign out against medical advice) because of suspicion and fear.

3. Intervention:
   a. To counteract fear, provide straightforward explanations of tests and procedures, including history-taking.
   b. Warn about possible side effects; explain changes in treatment, and offer reasons for delays.
      (1) A written treatment plan may help enlist cooperation.
   c. Appealing for tolerance may be helpful.

16.6   NARCISSISTIC

1. Definition:
   a. Works at establishing superiority over others and has been called the "entitled demander."
   b. Talks about accomplishments or claimed accomplishments.
   c. Shows a general attitude of arrogance.
   d. Sensitive to criticism, which may provoke either rage, humiliation, or both.
   e. Difficulty feeling dependent on others, because this would imply others' superiority.
   f. Interpersonal relationships are characterized either by disruption (because of inability to accept criticism) or control.
2. Impact on medical care:
   a. The narcissistic patient:
      (1) Experiences a damaged sense of superiority in accepting the sick role; "sickness" involves being placed in an inferior position.
      (2) Makes disparaging remarks about providers as a defense.
      (3) Astutely notices professional weakness and disqualifies providers as not "good enough."
      (4) Often demands referral to a specialist.
      (5) May provoke an argument or power struggle.
3. Intervention:
   a. Treating the narcissistic patient involves maintaining a balance between two positions:
      (1) If the physician appears too controlling or powerful, the patient cannot tolerate the relative inferiority and weakness;
      (2) If patient feels the physician is not special, he or she feels devalued and worries about getting special treatment.
   b. Convey unassuming self-confidence.

16.7   SCHIZOID

1. Definition:
   a. Keep to themselves, are not intrusive, and are rarely thought to be a problem.
   b. Prefer to live apart from others, and describe themselves as "loners."
   c. Occupations often involve little interpersonal contact.
   d. If, in addition to social isolation there are additional eccentricities in communication or behavior, the schizoid patient may be classified as *schizotypal personality disorder.* Such eccentricities may include:
      (1) Magical thinking (telepathy or clairvoyance)
      (2) Referential thinking ("everything going on pertains to me")

(3) Odd communication (wandering or metaphorical speech).

   e. The schizoid patient does not seem to care about social contacts. If the social isolation is caused by a fear of rejection, with an underlying desire for acceptance, the patient may be an ***avoidant personality.***

2. Impact on medical care:

   a. The schizoid personality:

     (1) Is uncomfortable by forced contact with medical providers.

     (2) Deals with anxiety by withdrawing

       (a) Emotional or physical disorders may go unreported.

     (3) May prompt well-meaning providers to draw them out, increasing the distress.

3. Intervention:

   a. Do not try to resocialize these patients.

   b. Rely on diagnostic thoroughness to avoid overlooking disorders that the patient is reluctant to volunteer.

16.8   ANTISOCIAL

1. Definition:

   a. An extended history of multiple antisocial behaviors beginning before age 15 and continuing into adulthood.

     (1) Before age 15, shows several of the following: truancy, expulsion from school, delinquency, running away from home, persistent lying, vandalism, early sexual behavior, or substance abuse.

     (2) After age 15, shows: arrests, assaults, thefts, debt defaulting, illegal occupations, itinerancy, or poor occupational performance.

   b. Previously classified as "sociopaths" or "psychopaths."

   c. Subgroups include: "emotionally unstable character disorder," and "episodic dyscontrol syndrome" (which may be responsive to lithium and/or diphenylhydantoin [Dilantin], respectively).

2. Impact on medical care:

   a. The anti-social personality:

     (1) Substance abuse leads to lying or stealing drugs.

     (2) Makes persistent, inappropriate demands.

3. Intervention:

   a. To avoid being manipulated, document objective physical signs in managing clinical problems.

   b. Provide straightforward confrontation with a reasonable treatment plan. Provide clear boundaries and consequences.

   c. Be aware that these patients make the physician feel guilty for not providing what they want.

   d. Treatment of substance abuse is best handled by well-organized treatment systems.

16.9   BORDERLINE

1. Definition:

   a. Relationships (including with physicians) are unstable and intense, alternating between intense dependence and rejection.

   b. "Splitting" is common: a very positive relation with one member of the treatment team, and a very negative relation with another. When team members find themselves fighting with each other, suspect a borderline patient is involved.

c. Behavior is impulsive, self-damaging, and usually manipulative, involving areas such as substantive abuse, eating, spending, fights, accidents, wrist-slashing, or overdosing. Often these acts are an attempt to manipulate someone.

d. Affect is inappropriately intense and unstable with outbursts of anger, depression, or anxiety. In between, there may be chronic feelings of emptiness or boredom (often confused with depression) with an absence of self-satisfaction.

e. Identifying disturbance is seen in several areas such as self-image, gender identity, values, and loyalties. These patients often have problems tolerating being alone.

f. Brief psychotic experiences may occur, which most commonly involve paranoia or feelings of unreality.

2. Interaction with the medical system:
   a. Borderline personalities:
      (1) Initially appear attractive and hopeful. It is not unusual to hear, "You are the best doctor I have ever had."
      (2) Inevitably become angry and disappointed.
      (3) Often make suicide attempts. Evaluation and disposition is complex because of the need to assess chronic suicidal behavior (see Chapter 13).
      (4) Make treatment difficult because of self-destructive tendencies and instability.
      (5) Exhibit intensification of pathologic behavior at any suggestion of rejection or termination.

3. Intervention:
   a. Maintain balanced, realistic expectations.
   b. Do not use "borderline" as a pejorative term.
   c. Understanding the stable pattern of instability may put a perspective on a frustrating situation.
   d. Be realistic about what is possible.
   e. Provide clear and consistent boundaries and limits.
   f. Communication should be simple and straightforward.
   g. A single clinician should be in charge of all phases of therapy to avoid splitting.
   h. Avoid being blackmailed by the patient's implicit or stated demands. Instead, reassure the patient that the best possible treatment will be provided.
   i. When behavioral problems emerge, calmly review the therapeutic goals and boundaries of treatment.
      (1) Such limit-setting is definitely necessary but in the short run may lead to new complaints, noncompliance, outright hostility, a suicide attempt, or termination of treatment.
   j. Do not underestimate the significance of going on vacation or transferring the patient to another doctor. Prepare the patient for referral early on and be prepared for reactions, which may be interpreted and contained.
   k. Role of psychotropics:

(1) Antianxiety agents: Benzodiazepines often lead to a dependence problem and occasionally to disinhibition. Buspirone may be a more sensible approach for chronic anxiety.

(2) Antipsychotic agents: These agents play a role episodically during periods of psychotic disorganization. Maintenance is usually not necessary and should be avoided because of risk of tardive dyskinesia.

(3) Mood stabilizers: In patients with mood instability, it can be tempting to provide a trial of lithium or divalproex (Depakote). Both medications require reasonable compliance and monitoring and may be too problematic in difficult borderlines.

(4) Antidepressants: A high rate of depression co-morbidity occurs in borderlines. When present, it should be treated with an antidepressant. The tricyclics tend to have a higher overdose liability and potential lethality; for this reason it may be better to use an SSRI (see Chapter 6).

16.10   LONG-SUFFERING, SELF-SACRIFICING (MASOCHISTIC)

1. Definition:
   a. While not in the DSM system, the long-suffering, self-sacrificing personality type warrants consideration because it frequently presents clinical problems.
   b. Has been called "manipulative help rejecters" and has features of the "pain-prone patient."
   c. Regards sacrifice as the necessary burden of life, and little is done for personal pleasure. Very often, those who are supposed to "benefit" from their sacrifices feel guilty and frustrated.
2. Impact on medical care:
   a. The masochistic personality:
      (1) Never acknowledges anything positive about what is done for them.
3. Intervention:
   a. There may be no way to alter this self-pitying behavior.
   b. Recognize the problem as a lifelong style.
   c. It may be worthwhile to confront the patient in a nonrejecting way by pointing out the negative behavior.
   d. It may help to suggest that recovery is another burden. This allows continued complaining while behaving more positively. One might say, "It seems that in a life of trials, you have one more burden to take on."
   e. Suggest that the patient work on recovery for the sake of someone else (e.g., the children).

16.11   PASSIVE AGGRESSIVE

1. Definition:
   a. Although not a DSM category, this type of patient is also commonly encountered and is characterized by:
      (1) Angry reluctance when having to do things
      (2) Calculated inefficiency (procrastination)

  (3) Innumerable demands which, if met, never satisfy the person
  (4) A pervasive sense of underlying resentment
  (5) Disguised hostility.
2. Impact on medical care:
  a. The passive-aggressive personality:
    (1) Has a need to gain attention and is angry at the lack of attention
    (2) Ends up in a chronic state of dissatisfaction, frustration, and angry resentment about medical care
    (3) Holds a conviction of being treated poorly, reinforced when the doctor loses patience with the constant sense of dissatisfaction
    (4) May seek litigation, and complain to administration and directors about care.
3. Intervention:
  a. Accept that the complaining and dissatisfaction will not change
  b. Provide and document a solid standard of clinical care
  c. Guard against doing too little (i.e., digging in your heels to a dissatisfied customer) or going too far as a defensive measure.

References

Casey PR, Tryer P: Personality disorder and psychiatric illness in general practice, *Br J Psychiatry* 156:261-265, 1990.

Coccaro EF, Kavoussi RJ: Biological and pharmacological aspects of borderline personality disorder, *Hosp and Comm Psychiatry* 42(10):1029-1033, 1991.

Elliot RL: The masochistic patient in consultation-liaison psychiatry, *Gen Hosp Psychiatry* 9:241-250, 1987.

Frances A, Widiger TA: Treating self-defeating personality disorder, *Hosp and Comm Psychiatry* 39(8):819-821, 1988.

Groves JE: Borderline personality disorder, *N Engl J Med* 305:259-262, 1981.

Groves JE: Taking care of the hateful patient, *N Engl J Med* 298:883-887, 1978.

Gutheil TG: Medicolegal pitfalls in the treatment of borderline patients, *Am J Psychiatry* 142:914, 1985.

Kroessler D: Personality disorder in the elderly, *Hosp and Comm Psychiatry* 41(12):1325-1329, 1990.

Reich JH, Green AI: Effect of personality disorders on outcome of treatment, *J Nerv Ment Dis* 179:74-82, 1991.

Shea MT, Pilkonis PA, Beckham E et al: Personality disorders and treatment outcome in the NIMH treatment of depression collaborative research program, *Am J Psychiatry* 147:711-718, 1990.

Siever LJ, Davis KL: A psychobiologic perspective on the personality disorders, *Am J Psychiatry* 148(12): 1647-1658, 1991.

Stoudemire A, Thompson T: The borderline personality in the medical setting, *Ann Intern Med* 96: 76-79, 1982.

Behavioral Problems in Alzheimer's Disease: Psychopharmacologic Management

17

The following are goals of this chapter:
1. To review the prevalence of behavior problems associated with Alzheimer's disease.
2. To review etiologic factors that contribute to these problems.
3. To review management of each problem with some emphasis on appropriate use of psychopharmacology.

17.1 INTRODUCTION

1. Alzheimer's disease (AD) is an increasingly common national health problem. It is estimated to be present in about 3% of those age 65 to 74; 19% of those 75 to 84; and 47% in those over age 85.
2. Chapter 3 provides an overview of the differential diagnoses of dementia.
3. Chapter 4 provides an overview of the medical evaluation of dementia.
4. This chapter focuses more specifically on AD, with an emphasis on the psychopharmacologic management of its behavioral symptoms (see Table 17.1).

17.2 BEHAVIORAL SYMPTOMS

1. **Psychotic symptoms:**
   a. Delusions (occur in 30% to 40%)
      (1) People are stealing things
      (2) Interacted with a dead person
      (3) Family are imposters
      (4) Spouse is unfaithful
      (5) Somatic symptoms
      (6) Abandonment.
   b. Hallucinations (occur in 15% to 30%)
      (1) Seeing/hearing a dead person
      (2) Seeing/hearing an unfamiliar person
      (3) Seeing animals
      (4) Seeing intruders
      (5) Hearing voices
      (6) Smelling something.
   c. Neuroleptics are appropriate to use to treat psychotic symptoms accompanying AD.

Table 17.1   Prevalence of behavioral symptoms in Alzheimer's disease

Symptom	Prevalence
Delusions	30%
Hallucinations	25%
Depression	40%
Paranoia	35%
Aggression	25%
Sleep disturbances	20%
Wandering	18%
Inappropriate behavior	18%

Table 17.2   Use of neuroleptics for psychotic symptoms of Alzheimer's disease

Side Effects	Haldol	Mellaril	Clozapine
Extrapyramidal	++++	+	0
Sedation	+	+++	++
Neuroleptic malignant syndrome	+	+	+/−
Orthostasis	0	+++	++
Anticholinergic	0	+++	++

(1) Chapter 11 reviews the detailed use of neuroleptics. Table 17.2 summarizes issues involved with their use with AD patients.

(2) Thioriadazine is commonly used because of low potential for extrapyramidal side effects (EPS).

    (a) Sedation and anticholinergic side effects are limiting factors.

    (b) Patients can generally tolerate total daily doses of less than 100 mg.

(3) The high potency neuroleptics are generally too likely to cause EPS.

(4) The atypical neuroleptic clozapine may have a role in psychotic AD patients because it does not cause EPS.

2. **Depression:**

  a. Significant symptoms in 5% to 50%

    (1) Tearful episodes

    (2) Poor appetite

    (3) Mood fluctuations

    (4) Withdrawn behavior

    (5) Major depression (in up to 20%)

    (6) Drug-induced depressive syndromes (see Box 5.3).

  b. Use of antidepressants

    (1) Chapter 6 provides detailed information on the use of antidepressants.

    (2) Table 17.3 summarizes issues pertinent to their use in AD.

Table 17.3 Issues in the use of antidepressants in patients with Alzheimer's disease

Side Effect	Trigyclics	SSRIs/SNRI	Nefazodone
Cardiac	+++	0	0
Anticholinergic	+++	0	0
Sedation	+/+++	+	+
Activation	+	++	0
Orthostasis	++	0	0
GI	+	++	+

3. **Anxiety** (5% to 35%)
   a. Etiology:
      (1) Anxiety secondary to some medical problem is the most common cause (see Boxes 8.2 and 8.3)
      (2) Fearful anticipation is common
      (3) Longstanding anxiety (e.g., generalized anxiety disorder) continues into old age
      (4) Anxiety symptoms (panic or obsessive-compulsive) may emerge during episode of depression.
   b. Treatment:
      (1) Chapter 9 provides details on use of antianxiety agents
      (2) Table 9.3 provides a summary of issues involving benzodiazepiones vs azapirones
         (a) In general, azapirones lack the sedative side effects of benzodiazepines and are preferable for generalized anxiety.
4. **Sleep disturbance:** (see Chapter 10)
   a. Common causes in the elderly:
      (1) Caffeine use should always be considered
      (2) Environmental causes should be eliminated
         (a) Noise
         (b) Lights
      (3) Nocturnal myoclonus (about 15% prevalence)
      (4) Restless legs (about 5% prevalence)
      (5) Sleep apnea (affects 25% to 70%)
      (6) Sedative-hypnotic dependence.
   b. Treatment:
      (1) See Chapter 10.
   c. Omnibus Budget Reconciliation Act (OBRA) regulation on the use of hypnotics:
      (1) Use of hypnotics in nursing homes requires:
         (a) Documenting a differential diagnosis
         (b) Documenting that the medication improved function
         (c) Medication cannot be used for more than 10 days without documenting an attempt to reduce it.
5. **Eating disturbances:**
   a. Inadequate nutrition is found in 20% to 60% of older patients in nursing homes.
   b. A serum albumin of less than 3.5 g/dl indicates protein depletion.

    c. Drug-induced anorexia:
        (1) Digoxin
        (2) NSAIDs
        (3) Theophylline
        (4) HCTZ.
    d. Drug-induced hypogeusia (loss of taste):
        (1) Allopurinal
        (2) Clindamycin
        (3) Antihistamines.
    e. Drug-induced vitamin/mineral deficiencies:
        (1) Diuretics . . . . Zinc
        (2) Salicylates C
        (3) Anticonvulsants . . . . D, folate
        (4) Tetracycline . . . . calcium, iron
        (5) Mineral oil . . . . A, D
    f. Causes of weight loss in ambulatory geriatric patients:
        (1) Unknown: about 25%
        (2) Depression: about 20%
        (3) Cancer: about 15%
        (4) Other GI disease: about 10%
        (5) Hyperthyroidism: about 10%
        (6) Secondary to medications: about 10%
        (7) Neurologic abnormalities (AD;CVA): about 7%
        (8) Other (e.g., TB, poor eating habits): about 5%.

6. Incontinence

    a. About 40% to 60% of older patients in hospitals and nursing homes and 25% in the community have incontinence.
    b. Drug-induced overflow incontinence:
        (1) Anticholinergics
        (2) Smooth muscle relaxants
           (a) Nifedipine
        (3) Alpha-adrenergic agonists
           (a) Phenylpropanolamine.
    c. Drug-induced urge incontinence:
        (1) Diuretics
        (2) Lithium
        (3) Tamoxifen.
    d. Drug-induced oversedation:
        (1) Benzodiazepines
        (2) Neuroleptics.
    e. Nondrug differential diagnosis of incontinence is summarized by the well-known mnemonic DIAPERS:

D	*D*elirium and *D*ementia
I	*I*nfections
A	*A*trophic vaginitis, urethritis, atonic bladder
P	*P*sychiatric disorders (e.g., depression), prostatism
E	*E*ndrocrine abnormalities (e.g., diabetes, hypercalcemia, hypothyroidism)
R	*R*estricted mobility
S	*S*tool impaction (causes up to 10% of incontinence in nursing homes)

7. **Mobility impairment:**
   a. A large number of medical conditions contribute to mobility impairment including:
      (1) Neurologic diseases:
         (a) CVA
         (b) Parkinson's
         (c) Normal pressure hydrocephalus
         (d) Neuropathy
         (e) Subdural hematomas
         (f) B_{12} deficiency
         (g) Cervical spondylosis
      (2) Unsuspected fractures
      (3) Arthritis
      (4) Delirium and dementia
      (5) Depression
      (6) Fearfulness.
   b. Drug-induced causes of mobility impairment:
      (1) Dopamine blockers
         (a) Neuroleptics
         (b) Metoclopramide
      (2) Hypotension
         (a) Diuretics
         (b) Vasodilators
         (c) Tricyclics
      (3) Muscle weakness
         (a) Steroids.
8. **Cognitive impairment**
   a. Drug-induced:
      (1) Anticholinergics
      (2) Bendzodiazepines
      (3) Digoxin
      (4) Dopamine agonists
      (5) H2 blockers
      (6) Lidocaine
      (7) Narcotics
      (8) Phenytoin
      (9) Salicylates
      (10) Theophylline.
   b. Other causes:
      (1) Impaired sensory organs
         (a) Vision
         (b) Hearing
      (2) See Boxes 3.1 and 3.2 for medical and medication causes.
   c. Drugs to treat cognitive impairment:
      (1) *Antidepressants* help with "pseudo-dementia" (cognitive impairment secondary to depression).
      (2) *Cholinergic agents* (Rationale: to counteract decreased cholinergic function):
         (a) Studies have looked at lecithin, physotigmine, bethanecol without success.
         (b) Tacrine (a cholinesterase inhibitor).

(*i*) Some evidence for slowing decline in cognitive function in AD patients with mild to moderate disease.

(*ii*) Nausea and vomiting are most common side effects: LFTs need to be monitored. Taking the drug with meals can reduce these side effects. ALT elevations return to normal after drug discontinuation. If ALT rises to greater than three times normal, the drug dose should be reduced until levels fall within normal limits. Patients can then be resumed on titration with continued monitoring.

(*iii*) Tacrine can prolong succinylcholine effects and therefore should be discontinued before ECT.

(*iv*) Patients at risk for ulcers should be watched closely for active or occult GI bleeding, because tacrine increases gastric acid secretion.

(*v*) Tacrine can increase theophylline levels.

(*vi*) Initial dose is 10 mg qid, maintained for 6 weeks, while monitoring ALT levels weekly. If tolerated, doses can be increased by 40 mg/day at 6-week intervals up to 160 mg/day.

(3) *MAOIs:* Pilot data indicate potential benefit from L-deprenyl (a selective type-B MAOI).

(4) *Opioid antagonists* (Rationale: opioid agonists impair learning and conditioned avoidance behavior):

    (a) Studies of naloxone and naltrexone have not been productive.

(5) *Ergoloid mesylates* (Hydergine)

    (a) Hydergine (a mixture of four ergot alkaloids) is FDA approved for the treatment of cognitive decline

    (b) Acts as a vasodilator (alpha-adrenergic antagonist), though this may have nothing to do with its effects

    (c) May enhance cerebral metabolism

    (d) Partial agonist for dopamine and serotonin

    (e) Best results with higher doses (e.g., up to 4.5 mg/day) over long durations (months).

(6) *Vasopressin* (Rationale: improves memory and learning in animal models)

    (a) No demonstrated efficacy in humans to date.

(7) *Lithium* (Rationale: increased RBC choline and may increase neuronal choline)

    (a) No efficacy data.

9. **Physical agitation**

a. *Symptoms:*

    (1) Physical outbursts

    (2) Verbal outbursts

    (3) Motor restlessness

    (4) Threatening behaviors

    (5) Wandering

    (6) Purposeless activity

    (7) Inappropriate activity.

b. *Drugs that produce agitation* (see Box 17.1).

c. *Other common medical causes of agitation:*

Box 17.1   Drugs that Produce Agitation

Stimulants	Sedatives	Anticholinergics
Caffeine	Alcohol	Trihexyphenidyl
Phenylpropanolamine	Barbiturates	(Artane)
Pseudophedrine	Benzodiazepines	Diphenhydramine
Phenylpropanolamine	Narcotics	(Benadryl)
		Benztropine
		mesylate
		(Cogentin)
		Oxybutynin
		(Ditropan)
		Propantheline
		(pro-Banthine)
		Tricyclics

Dopaminergics	Miscellaneous
Bromocriptine	Digoxin
Neuroleptics	H2 antagonists
Metoclopramide	Phenytoin
Levodopa-carbidopa (Sinemet)	Salicylates
Amantadine (Symmetrel)	Steroids

(1) Stroke
(2) Delirium
(3) Traumatic brain injury
(4) Parkinson's disease
(5) Brain tumors
(6) Infectious disease
(7) Metabolic disorders: thyroid disorders, hypoglycemia, vitamin deficiencies.

d. *Drugs used to treat agitation* (see Table 17.4).
   (1) Neuroleptics (see Table 17.2)
      (a) Limiting factors are EPS, sedation, tardive dyskinesia.
   (2) Benzodiazepines (see Table 9.3)
      (a) Limiting factors are sedation and cognitive impairment.
   (3) Beta-blockers:
      (a) May be helpful in some aggressive AD patients.
      (b) May be helpful in reducing episodic aggression after head injury.
      (c) Propranolol is often used in high doses, such as over 300 mg/day.
         (*i*) Start on low doses (such as 20 mg tid PO) and gradually increase while monitoring pulse and blood pressure.
         (*ii*) Problematic in the elderly because of the cardiovascular side effects.
         (*iii*) Diabetes, asthma are also contraindications.

Table 17.4   Drugs to treat agitation in dementia

Drug Group	Issues in use
Neuroleptics	Extrapyramidal side effects
Benzodiazepines	Sedation Cognitive impairment Psychomotor impairment
Beta-blockers	Hypotension Bradycardia
Buspirone	Slow onset
Trazodone	Sedation
Carbamazepine	Nausea
Valproate	Sedation Dizziness Tremor
Lithium	Tremor GI upset Confusion

(4) Serotonin agonists
    (a) Buspirone:
        (i) There is increasing data that buspirone may be effective.
        (ii) Start at 5 mg tid PO. If the patient becomes more anxious at this dose, halve the amount. If no response after 3 weeks, titrate up to 20 mg tid.
        (iii) Side effects are nausea, nonvertiginous lightheadedness, and dull headache.
        (iv) The effect may appear within days but usually takes several weeks.
    (b) Trazodone:
        (i) Can have an acute effect on calming agitated AD patient.
        (ii) Dose varies between 25-100 mg, depending on the size and physical status of the patient.
        (iii) In addition to acute sedation, maintenance over 3 to 6 weeks may decrease agitation, using doses of 25-50 mg tid.
        (iv) Limiting factors are sedation and orthostasis.
    (c) Selective serotonin re-uptake inhibitors (SSRIs) (e.g., fluoxetine, paroxetine, sertraline):
        (i) There is little evidence that these drugs can decrease agitation; however, insofar as they augment serotonin

Table 17.5   Issues in use of anticonvulsants

Anticonvulsant	Monitor	Side Effects
Carbamazepine	CBC LFTs Drug level	Nausea Dizziness Ataxia Sedation Pancreatitis Cardiac
Valproate	LFTs Drug level	Nausea Tremor Ataxia

function, they may be a possible alternative in usual antidepressant doses.

(5) Anticonvulsants: carbamazepine and valproic acid (see Chapter 7 and Table 17.5):

   (a) There is some evidence of effectiveness, usually in patients with possible underlying seizure problems (previous head injury, epileptic-like episodic behaviors; history of stroke; history of seizures).

   (b) Start at low doses and gradually build up to usual anticonvulsant plasma levels.

   (c) Carbamazepine:

      (i) Limiting factors are nausea, drops in WBC, and sedation (also see Chapter 7).

   (d) Valproic acid:

      (i) Limiting factors are nausea and occasional increases in LFTs (also see Chapter 7).

(6) Lithium:

   (a) There are case reports of lithium being helpful in decreasing agitation in AD.

   (b) Consider for patient with mood swings or history of mood swings, even in absence of formal bipolar diagnosis.

   (c) Issues in its use include:

      (i) Side effects:

         (a) Tremor

         (b) GI upset

         (c) Diabetes insipidus

         (d) Confusion

         (e) Hypothyroidism.

      (ii) Monitor levels carefully:

         (a) Should not generally exceed 1.0 mEq/l

         (b) Effects may occur at lower levels.

      (iii) Lithium is cleared by the kidneys; therefore, be cautious with renal impairment.

        (*iv*) Initial doses generally 150 mg tid. (See Chapter 7 for details on use of lithium.)

e. *Non-medication approaches to reducing agitation in AD patients:*
    (1) Relaxation: engage patients in regular practice of relaxation.
    (2) Try to determine triggers for agitation (e.g., a particular person, situation, or setting).
    (3) Use adequate staffing to allow for pacing or other temporary restlessness.
        (a) This may avert escalation reactions to being confronted or restrained.

f. *OBRA regulations*
    (1) Congress enacted legislation to improve the quality of care in nursing homes as part of the 1987 Omnibus Budget Reconciliation Act (OBRA).
    (2) These guidelines mandate patient assessment and limit psychotropic drug use involving benzodiazepines, neuroleptics, and sedative-hypnotics.
    (3) Guidelines for **short-acting benzodiazepines** (e.g., lorazepam, oxazepam, alprazolam). If you intend to prescribe one of these drugs, you must document:
        (a) Differential diagnosis of symptoms (e.g., consider organic causes, depression).
        (b) Number and nature of symptoms being treated (if such symptoms are considered secondary to dementia).
        (c) That the medication results in some functional improvement.
        (d) A gradual reduction of medication after every 4 months, until such reduction attempts have failed twice within a year.
    (4) Guidelines for the use of **long-acting benzodiazepines** (e.g., diazepam, chlordiazepoxide, clonazepam, clorazepate). If you plan to use one of these medications, you must document:
        (a) Failure with a short-acting benzodiazepine.
        (b) A differential diagnosis.
        (c) Maintenance or improvement in function.
        (d) A gradual reduction after every 4 months until such attempts have failed twice within a year.
    (5) Guidelines for the use of **hypnotics** (e.g., flurazepam, estazolam, triazolam, temazepam). If you intend to prescribe a sleeping pill, you must document:
        (a) A differential diagnosis.
        (b) That the medication results in improved function.
        (c) An attempt to reduce the dose if you use the medication for more than 10 days.
    (6) Guidelines for the use of **neuroleptics:**
        (a) OBRA guidelines do not apply to use of neuroleptics for psychiatric diagnoses, such as schizophrenia or organic psychotic disorders.
        (b) You cannot prescribe neuroleptics for wandering, anxiety, unsociability, uncooperativeness, poor self-care, and agitated behaviors that are not a danger.

(c) The guidelines are meant to apply to behavioral control of agitated behavior associated with dementia.
(d) If you use a neuroleptic in those circumstances, you must document:
- (*i*) Number and content of episodes.
- (*ii*) Failure of other means of control.
- (*iii*) That the symptoms present some danger or functional loss or are of psychotic nature.
- (*iv*) Reassessment of the orders and treatment plan if prn neuroleptics are used more than twice in a 7-day period.
- (*v*) Side effects, including:
  - (*a*) Tardive dyskinesia
  - (*b*) Orthostasis
  - (*c*) Akathisia
  - (*d*) Parkinson's symptoms
  - (*e*) Cognitive/behavioral impairment.
- (*vi*) Gradual dose reduction unless you document two failed attempts to taper within a 1-year period.
- (*vii*) Reasons for exceeding OBRA dose guidelines (examples of dose guidelines include: haldol 4 mg/day; mellaril 75 mg/day; trilafon 8 mg/day):
  - (a) Prescribing outside the guidelines is allowed as long as there is good clinical reasoning documented. Simply listing a symptom is not enough.

References

Arrigo A, Casale R, Giorgi I et al: Effects of intravenous high dose co-dergocrine mesylate (Hydergine) in elderly patients with severe multiinfarct dementia: a double-blind, placebo controlled trial, *Curr Med Res Opin* 11: 491-500, 1989.

Barnes RE, Veith R, Okimoto J, et al: Efficacy of antipsychotic medications in behaviorally disturbed demented patients, *Am J Psychiatry* 139: 1170-1174, 1982.

Colenda CC: Buspirone in treatment of agitated demented patient, *Lancet* 1:1169, 1988.

Davis KL, Thal LJ, Gamzu ER et al: A double-blind, placebo-controlled multicenter study of tacrine for Alzheimer's disease, *N Engl J Med* 327:1253-1259, 1992.

Evans DA, Funkenstein H, Albert MS et al: Prevalence of Alzheimer's disease in a community population of older persons, *JAMA* 262(18):2551-2556, 1989.

Gleason R, Schneider LS: Carbamazepine treatment of agitation in Alzheimer's outpatients refractory to neuroleptics, *J Clin Psychiatry* 51:115-118, 1990.

Goldberg RJ: The use of buspirone in geriatric patients, *J Clin Psychiatry.* In press.

Greenwald BS, Marin DB, Silverman SM: Serotoninergic treatment of screaming and banging in dementia, *Lancet* 2: 1464-1465, 1986.

Helms PM: Efficacy of antipsychotics in the treatment of the behavioral complications of dementia: a review of the literature, *J Am Geriatr Soc* 33: 206-209, 1985.

Leibovici A, Tariot PN: Carbamazepine treatment of agitation associated with dementia, *J Geriatr Psychiatr Neurol* 1: 110-112, 1988.

Maletta GJ: Pharmacologic treatment and management of the aggressive demented patient, *Psychiatr Annals* 20: 446-455, 1990.

Mendez MF, Martin RJ, Smyth KA et al: Psychiatric symptoms associated with alzheimer's disease, *J Neuropsychiatry* 2: 28-33, 1990.

Nicholson CD: Pharmacology of nootropics and metabolically active compounds in relation to their use in dementia, *Psychopharmacology* 101:147-159, 1990.

Pinner E, Rich C: Effects of trazodone on aggressive behavior in seven patients with organic mental disorders, *Am J Psychiatry* 145: 1295-1296, 1988.

Reifler BV, Tevi L, Raskind M et al: Double-blind trail of imipramine in Alzheimer's disease patients with and without depression, *Am J Psychiatry* 146: 45-49, 1989.

Schneider L, Pollock V, Lyness S: A meta analysis of controlled trials of neuroleptic treatment in dementia, *J Am Geriatr Soc* 38:553-563, 1990.

Schneider LS, Sobin PB: Non-neuroleptic medications in the management of agitation in Alzheimer's disease and other dementia: a selective review, *Int J Geriatr Psychiatry* 6: 691-708, 1991.

Skoog, I, Nilsson L, Palmertz B et al. A population-based study of dementia in 85 year olds, *New Engl J Med* 328:153-8, 1993.

Tiller JWG, Dakis JA, Shaw JM: Short-term buspirone treatment in disinhibition with dementia, *Lancet* 2: 510, 1988.

Weiler PG, Mungas D, Bernick C: Propranolol for the control of disruptive behavior in senile dementia, *J Geriatr Psychiatr Neurol* 1: 226-230, 1988.

Yudofsky SC, Silver JM, Hales RE: Pharmacologic management of aggression in the elderly, *J Clin Psychiatry* 51(10) suppl: 22-28, 1990.

Eating Disorders and Nicotine Dependence

18

The following are goals of this chapter:
1. To define anorexia nervosa and bulimia nervosa.
   a. To review the laboratory assessment and differential diagnosis of these two disorders.
2. To review treatment approaches to these two disorders.
3. To review the pharmacology of nicotine.
4. To review the relationship of smoking to psychiatric disorders.
5. To review the treatment of nicotine dependence.

18.1 ANOREXIA NERVOSA

1. Definition:
   a. Refusal to maintain minimal normal body weight
   b. Intense fear of gaining weight or becoming fat, even though underweight
   c. Disturbance in self-perception of weight, body size, or shape
   d. In females, absence of at least three consecutive menstrual cycles.
2. Epidemiology:
   a. 95% of cases are women
   b. Most cases develop during adolescence.
3. Etiology:
   a. There are many theories, but no known etiology.
4. Recognition:
   a. Patients use two methods to control weight:
      (1) Restrictive approach uses low calorie intake and exercise.
      (2) Bulimic approach alternates binging and starvation (along with purging and laxative and/or diuretic abuse). Purging may occur in up to 70%.
      (3) 50% of patients also meet criteria for bulimia (see next section), raising the term *bulimarexia* or *bulimia nervosa*.
   b. Symptoms:
      (1) Extreme fear of gaining weight
      (2) Obsessive-compulsive behaviors are common
      (3) Poor social adjustment with some areas of high functioning (e.g., intellectual)
      (4) Odd food habits (hoarding, hiding)

      (5) Hyperactivity is common with compulsive, extreme training programs

      (6) Mood and sleep disturbances are not uncommon.

  c. Physical signs:

      (1) Emaciated physical appearance

      (2) Dry yellowish skin, along with some hair loss

      (3) Loss of tooth enamel and scarring of the back of the hand from inducing vomiting

      (4) Neuropathies and seizures may be an outcome

      (5) Cardiomyopathy (especially with concurrent use of ipecac), showing CK abnormalities along with nonspecific ECG changes.

  d. Laboratory abnormalities (see Box 18.1).

  e. Medical disorders (see Box 18.2).

5. Differential diagnosis:

  a. Normal thinness. Anorexia nervosa is a distinct disorder and is not simply the low end of the normal weight distribution.

  b. Medical disorders:

      (1) Hypothalamic disease (growth hormone deficiency may result in diminished appetite)

      (2) Diabetes mellitus (there seems to be an increased statistical association)

      (3) Addison's disease (cortisol insufficiency may be associated with early satiety)

      (4) GI disorders

         (a) Malabsorption

         (b) Inflammatory bowel disease

      (5) Genetic disorders

         (a) Turner's syndrome

         (b) Gaucher's disease.

Box 18.1   Screening Laboratory Evaluation of Eating Disorder Patients

1. CBC
2. Glucose
3. Electrolytes
4. BUN, creatinine
5. Calcium
6. Magnesium
7. Phosphate
8. Serum osmolality
9. Liver function
10. Amylase
11. Urinalysis (with electrolytes)
12. ECG
13. Bone density
14. Thyroid function

Box 18.2   Medical Disorders in Patients with Eating Disorders

Hematologic

Anemia (low iron, B_{12}, folate)
Leukopenia
Thrombocytopenia
Coagulopathies

Gastrointestinal

Pancreatitis
Nonspecific LFT changes
Steatohepatitis

Endocrine

Hypothalamic amenorrhea
Euthyroid sick syndrome
Osteoporosis
Abnormal LH and FSH levels

Renal/electrolytes

Hyponatremia
Hypokalemia
Diabetes insipidus
Metabolic acidosis
Metabolic alkalosis
Azotemia

Cardiovascular

Nonspecific ECG changes
Bradycardia
Arrhythmias

---

  c. Psychiatric disorders
    (1) Major depression with poor appetite
    (2) Obsessive compulsive disorder with focus on food
    (3) Psychotic disorder (e.g., schizophrenia or paranoid disorder, where food is feared as part of a delusion)
    (4) Phobic disorders where food is avoided
      (a) Swallowing phobia occurring after a choking episode
      (b) Food fears after oral surgery
      (c) Fear of vomiting in public (as a component of an agoraphobia disorder)
    (5) Tourette's disease (may have accompanying anorexia).
6. Treatment:
  a. Hospitalization:
    (1) This is one of the most important decisions a clinician has to make, especially because the consequences of this disease can be fatal.
    (2) Criteria for hospitalization include:
      (a) Behavior that is dangerous to the person's health, that is out of control, and that cannot be managed as an outpatient (e.g., suicidal behavior, severe depression, psychotic decompensation) (binging-purging out of control)
      (b) Weight loss of >30% over 6 months
      (c) Hypokalemia <3 meq/L or other electrolytes disturbance not corrected by oral supplementation
      (d) ECG changes (especially arrhythmias)

Box 18.3   Example of Refeeding Protocol

1. Contract with patient for a weight goal. Goal should not exceed 1-2 pounds in the first week and 3-5 pounds afterwards.
2. Begin 800-1200 kcal in frequent small meals (to avoid bloating sensation).
3. Increase calories to 1500-3000 depending on height and age (consult with nutrition service).
4. Add, as necessary, vitamin and mineral supplements.
5. In severe cases, TPN must be used (starting at 800-1200 kcal/day).

       (e) Severe hypothermia or dehydration
       (f) Laxative/diuretic abuse that cannot be controlled as outpatient.
    (3) Interventions in the hospital include:
       (a) Identification and management of medical problems.
          (*i*) Monitoring vital signs, ECG, hydration, electrolytes.
       (b) Bed rest with supervised feedings using constant observation.
       (c) Refeeding protocol (see Box 18.3):
       (d) Complications of refeeding:
          (*i*) Edema (use support stockings, leg elevation, salt restriction)
          (*ii*) Abdominal distention and bloating. Use reassurance. May also try metoclopramide 5 mg PO bid
          (*iii*) Congestive heart failure: patient may require diuretics and careful medical management.
       (e) Setting weight goals and patient involvement in a program with positive behavior reinforcements.
       (f) Forced feeding should be used in patients with medically serious status.
       (g) Medications:
          (*i*) Cyproheptadine may stimulate appetite (initial doses of 8 mg/day PO may be increased to 32 mg/day)
          (*ii*) Antidepressants should be used if depressive symptoms exist
          (*iii*) Neuroleptics in low doses may be tried for those patients whose preoccupations seem to be of psychotic proportions
          (*iv*) Short-term anxiolytics may help some very anxious patients if given before mealtime
          (*v*) There have been some case reports of the use of naltrexone (50-150 mg/day) to assist in weight gain.
       (h) Family intervention is almost always necessary because of the pathological family dynamics that usually develop around the eating problems.

7. Prognosis:
   a. This disease may have a mortality rate of 5% to 20%.
   b. Most patients will improve with treatment, though the illness may be relapsing.
   c. Favorable prognostic indicators:
      (1) Earlier age at onset
      (2) Return of menses
      (3) Good premorbid school/work history.
   d. Negative prognostic indicators
      (1) Recurrent illness
      (2) Hospitalizations
      (3) Male
      (4) Co-morbidity of anorexia
      (5) Co-morbid psychopathology
      (6) Family pathology.

18.2 BULIMIA NERVOSA

1. Definition:
   a. Recurrent episodes of binge eating (several/week for several months)
   b. Feelings of lack of control over binging behavior
   c. Regular episodes of self-induced vomiting, use of laxatives or diuretics, fasting, or vigorous exercise to prevent weight gain
   d. Persistent over-concern with body shape and weight.
2. Epidemiology:
   a. Some binge eating is extremely common in adolescents (about 90% of cases are women).
   b. Some bulimic features are present in 5% to 25% of the young adult population.
3. Clinical recognition:
   a. Uncontrollable binging episodes.
      (1) Foods consumed are usually high in carbohydrates and fats and may exceed 5000 kcal per episode.
   b. Food buying and binging are often done in secret and may occur anytime.
   c. Binging usually alternates with purging, terminating a binging episode with forced vomiting. Urine screens for laxative and diuretics may be helpful. Diuretics generally also increase urine electrolytes.
   d. Co-morbid emotional difficulties are common:
      (1) Feelings of guilt
      (2) Concurrent depression (in up to 70%)
      (3) Other impulse control problems may co-occur, including substance abuse (involving 30% to 40%) in males
      (4) Sexual dysfunction is also common
      (5) Obsessive-compulsive symptoms in up to 30%
      (6) Panic disorder in up to 20%.
   e. Medical complications (seen in up to 40%):
      (1) Electrolyte imbalances
      (2) Metabolic acidosis
      (3) Increased BUN
      (4) Esophageal tears

    (5) Decalcification of teeth

    (6) Parotid swelling, with increased amylase (usually elevated in binge-purge patients and not in restrictive anorectics). Serial amylase level may help detect covert purging

    (7) Altered thyroid and cortisol function.

4. Differential diagnosis:

    a. Anorexia nervosa (see last section)

    b. Major depression

    c. Bipolar affective disorder

    d. Adjustment disorder (bulimia as a reaction to a stress)

    e. Klein-Levin syndrome: hypersomnia and hyperphagia

    f. Kluver-Bucy syndrome: visual agnosia, hypersexuality, hyperphagia

    g. Compulsive hyperphagia has been reported in patients with seasonal affective disorder.

5. Medical evaluation:

    a. Electrolytes

    b. Glucose

    c. Thyroid function tests

    d. Neuroimaging of pituitary

    e. CBC

    f. ECG.

6. Treatment:

    a. Medical stabilization is the first priority

    b. Behavioral therapy (and nutrition education) with scheduling and positive reward mechanisms

    c. Group therapy with other bulimics may be helpful

    d. Family therapy is usually needed to assist the family in how best to interact with the patient.

    e. Medication

        (1) A trial of anticonvulsants (phenytoin or carbamazepine in usual anticonvulsant doses) may help a subgroup of patients with abnormal EEGs even without a formal seizure disorder. Plasma levels should be monitored carefully.

        (2) Use of tricyclic antidepressants (after correction of underlying electrolyte and ECG abnormalities) may be helpful to treat co-morbid affective symptoms but have also been reported as helpful even in patients without identifiable depressive symptoms.

        (3) Some preliminary studies indicate possible beneficial effects of naltrexone in reduced binging and purging.

7. Prognosis:

    a. Up to 50% recover, about 25% remain unimproved in follow-up. Mortality may be 5% to 15%.

    b. Treatment of psychiatric co-morbidity is important to outcome.

18.3   NICOTINE DEPENDENCE

Prevalence and Significance

1. Cigarette smoking remains the most important preventable contributor to death, disability, and unnecessary health expenditures in the U.S.

2. Over 50 million adult Americans still smoke (28%).

Nicotine Pharmacology

1. Nicotine from tobacco smoke is rapidly absorbed and achieves maximum brain concentrations within 1 minute.
2. Since tolerance develops, people have to smoke more to obtain the desired effects of nicotine.
3. Effects of nicotine:
   a. Skeletal muscle relaxation
   b. Brain activation with increases in serotonin, endogenous opioids, catecholamines, and vasopressin
   c. Stimulates the brain's "reward center" through effects on dopamine pathways in the mesolimbic system
   d. Increases attention, memory, and learning
   e. Anxiolytic
   f. Decreases negative affect
   g. High doses can produce cocaine-like stimulation
   h. Suppresses appetite.
4. Addictive properties of nicotine:
   a. Nicotine produces physiologic changes, which account for tolerance, physical dependence, and withdrawal.
   b. Nicotine withdrawal syndrome:
      (1) Timing: appears within 2 hours of cessation of smoking and peaks within 24 to 48 hours. The syndrome may last days to weeks, with great individual variation.
      (2) Symptoms:
         (a) Nicotine craving
         (b) Irritability, anger
         (c) Anxiety
         (d) Difficulty concentrating
         (e) Restlessness
         (f) Decreased heart rate
         (g) Increased appetite/weight gain (smoking cessation is associated with an average weight gain of about 6 pounds)
         (h) Depression.
5. Drug interactions:
   a. Nicotine accelerates the metabolism of many drugs, including many (but not all) tricyclic antidepressants, benzodiazepines, and possibly some neuroleptics.

Smoking and Psychiatric Disorders

1. Psychiatric patients are more likely than the general population to smoke
2. Smokers have higher levels of depression
3. Patients with depression who smoke are less likely to quit
4. Depression may be a strong predictor of relapse in people who try to quit smoking
5. Substance abusers have a high rate of smoking
6. Alcohol use is associated with more difficulty in trying to quit smoking.

18.4 TREATMENT OF NICOTINE DEPENDENCE

The best treatment programs combine pharmacologic with cognitive-behavioral and social therapies.

Box 18.4   Drugs Whose Metabolism is Accelerated by Nicotine

Caffeine
Clomipramine
Clorazepate
Desmethyldiazepam
Imipramine
Lidocaine
Oxazepam
Pentazocine
Phenacetin
Propranolol
Theophylline

---

1. **Pharmacologic approaches**
   a. *Nicotine resin complex* (nicotine gum) (Nicorette)
      (1) Limited effects in producing long-term abstinence, especially when used without a cognitive-behavioral intervention.
      (2) Most frequent side effects are hiccups, nausea, anorexia, oral/jaw soreness, GI distress.
      (3) Nicotine gum users can become dependent on the gum instead of smoking.
      (4) Instructions for use:
         (a) Do not use with cigarettes
         (b) Use as a substitute for smoking
         (c) Chew slowly and "park" the gum to titrate release of nicotine, to simulate smoking
         (d) One piece substitutes for about two cigarettes
         (e) Establish a maintenance level for 2 to 3 months, then slowly decrease
         (f) Avoid acidic drinks (coffee, juice) before and during gum.
   b. *Nicotine transdermal patches*
      (1) Has the advantage of once/day application.
      (2) Can be used with patients who would have trouble following the instructions for chewing nicotine gum.
      (3) Disadvantage is that some patients are helped by more of a direct substitute (the patch is abstract).
      (4) Side effects include:
         (a) Skin irritation (causes discontinuance in up to 5%)
         (b) Insomnia and disturbing dreams
         (c) Cardiac arrhythmias if combined with smoking in susceptible patients with coronary disease.
      (5) Options available:
         (a) Habitrol and Nicoderm—7, 14, 21 mg released over 24 hours
         (b) Usual treatment involves 4 to 6 weeks at the 21 mg level, followed by 2 to 4 weeks at 14, then 7 mg levels

        (c) Use lower starting dose in patients with coronary disease, weight under 100 pounds, or those who smoke less than half a pack/day.

  c. *Clonidine*
- (1) Has been shown to attenuate nicotine withdrawal symptoms and has been used as an adjunct to smoking cessation programs
- (2) Usually used in doses of 0.1-0.3 mg/day for 2 weeks, then tapered
- (3) Side effects include dizziness, lightheadedness, sedation, dry mouth.

  d. *Antidepressants*
- (1) May be effective adjuncts in smoking cessation programs (especially given the high co-occurrence of depressive symptoms).

  e. *Buspirone*
- (1) May be a useful adjunct to cessation, especially in patient with co-occurring generalized anxiety symptoms.
- (2) Should be started 2 weeks before the nicotine tapering program. Doses of 10 mg tid PO should be used for most patients.

2. Cognitive-behavioral treatments
  a. This component is essential to any treatment program; it usually involves three stages:
- (1) Preparation:
  - (a) Review reasons and readiness for quitting
  - (b) Establish a target quit date
  - (c) Keep a daily diary to establish baseline levels as well as what prompts smoking.
- (2) Quitting:
  - (a) Self-management (stimulus control)
  - (b) Identify, alter, or avoid cues that trigger smoking
  - (c) Substitute another stimulus for cues that cannot be avoided
  - (d) Aversion strategies have sometimes been used:
    - (*i*) Increase usual smoking rate to the point where it becomes distasteful.
  - (e) Nicotine fading:
    - (*i*) Gradually switching brands to ones with lower nicotine content.
- (3) Maintenance:
  - (a) Identify high-risk relapse situations
  - (b) Rehearse steps to deal with those situations
  - (c) Avoid seeing a slip-up as a total failure
  - (d) Get involved in other rewarding activities.

References

Abelin T, Muller P, Buehler A et al: Controlled trial of transdermal nicotine patch in tobacco withdrawal, *Lancet* 1:7-10, 1989.

Anda RF, Williamson DF, Escobedo LG et al: Depression and the dynamics of smoking, *JAMA* 264:1541-1545, 1990.

Benowitz NL: Pharmacologic aspects of cigarette smoking and nicotine addiction, *N Eng J Med* 319:1318-1330, 1988.

Covey LS, Glassman AH: A meta-analysis of double-blind placebo-controlled trials of clonidine for smoking cessation, *Br J Addict* 86:991-998, 1991.

Cummings KM, Giovino G, Jaen CR et al: Reports of smoking withdrawal symptoms over a 21-day period of abstinence, *Addict Behav* 10:373-381, 1985.

Fagerstrom KO: *Efficacy of nicotine chewing gum: a review.* In Pomerleau O, Pomerleau CS, eds: *Nicotine replacement: a critical evaluation,* New York, 1988, Alan R Liss.

Fiore MC, Novotny TE, Pierce JP et al: Methods used to quit smoking in the United States, *JAMA* 263:2760-2765, 1990.

Gawin F, Compton M, Byck R: Buspirone reduces smoking, *Arch Gen Psychiatry* 46:288-289, 1989.

Glassman A, Jackson WK, Walsh BT et al: Cigarette craving, smoking withdrawal and clonidine, *Science* 126:864-866, 1984.

Glassman AH, Helzer JE, Covey LS et al: Smoking, smoking cessation and major depression, *JAMA* 264:1546-1549, 1990.

Hall RCW, Hoffman RS, Beresford TP et al: Physical illness encountered in patients with eating disorders, *Psychosomatics* 30:174-191, 1989.

Hjalmarson AI: Effect of nicotine chewing gum in smoking cessation, *JAMA* 252:2835-2838, 1984.

Mitchell JE, Seim HC, Colon E et al: Medical complications and medical management of bulimia, *Ann Intern Med* 107:71-77, 1987.

Prochaska JO, Goldstein MG: Process of smoking cessation: implications for clinicians. In JM Samet JM, Coultas DB, eds, *Clin Chest Med* 12:727-735, 1991.

Transdermal nicotine study group: transdermal nicotine for smoking cessation: six month results from two multicenter controlled clinical trials, *JAMA* 266:3133-3138, 1991.

Index

To help us publish the most useful materials for today's health care providers, we would appreciate your comments on this book. Please take a few moments to complete the form below, and then tear it out and mail to us. Thank you for your input.

Goldberg: *PRACTICAL GUIDE TO THE CARE OF THE PSYCHIATRIC PATIENT*

1. How are you using this book? _____

2. Was this book useful? Please explain.

___ yes ___ no _____

_____

3. What influenced your decision to buy this book? (*check all that apply*)

___ required/recommended by instructor ___ bookstore display
___ recommended by student ___ journal advertisement
___ other

Are you interested in doing in-depth reviews of our publications? ___ yes ___ no

NAME: _____

ADDRESS: _____

_____

TELEPHONE: _____

BUSINESS REPLY MAIL

FIRST CLASS MAIL   PERMIT No. 135   St. Louis, MO.

POSTAGE WILL BE PAID BY ADDRESSEE

CHRIS REID
MEDICAL EDITORIAL
MOSBY-YEAR BOOK, INC.
11830 WESTLINE INDUSTRIAL DRIVE
ST.LOUIS, MO 63146-9987